BEING ENOUGH

Breaking the Walls
Between Teenagers and Parents

insights from a teen

SAMEEP MANGAT

TABLE OF CONTENTS

INTRODUCTION

Sameep

I am a teenager.

I am 16 years old.

I may have never worried about having enough, but I have always worried about being enough.

I do not worry about my stomach caving in because I couldn't afford dinner, but rather my stomach spilling out over my jeans because I have eaten too much lunch. I do not worry about whether my house will be foreclosed on by the time I return from school, but rather whether I'll be able to find the courage within myself to step outside my house in the first place. I do not worry about people refusing to be friends with me because I'm poor but rather people refusing to be friends with me because I do not fit the societal mold of an ideal girl.

My name is Sameep, and I'm the so-called "author" of this book, although I think the real writers are the people who have helped shape every chapter of this novel. I think if we're to understand each other, you need some context about me, so here goes. I'm just your average teenager with an obsession for video games, everything Disney, and fluffy dogs. I live for late-night runs; I'm a total musical theater geek; and I love sitting in old bookshops to read. If I were stranded on an island, I would proba-bly bring speakers to blast rap music, a bunch of pens and paper to write stories, and a ton of breadsticks. You'll find me playing soccer during a free period or singing my heart out as I bang away on a piano with all the scrappy techniques that I learned and then pretty much forgot after third grade. So, there are a few basics of me, but you'll discover much more as you read through these chapters.

Thankfully, I am privileged enough to receive an education, so I grew up learning in a safe school environment. Along my road to and through high school, I have realized that the issues we face as teenagers are complex and often misunderstood by adults. We're sent into the world with the idea that if we're not curing cancer or changing the world in some fundamental way, we're failing. Despite technological advancements and expanding avenues of communication through social media, I feel like our society has a deeply ingrained emotional scarcity that makes people feel alone, maybe even more than before social media. A person could have 800 Facebook friends, but only a few who he or she can call up in the middle of the night to talk.

Teenage drama has taken over our lives, and the desire to fit in is an ever-present issue. In the snap of a finger, the most popular girl can become the most hated girl, and the social hierarchy of high school rearranges. Within seconds, gossip can spread like wildfire, destroying reputations and leaving pain in its wake. Every day, fights break out in the locker room about football positions, and girls cry softly in the school bathroom as they puke up their food.

You may be wondering why I didn't do anything about these situations before now.

Let me tell you, I have tried, and I'm still trying my best. I started an anonymous advice Tumblr blog (helpugetthru.tumblr.com). It wasn't long before hundreds of questions poured in. I collected answers from my own experiences, the experiences of people around me, and online sources, and I spent hours every night providing the best solution that I could muster to answer each problem. But that wasn't enough. And so I compiled songs and photos into a single area that changed depending on how someone was feeling. What better way to appeal to a technologically advanced generation than with technology? That was how I designed the mobile iOS app, Aura (http://aura-app.me) to track moods and happiness and provide easily accessible resources, such as jokes, tips, quotes, songs, videos, and compliments, for different emotional states.

Ultimately I realized that more conversations centered on the issues teens face, such as mental health, self-esteem, and body image, were necessary. We can do a lot to try to fix the issues around us, but work has to be done to stop destructive habits and situations from developing in the first place. And that, ladies and gentlemen, is why I'm writing this book.

When starting this process, I recognized that I didn't know everything. It took hundreds of hours of research and organizing material in order to provide substantial insight that was not simply experience. This book is not an encyclopedia of teenager issues, and I'm not trying to pass it off as one. There are so many issues in the world today that pertain to adolescents; these are just the ones that I thought were important to mention. I do not think this book has the world's answers or the solutions to every problem; it is neither comprehensive in depth nor exhaustive in scope. This is just my way of offering my perspective – one teenager's perspective – on the issues that I see around me.

Each chapter of the book touches a teenager issue, and the topics are arranged alphabetically. Each chapter follows a very similar structure in order to create an organized display of the information.

- Excerpt/Story

- Statistics/Facts

- Tips for Teens

- Tips for Parents

Most of the chapters revolve around four fundamental themes: communication empathy, love and compassion, and judgment. Keep a look out for these, as they will be talked about in length at the end of the book as the basis for any functioning family.

Feel free to skip through to the chapters that actually pertain to the topics that are relevant to your life. How you read this book is your choice. Flip through it in one sitting, use a highlighter, scribble down margin notes, or don't read parts of it at all; it's all up to you and what you hope to gain or need from reading it. I don't think there is only one correct or most beneficial way to use this book; the best way is the way that best suits you.

For far too long, it's been parents telling other parents how to parent. It's been parents who have limited empathy for what teens actually experience, and parents who are trying to find the perfect formula for concocting the perfect child. I'm hoping – no, praying – that this book serves to equip parents and teens alike with the weapons of knowledge and guidance to combat the challenges teenagers face and the struggles of the teenage years. Necessary conversations about issues covered in this book have been swept under the rug for far too long. I've had enough of watching people build walls around themselves as a form of protection. It's time to start the conversation. It's time to break these walls down.

Parents, I am asking you to take advice from a teenager. Crazy request, I realize. But your child is not a recipe or a formula, a mathematical equation, an SAT score, or a sport. Your teen is human, and they deserve to be treated as such. I understand much of the content discussed in this book may be shocking. Even my parents were astounded to realize how much went on behind the scenes in my teenage life. Keep an open mind as you read the book so that you can better understand what teenagers go through, and you can foster open communication in your family. You care, you want to do it all right, but I hate to break it to you: you're not going to be the perfect parent, and your kid isn't going to be the perfect kid. But that doesn't mean you can't be a beneficial parent who grows alongside your teenager and constantly improves. It's a learning process; we're all in the same boat.

Teens, I get it. We go through some grueling, painful years in high school. Even prom queens or star quarterbacks experience disappointments and frustrations during high school. There are always more people to please, more parties to attend, and better grades to get. We're told who to be, and that's not okay. No matter who you are, I hope you can relate to the stuff in this book and learn to communicate better with your parents. Quite honestly, your parents might be making you read this, but I still hope you enjoy it and benefit from it. Pop some headphones in; turn up that rap, indie, or pop; and let's do this. Take some breaks if you have to and go play some Black Ops or 2k. This book will be waiting when you come back.

This book has made me aware. It's made me look at the world with a different perspective and helped me better understand both my parents and even myself. I hope it does the same for you. Honestly, if this book helps even one family – even one person – then I've achieved what I set out to do.

Good luck, my friend.

Bon voyage.

I'll see you on the other side.

1

Academic Pressure

"So you're going to Stanford or an Ivy too, huh?"

I looked up to see what seemed like a thousand beady eyes gazing at me.

One of our family friends continued, "I mean, after all, your brother goes to Stanford."

I slumped further down into my seat, melding into the plastic that was supporting me and keeping me from liquefying into a puddle on the floor. Forcing out a laugh, I choked out a "yea!" I focused my attention on a scratch etched into the third tile of concrete.

This conversation became a common occurrence in my life once my brother was admitted into one of the highest ranked colleges of the nation. Parents whispered, "Stanford" with reverence and respect into my ear, while students shouted it with possessiveness and contempt, as if stealing the word would guarantee that I would not follow in my brother's footsteps.

I was left with a responsibility and a duty to uphold. My only purpose, it seemed, was to achieve the highest grade point average (GPA) possible, which would guarantee me admission into a highly ranked university and in turn a one-way ticket to a bright and successful future. Ingrained in me was the belief that if I did not get straight A's, I was a disappointment.

I went to bed at 2:00 A.M. those nights, those terrifyingly dreary nights full of caffeine and cold water face washes. I remember staying up until 2:30 A.M., cramming for the history test the next day. I got three and a half hours of sleep because I couldn't bear the idea of getting a "B." A "B" stood for brat. A "B" stood for burden. A "B" stood for brainless. But an "A"? An "A" represented accomplishment. An "A" meant admirable. An "A" was an advantage. For me, anything less meant I was a failure and proof that my parents had only raised one kid right, and that kid wasn't me.

My school has one of the highest academic standards, in my opinion, and is filled with a plethora of intelligent and competitive students. Now, of course, there are a variety of sports, extracurricular activities, and customization options that I could've considered, but I chose a challenging course load with multiple advanced placement (AP) classes, activities that devoured my afternoons, and a demanding performing arts program. I broke down weeping some nights over the stress I felt. I was pretty sure that my gravestone would have read: "Death by Stress."

For some, it's the worry of getting enough credits to graduate high school. For others, the stress comes from pressure to become valedictorian then competing with all the other valedictorians of other schools for entrance into Harvard or Stanford or another Ivy League school. We all struggle through unavoidable stresses, whatever the source. But the toll it takes is evident. It's suddenly less about learning and more about the grade or an Ivy League school.

High school students are told to get at least eight hours of sleep a night, but once sports, performing arts, robotics, and then four hours of homework are piled on each night, a student is lucky to get five hours of sleep. Black circles under eyes and brain-pounding headaches are closer to the norm than eight hours of sleep.

This academic pressure caused by parents, institutions, and students surrounds teens and guides every movement and decision. The world is competitive. Every year there are more applicants to the top universities, and the acceptance rate drops. Stanford has an acceptance rate that's around 5%. Ten-year-olds are developing life-changing apps, and tweens are building careers on social media sites. How are teenagers supposed to rival that? It's obvious no one is interested in failing, even if it means sacrificing health to succeed.

Every generation has felt this kind of academic pressure, but I feel that especially recently, the stakes have risen. Pressure for satisfactory grades for admission into a quality college, social media overload, and a constant fear of parental disappointment lurks behind every decision and choice. This stress fuels panic attacks, anxiety, and burnout, which many students experience.

I go to a prestigious private school in California with a particularly rigorous course load and extensive competition. At my school, taking seven or eight AP classes by the end of high school is the norm. At my school, the average SAT score is above 2100, and the admission rates into Stanford, universities of California (UCs), and Ivy League schools are outstanding.

I chose this high school because I desired a challenging education. I knew that by pressuring myself, I would be able to push myself and shine in a way that promoted my excellence. Some students even prosper in this type of environment. They're motivated and driven enough that they welcome the challenge because it gives them an opportunity to achieve their full potential. So by no means does this idea of extreme academic pressure apply to everyone. I'm simply speaking from my own experiences at a rigorous high school.

Statistics

The impact of rising academic pressure affects the entire world. The pressure to meet expectations for many students makes suicide seem better than being a disappointment to parents or family.

American teenagers are the most stressed-out age group in the United States according to an American Psychological Association "Stress in America" Survey (2013).

Polls show that academic pressure harmfully impacts teenage development. For example, a National Public Radio poll found that 40% of parents claim that the stress their teenager is experiencing is academic rather than social ("School Stress," 2013).

Most high school students consider cheating okay because it's an alternative to failing, so it alleviates stress. According to a national survey by Rutgers' Management Education Center, 50% of a 4,500 high school student survey group thought that copying from another student didn't count as cheating (Slobogin, 2002). Cheating guarantees a similar grade as classmates and requires half the effort. Now, of course, it's ethically wrong, but that doesn't stop students from partaking in it.

Academic pressure, just like all other types of pressure, is even detrimental to mental health. I've seen students pulled out of school because academic pressure was too much and worsened their mental illnesses. A survey by the APA and NPR found that nearly half of all teens – 45% – said they were stressed by school pressure ("School Stress," 2013). I've seen the toll academic pressure takes on classmates. Panic attacks and mental breakdowns are common in a high intensity environment where being "average" isn't good enough.

What are sources of academic pressure?

That's a complicated question, since it varies, depending on the individual. The following are some scenarios:

Parents are the most common source of pressure in a teenager's life. Parents aren't necessarily doing anything wrong, but their drive and desire for their teen to do well and succeed in life can come off as controlling.

I come from an immigrant family where superior grades and a high-caliber education are expected of me. My parents used their educations to work their way up the social ladder of life. They believe that education leads to more opportunities and more success, since that's how it's worked for them. It's a very similar scenario for a lot of other children of immigrant parents. The parents built something out of nothing and want to make sure to provide the best that they can for their children.

For me, it's not so much about the shame of getting bad grades, but rather the consequences that would follow getting bad grades. Failing a test would result in grounding, and the worst of all, a silent grunt of disapproval that would leave me reconsidering my entire life and career. Sometimes I hid scores like a "B" for fear of being reprimanded.

As I've gotten older, my parents have stepped away from my grades and stopped caring as much. Of course, they still paid attention to ensure I wasn't slipping, but they no longer monitored every grade or checked every homework assignment. It was something to which my parents and I both adapted, and they learned how to distance themselves from my academic life and let me make my own mistakes.

Siblings can leave a pretty hard act to follow. As I talk about in Chapter 15, having a sibling meant I was faced with standards that I often had to meet. I had to obtain the similar GPA, impress my teachers just as much as he did, and maintain a pristine academic track record.

This also meant people punching me playfully in the shoulder and saying things like: "Next in line for Stanford, huh?" If I produced anything less, I'd be the child who didn't make it to a top university, the child who wasn't as good, or the child who didn't turn out right. Most of this was in my head, but it was still a pressing fear of mine and it motivated me to study hard and try hard in everything that I did. Just being affiliated with the name of a sibling can be stressful. Add a sibling's successful admission to a high-ranking college into the mix, and the pressure gets a whole lot more intense.

College is a very high stake. The reality, as college counselors like to tell us, is that without adequate grades, a student won't get admission into a top tier college. Without "good grades," a student won't be considered, no matter what other extracurricular activities they have. You could be the best basketball player in the nation, and yet with a 2.0 GPA, a top school may be out of reach.

My childhood was all about an elite college, which sprouted from my environment. I watched my brother and his friends go through the admissions process. By the age of twelve, before I had even finished the entire Harry Potter series, I knew the exact grade point I needed and how to write a college essay. It was understood—at least by me—that in order to prove my self-worth and make my parents happy, I had to get into a good college.

Peers are also a source of academic pressure. Academic pressures are not contained only in the classroom environment. Walk through the halls of any academic school during lunch, and you'll most likely hear any of the following:

"Did you get 45 as the answer to question number 10 on the math test?"

"Was the physics test hard?"

"I have a 'B' in that class! My parents are going to kill me!"

"What grade did you get on the English essay?"

There's a huge focus on academics and letter grades. There's no escape, and the competition of hearing other students' grades only adds to the stress.

It's all about outshining the competition. I would get drilled on the number of AP classes I was taking from other students so that they could ensure that they could take more. Competition fuels hungry minds and amps up the stress to the max. It happens at every school, depending on the environment and an individual student's clique.

Teachers have standards as well in most high-ranking schools and unintentionally phrase discussions about academics so that it's implied that anything below a "B" is below expectations. Countless times, I've heard the phrase "Some of you will get B's in this class, and be incredibly disheartened," and although they don't mean it in a negative way, it can come across as a requirement to get an A or move down to an easier class. It's always been about reaching your full potential and trying to make sure you're doing your best.

Self-fostered. A lot of academic pressure ends up being self-fostered. I pressure myself into the mindset that without good grades, my future won't be as bright as it could be. I take it upon myself to deem myself worthless if I don't hit my own standard. I declare myself a disappointment when I don't live up to my own dreams. I use external means of validation such as grades to attribute a value to myself. I assume that getting good grades and receiving admission into a top tier university will bestow upon me respect and honor. I convince myself over time that the only way I will rise above a mediocre life and make an impact is if I work hard and get into a university that provides me with good education, a network of intelligence, and opportunities.

I wanted to challenge myself and prove my intelligence, so I loaded up with APs and some of the most difficult classes I could take. I've spent nights toiling under an artificial yellow light, praying that I would be able to finish the 20-page paper due the next day before the sun peeked out behind the mountains outside my hazy windows.

The first thing I still think when I look at my report card is "what will my parents say?" And even though they likely won't reprimand me, it's still a fear that remains cemented in my mind. My parents pay so much for my education, and the thought of not producing suitable return frightens me. A lot of us have these instinctual fears, and even if they're irrational, they stay with us because we grow up believing them. It can be hard to get rid of them, even if they no longer pertain to the situation.

TIPS FOR TEENS

I wish I could tell you to simply avoid the pressures of school, but that's not a reality for most of us. School is a permanent aspect of adolescence, but a teenager can learn to better cope with the stress. The challenges of high school prepare us to take on the real world and give us a platform to build our future.

Tip #1: Time management

I remember classes on study skills in lower school, which I never took seriously. But sometimes I wish I had paid more attention. In order to conquer homework in a timely fashion, learn how to balance time with extracurricular activities and schoolwork. Plan out the week and get ahead on work on the weekends. Try to be efficient and eliminate distractions. Here are some tips that have worked for me in the past:

Use a planner. I like to use a whiteboard and plan out my week and then on a large scale, on a monthly board. On the monthly board, I write down big tests and events, while on the weekly board, I write everything. Whenever I finish an assignment or take a test, I mark that off my board. At the end of the week, I wipe off the entire board, and it leaves me with a sense of accomplishment.

Finish as much work as you can at school. I'm not saying spend lunch cooped up in the library, trying to finish work. That'll reduce social interaction, and that's not good. Rather, use a free period to get ahead on the homework for the night. Especially if you have extracurricular activities after school, finishing as much homework during the day as possible will ease up your load.

Have a clean, peaceful environment to work. Work happens more slowly in a dirty or disorganized environment. A cluttered desk means a cluttered mind.

Listen to music if it helps you work. Certain types of music motivate me. When I'm studying for a test, I typically listen to songs that I've memorized, so I don't have to think about the lyrics, or I listen to piano. When I'm writing essays, I listen to hardcore rap, and when I'm doing homework, I listen to R&B. Pick music that works for you and with your tastes.

Take breaks to increase efficiency. Working your mind for too long without any breaks will tire you, and information processing will slow. Take regular breaks and remember to stretch and grab a glass of water every half hour.

Tip #2: Reach out to teachers

You'd be surprised how accommodating many teachers can be. If you're having a particularly stressful week, chat with them about options regarding rescheduling tests or turning in assignments at a later date with no penalty. The more responsibility you take in your own academic course load, the more impressed they're likely to be, which will make them more understanding of a situation. Come in for extra help to get guidance on class material to prove how dedicated you are to truly learning rather than just getting good grades. Reach out to parents and counselors for additional help if needed.

Tip #3: Don't overbook yourself

Be aware of how much you can handle. Don't pile on work. As much as you might want to be a super hero, just take it easy. Start off with a few activities and wait until you get the hang of managing time before adding more activities into the mix. If it ever gets too stressful, ease back and cut down on unnecessary activities that take up time without adding any value. Focusing exclusively on the future and getting stuff done can accumulate pressure until you're at a breaking point. Be aware and watch out.

Tip #4: Don't doubt your self-worth

Not everyone is academically strong. Testing systems cater to a conventional measurement of intelligence. Some brilliant people don't test well because testing anxiety hinders them from tapping into their capabilities and creativity. Doing well on standardized tests holds no correlation with intelligence. No two people are the same. You are unique, with unique strengths and challenges. You do not have to match another person just to obtain validation or self-worth.

Tip #5: Keep the big picture in mind

It can be hard to look at the big picture in any given moment, but try to keep in mind that in the end, that one test isn't going to matter. You're going to forget about it, and it probably won't make a big impact on the final class grade. The stress will pass. Just remember to focus on the present and keep moving.

Grades don't define the future or where life will lead. Many individuals who have dropped out of college have ended up just fine. (I am in no way implying that you should; it's just something to keep in mind.) Do the best work possible then whatever happens, happens. Don't stress out about one bad grade. Chances are it won't matter in the long run. I try to allow one shoddy grade per subject before I freak out.

Tip #6: Strike a balance

Take challenging courses within capability so that you're not spending all night trying to keep up. Take classes that you're passionate about, not what parents or friends say or suggest to take. Enjoying the subject will be motivation to work harder.

It's important to remind yourself that some pressure is a necessity. "Pressure makes diamonds," as the adage goes, so just remember to find the sweet balance of challenge.

Tip #7: Get a tutor

Hire a tutor if you need help. It can be very helpful to have someone to thoroughly explain certain subjects with which you struggle, since getting extra attention from a teacher can be difficult. If extra help sessions during school are available, go to the teacher and ask for help on specific topics. Some of the best students I know have tutors who help them explore concepts more deeply, allow them to better understand the material, and aid them to excel on tests.

One of my friends used to be terrified of admitting to the people that she needed a tutor. She'd disappear on random occasions and when prompted, would quickly squeak, "got to finish some work" and scamper off to her backpack. When she admitted the truth to me, I could tell she was embarrassed, but hiring a tutor is smart. Since then, my friend has realized the value of having a tutor and proudly suggests one whenever her peers are struggling with a certain subject.

Tip #8: Find stress relievers

Exercise regularly and find activities that release endorphins and calm you down. It may be playing a sport, hiking, or knitting. Maybe it's watching an episode of "New Girl" while sipping hot chocolate while wrapped up in a fuzzy blanket. Find what works and engage in these activities to help alleviate the stress from academics. Learn relaxation exercises like muscle relaxation techniques and breathing techniques, or get a massage.

Tip #9: Appreciate the work you've done

Sometimes we keep moving and forget to savor accomplishment. When you get an "A" for a test for which you thoroughly prepared, go out and celebrate. Treat yourself to something special. When you finish an essay, don't just save it and quit. Take a step back, scroll up, and look at the length of it. Be proud of it. Positive reinforcement works wonders at providing motivation to continue putting out good content.

Tip #10: Rely on Friends

Have group Skype nights to study for math and make it fun. Go out for a group dinner once your entire friend group finishes that really hard biology test. A good network of friends who you can rely on to study and who motivate you should also be the people with whom you celebrate accomplishments. These friends will be a positive influence and support. I can't count the number of times my friends and I have studied together by prepping a communal study guide and contributing whenever possible. It's nice to have someone to rely on, even if it's just someone to stay up with until 2:00 A.M.

TIPS FOR PARENTS

It's hard to watch a teenager struggle with academics, especially since stepping in directly and doing the work for them isn't an option. Academic motivation has to come from within a teenager. However, you can set up a positive environment for your teenager to prosper and guide them in ways to help them achieve.

Tip #1: Don't blame your kid

If you can see that your teens are trying their hardest, don't blame them for being unable to immediately produce the results. It might take some time, and if you reprimand them for not being good enough when they're trying their best, they may feel unworthy and feel as if they've disappointed you. Use positive parenting instead and start the conversation about how you guys can work together to get their grades up and find both fun and motivational methods of studying.

My brother and dad used to study in intervals when he was younger, sectioning off time to not only work on English and Math but also to chuck around a baseball outside.

Tip #2: Change the conversation

Change up topics at home. Make sure that the main focus around the dinner table is how they're feeling and how their day was, rather than how the history test was. They get enough of that at school. I can't count the number of times I've lashed out in irritation because my mom unknowingly asked how a test, about which I'd already been asked repetitively by my classmates, was. My mom might've just been asking because she saw me studying late for it, but I took it the wrong way out of frustration since my day had already been hectic. Try not to pry into grades. Build a trusting relationship and allow your teen to handle their own grades. If they need help, trust that they will ask.

Tip #3: Don't instill fear

Encourage kids to want good grades for themselves. Explain the reason why your family encourages exemplary grades, and how good grades will aid in their life. Make sure to elaborate on why this is the approach you take. Motivation to work will provide better results than punishment for less-than-stellar performance. Taking things away from your teen as punishment for poor grades or lacking performance is going to interfere with their learning and create more anxiety than benefits. Reward them for good grades instead of punishing them for bad ones.

Tip #4: Avoid college preferences

When a family member holds a special place in their heart for a certain college, it can be obvious. Don't be that parent. Don't dump dreams onto your kid and blur theirs.

My parents have always held a soft spot in their heart for Stanford, as it's not only close to home, but it's an environment that we know a lot about due to my brother. It's created a lot of subconscious pressure for me, since I feel like getting into Stanford would make my parents especially proud, even though they constantly tell me that they'll be happy as long as I'm happy in the college I choose. Try to avoid coercing your teenager into aiming for a certain college, as it'll build unnecessary pressure. Some parents may unintentionally reveal preferences that add personal pressure to achieve to an already stressful situation. It's important to reassure your teenager that where they end up happy will be the best place for them.

Tip #5: Stay calm

Put on a calm front, even if you're frustrated or anxious. Work with your teen to develop a plan about how to proceed and how to balance various activities. As the adult in the situation, you have to act like one and take control. You are the role model. Consider how success is defined in your family and try to make it about happiness and satisfaction rather than a number on a scale. Your teenager is not a number.

Tip #6: Avoid being a helicopter parent

Check in once in awhile, but don't be a worry wart. Don't email the teacher every week or month. Let your teen step up and take responsibility for grades and conflicts. You can help them deal with anxiety and help them with questions, but don't check every assignment or drill them about every test.

Tip #7: Remind them of healthy lifestyle choices

My mom always brings me fruits while I'm studying and massages my shoulders if I'm having a particularly rough week. Remind your child to exercise. Encourage them to sleep enough and join for a family meal where no one uses a phone. Creating a positive environment full of healthy mental and physical choices will aid your teen in doing better in school.

There's so much more to life than grades, and I think measuring progress and knowledge by a letter seems reductive. I've never enjoyed the idea of being defined by a GPA or a grade, but it is reality.

It's important that each individual find what education means. I don't think academic education determines how life turns out or determines how successful an individual will be. I think education is about opening as many doors as possible and accumulating the most opportunities possible. Education is neither a requirement nor a necessity for success or happiness.

In my opinion, education shouldn't be about tests or memorization, but rather the application of it to better understand the world. Education is not about gaining more knowledge and information but applying it to understand the meaning of life.

If I don't remember how to find the equation of a polar conic in twenty years, it's okay. I have a calculator. If I don't remember the name of the general who led the French and Indian War, it's okay. I have Google. If I don't know exactly where Venezuela is on a map, that's okay. I'll just buy a globe.

Albert Einstein once said, "Everybody is a genius. But if you judge a fish by its ability to climb a tree, it will live its whole life believing it is stupid" (Kelly, 2015, p. 80).

I couldn't agree more.

We're all different.

You might be a fish. I might be a sloth.

And that's 100% okay.

2

Anxiety

Breathe. The word echoed in my head as I repeated it softly to myself, the swarms of students bustling around me. I leaned against the wall, a sudden panic washing over me. My fingers shook, my heart thudded in my ears, and tears pricked my eyes. The pit of my stomach dropped, and a feeling of anxiety tickled my senses, tracing my skin.

My week had been absolute hell; I'd barely gotten sleep the night before, spending every minute reading and studying the pages of my sophomore history textbook or writing the 15-page lab report due for physics. The worst fight I'd ever had with one of my close friends had broken out the night before, and the words that she had yelled at me through the phone were still imprinted on my mind. I knew there was no going back. I knew that the friendship was over. This was unfixable. Our constant arguments had taken a toll, and I was broken, worn down.

The blur of backpacks passed me, and my vision glazed over. My grades were about to plummet. One more bad test grade would leave me with a "B" in this semester on my report card. Elite colleges would not accept me with a "B." I would be forgotten, just a name in the yearbook. That girl who had potential but never put it to use.

My breath quickened: I began hyperventilating.

Dumb. The thought kicked me in the face.

Disappointment. To my teachers, to my parents, to my friends.

Stupid. Why did it take me so long to understand everything?

Worthless. I didn't add value to anything.

Forgettable. I was just another face.

Disposable. This is why I had lost her as a friend.

The tears streamed down my cheeks, and I shut my eyes, trying to block out the world and the fuzziness that accompanied it. I wanted to run, but there was nowhere to run. I was nothing. I slumped to the ground, holding my head in my palms, trying to shake off the dread that was taking over.

"Hey, Sameep," a voice near me said and jerked me out of the black hole that my thoughts had pulled me into. A girl I vaguely recognized glanced at me with concern, her brow furrowed, and her mouth painted in a grim line. "Let's get you to the counselor," she spoke quietly, eyes brimming with understanding.

That was one of the first experiences I had ever with a panic attack. I had never before felt such an overwhelming sense of dread and fear that sent me spinning off into insanity. The walls had been closing in, and I had felt like I was suffocating. I couldn't figure out how to breathe. I might not have an anxiety disorder, and my panic attack could have been due to a lack of sleep, but even this instance was enough to scare me.

We've all experienced anxiety at some point or another. I've seen actors throw up before auditions or performances because of anxiety, and I've encountered peers with hands shaking so vigorously with apprehension that even air would slip through their fingers. When I'm stressed, I bite the inside of my mouth until it bleeds, which is a body-focused behavior that supposedly provides me with some sense of relief.

Anxiety disorders are serious mental health problems. Normal anxiety is short-lived, a passing phase that fades within hours. An anxiety disorder is ongoing panic, fear, and worry that threaten to destroy the ability to communicate, learn, and carry out everyday activities regardless of momentary security or calm.

Anxiety is very common and can be healthy in dealing with certain situations. A variety of triggers contribute to anxiety, such as certain environments, traumatic events, or an overload of stress or pressure. It's very difficult to control and without a personalized method of coping can overwhelm a person.

Anxiety often goes hand in hand with other illnesses, such as depression and eating disorders. According to Anxiety and Depression Association of America (ADAA), "Anxiety disorders are the most common psychiatric illnesses affecting children and adults. An estimated 40 million American adults suffer from anxiety disorders. Only about one-third of those suffering from an anxiety disorder receive treatment, even though the disorders are highly treatable" ("Understanding the Facts," 2014).

Anxiety disorders are easy to identify if panic attacks are a common occurrence; however, the minor side signs of anxiety are more difficult to spot, unless you're actively looking for them.

SIGNS OF ANXIETY IN TEENS

Parents, it's important to watch out for these signs and get your teenagers help if they need it. They may not always be open to talking about it, but by stepping in, you'll be doing them a huge favor.

Based on various reports published online, such as at WebMD, CRC Health, Village Behavioral Health, the following are some of the signs of anxiety ("What are anxiety," n.d.; Hurst, n.d.; "Causes, Symptoms," n.d.;):

Excessive worry about everything: friends, school, and academics. Paranoia takes over and creates an excessive need for approval by teachers and parents.

Physical health deterioration, including complaints about headaches, stomach aches, fatigue, chest pain, muscle tension, shortness of breath, trembling, sweating, and panic attacks.

Sleeping problems, such as difficulty falling asleep, staying asleep, or just obtaining true rest from a full night of sleep.

Low self-esteem leading to excessive self-criticism or self-doubt.

Perfectionism, such as rechecking school work or other chores many times.

Withdrawal from social situations and daily interactions with friends and family due to fear of judgment by others.

Mood swings and irritability.

Drug use or alcohol use to cope with and alleviate anxiety.

Types of anxiety problems

What most people are not aware of is that many types of anxiety disorders exist. The following are some specific examples and stats listed by ADAA ("Anxiety and Depression", 2016):

Generalized anxiety disorder (GAD) includes a lot of unnecessary worry over little things that can be easily solved. According to ADAA, "GAD affects 6.8 million adults, or 3.1% of the U.S. population, and women are twice as likely to be affected as men." This disorder involves fear about the future, often times being things that are uncontrollable such as divorce, natural disasters, mistakes, or death.

Panic disorder and agoraphobia. Panic attacks are usually the main identifier of this disorder. There is sudden overwhelming fear and alarm, and an individual may begin to feel the telltale signs of a panic attack: sweaty palms, racing heart, chest pain, a desire to flee, and difficulty breathing. Panic disorders affect a similar number of people as GAD (2.75% of U.S. population), and the likelihood for women to be affected is also twice as likely. Agoraphobia, on the other hand, relates much more to a fear of areas where escape or calling for help appears difficult. People with agoraphobia avoid these situations at all costs and are very concerned with escape routes wherever they are.

Social anxiety disorder. Judgment is a big part of adolescence, and many teens may have a fear of social interactions because they fear they will be humiliated by or in front of their classmates. Social anxiety affects 15 million, or 6.8% of the U.S. population, and starting at age 13, these individuals may avoid outings, school, or other social interactions.

Health anxiety is not classified as a disorder, but there is a lot of anxiety, especially in teens, surrounding health and body image. It can be excessive and obsessive and prompts the development of widespread anxiety.

Post-traumatic stress disorder (PTSD) results from a traumatic experience. This can result from hearing about the experience, watching it, or being directly involved in it. Especially for young adults and children, this disorder can be a difficult one to talk about with others, and it usually invokes triggering memories, thoughts, and flashbacks. In total, 65% of men and 45.9% of women who experience rape develop this condition. In children, sexual abuse raises the likelihood for developing PTSD.

Hoarding disorder causes individuals to hoard possessions, as they are unable to deal with giving them away, regardless of the emotional or monetary value. If prevented from saving or acquiring these items, individuals with this disorder will undergo extreme stress that impairs their social, cognitive, and daily life functions.

Separation anxiety disorder sufferers experience excessive anxiety after being separated from parents, friends, or individuals who they are close to. They may refuse to go to school, to leave the side of certain people, or even to sleep alone in their own bed.

Specific phobias are fears regarding a specific situation or object that causes anxiety. It may be uncontrollable and hinder normal interactive day-to-day activities. Some examples include fear of bugs, dogs, heights, and injections. It's normal for many children and teens to experience some degree of these phobias, but it can get out of hand, causing the individual to avoid common, everyday situations to ensure that they will be safe.

Obsessive compulsive disorder causes compulsions and ticks to develop so that a person can ease the anxiety that they feel in everyday situations that frighten them or make them feel uncomfortable. A flood of unwanted images or obsessions leads them to engage in compulsions in an attempt to relieve some of the discomfort, including repeated hand washing, mental and physical ticks, and consistent routines.

Body focused repetitive behaviors is a disorder that encompasses many common disorders such as hair pulling, skin picking, and a variety of other habitual behaviors like cheek biting, lip biting, or nail biting. Noticeable "battle scars" develop from these behaviors, which serve as a method of coping with excessive anxiety. There is a significant disruption in routine life and can lead to even more stress due to the harm being caused to an individual's appearance.

Statistics

Per the ADAA and National Institute of Mental Health ("Anxiety Disorders", 2016),

- Forty million Americans over the age 18 and 10% of teenagers are affected by anxiety.

- Two-thirds of the individuals who experience an anxiety disorder do not undergo treatment.

- Individuals with an anxiety disorder are six times as likely to be hospitalized for a mental disorder.

- 36% of people with social anxiety disorder go untreated for ten years before finally seeking help.

Types of treatment

Anxiety can be treated if the problem is pinpointed early enough and the individual undergoes treatment. Especially during high school, it can be easy to brush aside the problem of anxiety or stress and label it as a "passing phase," but this can aggravate the condition and make it even more difficult to deal with it.

Generally, a physician can diagnose a patient when there are ongoing symptoms that last for more than six months. Although this requires monitoring for symptoms such as restlessness, excessive nervousness about anything and everything, and fidgeting, the physician can begin to create a plan inclusive of therapy and medication. While medication focuses on chemical imbalances and mental triggers, therapy allows for an outlet for the patient and their anxieties and helps the therapist better comprehend how to treat the individual.

The therapy could include the following methods:

- Cognitive-behavioral therapy focuses on thoughts and feelings that cause anxiety and encourage healthier thinking through various coping methods.

- Biofeedback measures the body's response to anxiety through sensors and helps the physician better identify how an individual responds to changing stress levels.

- Stress management offers relaxation and breathing exercises such as yoga, meditation, acupuncture, tai chi, Qigong, and massages.

- Therapeutic programs that are specifically geared toward calming and managing anxiety and other mental issues can be therapeutic ("What are anxiety," n.d.).

TIPS FOR TEENS

Tip #1: Try to stay positive

It's quite a feat to calm down when you're having a panic attack or stressing about a situation or experience, but learn to think positively. In an anxious situation, talk out loud to yourself as if you're speaking to a friend and reason with yourself. Find rational explanations for your feelings and think about all the ways an experience could go well. If you're freaking out about an exam or an audition, give yourself a pep talk and think about successes rather than failure. Give yourself a different perspective.

Your feelings about a situation or individual may be intensified in the moment. Focus on the bigger picture and try to realize perspective: will this matter a year from now? Time moves on; this current experience will pass.

Tip #2: Find outlets

Maybe it's running; maybe it's a breathing exercise; maybe it's meditating, but whatever it may be, find a way to regulate anxiety. When I'm stressed out, I'll go for a jog at night while listening to my favorite music playlist and watching the sparkling city lights out in front of me. I know friends who have a GIF on their phone that calms them down when they look at it. Whatever it is, engage in an activity that calms you down. Painting, singing, acting, sports, or just lying in bed listening to music are all activities with potential to help you deal with anxiety.

Tip #3: Keep a trinket

I like having a rock in my pocket that I turn over in my hand whenever I'm stressed out. Feeling the cold slick of it against my skin is usually enough to pull me back to reality and is an inconspicuous way of creating a rhythm that centers me.

Find an object that means something to you and keep it close by so that in the event that you experience anxiety, you can use it to calm yourself down. My rock even has the word "happy" etched into it.

Tip #4: Talk to someone you trust

Having someone who will listen to you, especially when you're suffering from anxiety, is important. Anxiety disorders can cause irrationality, so explaining how you're feeling to a third party provides outside perspective. Although you may not agree with everything that person may say regarding the subject, they'll be able to offer a different viewpoint that may be just enough to change your thought process.

In addition, a confidant can get you out of embarrassing situations when anxiety sets in. Especially at high school, where almost everyone is judgmental, it's important to find a solitary place to recuperate from anxiety and surround yourself with people who only want the best for you.

Tip #5: Take a break from technology

Although technology can be very beneficial, it also causes anxiety. One picture or phrase on social media can trigger various emotions and aggravate anxiety. Step away from your phone and laptop and try to relieve your stress before you delve back into the world of media and electronic interactions.

Tip #6: Get help

Don't be afraid to seek help. Anxiety disorders are very common, and talking about anxiety with an adult or a trained professional will placate the apprehension you're feeling. You'll be able to lead a productive, satisfying life without fear of breaking down.

TIPS FOR PARENTS

Tip #1: Don't invalidate

If your teenager is experiencing anxiety, don't brush it away and pretend it's irrelevant. Explore the problem and ask them to talk about it. Sometimes, it's hard to tell whether a teen is just having a bad day, or if they have a disorder. Watch out for reoccurring symptoms and mark how long symptoms last. Your teen is probably going through a lot, and having someone tell him or her that it's "just a phase" may prompt feelings of worthlessness that can exacerbate the problem.

Tip #2: Positive reinforcement

Rather than negating emotions, compliment your teenager at random times to build up self-esteem. Lack in self-confidence worsens anxiety, so by utilizing "hypodermic affection" (genuine appreciation), you might be able to offset some of the stress they're experiencing.

Tip #3: Explore therapy

Your teenager may be completely opposed to this, but it's important to get help when it's necessary. Explore therapy options and see what works best. At the end of the day, you may have to take the lead on this because your teen might not acknowledge what's really going on.

"This too shall pass."

We've all heard the phrase. Some say that it originates from the following Persian fable:

Once upon a time, a sultan ruled over the Red Sea and the land surrounding it. During times of prosperity and wealth, this sultan was elated and proud, but the instant any complications arose, his thoughts became anxious and cumbersome, and he was unable to pull himself out of the depths of discouragement that seemed to overwhelm him. In order to deal with the problem, he sought out the wise Solomon, who explained the erratic behavior of the king and the process through which to deal with how he felt. The sultan was asked to return a month later, and when he did, Solomon handed him a box. Inside it was a ring with the Hebrew phrase "Gam zeh ya'avor" inscribed into it.

What does that mean? "This too shall pass."

And as simple as it is, it holds so much truth. What you're worried about, what you're stressing about, will eventually fade. Everything is going to turn out the way it is supposed to. It always does. Focus on one thing at a time and work through it slowly. It's easy to get ahead of yourself when you feel stressed. Thoughts can get away from you. It took reality checks and breathing reminders to learn how to tame my anxiety when AP classes got to be too much and drama was enveloping my mind. But after all of this, after learning how to juggle my life and balance the world around me, I've only gotten stronger.

So fight it.

Fight the anxiety.

Fight the dread.

Because I know you can do it. You're strong too.

Everything is going to be okay. All is well.

This too shall pass.

3

Bullying

"OW!"

"Sorry," I sighed, drawing my hand back from his face. He looked at me with fury still dancing in his eyes, blood dripping from his lips.

"I can't freaking believe this," he said and laughed, but no lightheartedness danced in the echo of the laugh. This was not a pleasurable laugh; it was one flooded with indignation and ignominy. It was a laugh soaked with revenge that made me fear for whoever had messed with him.

"What even happened?" I asked, grabbing his arm in a feeble attempt to pull him to the table, but he wouldn't budge, not even flexing a muscle as he resisted me. The eerie red that had stained his white shirt flourished into a crimson brown flower, and his grass-covered club soccer shorts rippled in the wind, catapulting tiny pieces of turf toward me. He was a statue, an ornate statue knocked off his perch and shattered into tiny scarred pieces under the university lights that bore into his back.

Bypassing my question, he growled into his palms, seemingly shaking the world around him.

I nearly screamed in exasperation. "Chance, if you don't tell me what happened, I can't help you. We were watching you during the game, and you looked fine."

He muttered to himself, looking straight past me with a glazed expression.

Finally, I broke the tension that threatened to crush me. "Okay. Fine. We don't have to talk. At least let me fix you before anyone else sees you."

He nodded once before I left to go into the girl's restroom by the field to get a wet towel to clean the blood on his face. I applied the towel to his face, dabbing gently on the cuts that littered his lips, interrupted only by his occasional grunts of agony.

"Holy shit," he yelped, arm darting out to clutch my wrist before I continued. "Just give me one second," he whimpered, as he turned his face to the side.

As if oblivious to his tears that had just materialized in a misty sheen, I whirled around, rustling through the makeup bag I had brought with me to find the perfect concealer. With a tender hand, I smeared the beige cream in streaks across his eyes, blending it into the blue that now shadowed his features.

"That'll do," I said and packed up the products and flung open the door without even bothering to look back. As the initial shock had worn off, the only emotion that engulfed my heart was rage.

"Sameep, wait!" Chance called out from behind me, awkwardly hobbling up as he gritted his teeth in pain.

The corners of his mouth perked up until he winced with discomfort, all hints of amusement fading. "They're just jealous, okay? It's fine. It really doesn't matter. They do this all the time."

I stared.

"Okay fine. Nick and Isaac," he said; his eyes fluttered shut almost instantly in regret, but I had gotten my answer. I sprinted away before he had even finished his words, and the world around me passed in a blurry stream.

The parking lot. That was where I stood with my friend, waiting for them to appear.

"Good game, dude," I heard his voice approaching, the one that'd I heard so often catcalling the girls that played soccer with him. He emerged, a sweaty mop of brown hair that fell into his dim blue eyes.

With a calculated swing, he scooped up his bag, nearly bumping into me. "What're you doing here? This isn't your school." Grabbing my neck, he pulled my ear close to his mouth. "But if you were looking for me, I'll put you down on my 'To Do' list." Nick pulled away and smirked as I shivered in repulse.

It was one thing to defend myself against bullies, but when bullies targeted the people I cared about, there was no stopping me. Courage pumped through my blood and adrenaline blurred my vision, as I carried myself with as much bravery I could muster. This was no longer a question about my safety. It was a question of my best friend's safety, which was something I would never stop fighting to ensure.

"Who the hell do you think you are, huh?" I demanded and slapped my palms onto his chest, pushing him away from me with all of my might. "News flash, buddy: You aren't a starter because you aren't as good as you think. Beating up your teammates won't do anything to change that."

Cuffing my wrists with his fingers, he peeled me away from him and shoved my elbows backward. I struggled to free myself from his claws, but all I could do was lean back as he wheezed in my face. "So this is about Chance, huh? Cute that he sends little female warriors to defend him. He shouldn't be on the club soccer team in the first place. Indians belong in math camps, not on the soccer field. He deserves whatever's coming for him."

Out of the corner of my eye, I spotted Isaac warily observing the situation at hand to determine if Nick needed his help. He didn't.

With all the malice and contempt she could muster, my friend slid up to him and whispered, "You're a sad human being. You want to know why? Because you bully the people you want to be."

Before Nick could reply, I wrenched my arms free, and we sprinted away.

We tend to ignore bullying when it's done in slight until there's an occurrence that forces us to turn our heads and acknowledge the reality. We need to stop allowing deliberate "accidents" and intentional "mistakes" to go unnoticed. Despite the increased amount of media attention on bullying and awareness of bullying, much goes on behind the scenes of every high school that should be addressed. Whether it's a couple of words thrown or two fists, bullying is still bullying, and it needs to be treated as such.

Victims of bullying are at risk for extremely low self-esteem, and this can pave the way for various mental disorders and even suicide. A study by Yale University reports that bully victims are between two and nine times more likely to consider suicide than nonvictims (Peart, 2008). As a result, many schools are making sure to address harassment as a topic. However, that doesn't deter bullies from taking action underhandedly or simply outside of school grounds.

Girls, in particular, find ways to bully one another in covert ways. One of my friends was lured into a bathroom by girls in her school that she considered her friends. They would pout and play with her hair, widening their eyes as they whispered, "If only you put your hair down. It looks so much better like this, huh?" Then they would make her count to ten in a game of hide and seek and abandon her in the bathroom, cackling as they ran away from her with malice and contempt. One thing's for sure: It's been five years since that incident, and she still gets nervous sometimes about putting her hair up.

Although bullying happens often, it shouldn't be a norm. There is a distinction between "common" and "normal." Bullying may be common and occur often, but that doesn't mean it should be considered a normal aspect of the teen years. There are often detrimental effects to bullying that carry over into adulthood and leave emotional scars that take a lifetime to heal. Bullying doesn't stop after high school. It continues into the adult life.

Managers bully employees; parents bully other parents. It's important to learn how to deal with bullies at a young age, because verbal, physical, or cyber harassment can happen to anyone anytime.

Types of bullying

It's apparent that there isn't simply one form of bullying; it can happen in a variety of ways, and it's important to know all of them so you can make the distinction ("Teenage Bullying" n.d.).

Physical bullying is when things get, well, physical, and it's one of the most common types of violence. The bully may attempt to do physical harm or push around the victim in an attempt to subdue him or her or impose dominance.

Verbal bullying is often accompanied by physical bullying. This type of harassment is communicated through belittling words or phrases that attack the victim. The bully succeeds in making the victim feel isolated and humiliated.

Cyber bullying encompasses verbal bullying that occurs on the Internet. Cyber bullying is achieved in numerous ways, ranging anywhere from a couple of rude comments on an Instagram post to an entire Facebook page devoted to telling the victim to commit suicide. The pervasiveness of this type of bullying leaves the victim particularly devastated as they may feel there is nowhere to run, and their home is no longer enough.

Bullying statistics

Below are some of the statistics published ("The Link," 2016):

- Every year, 3.2 million students experience bullying.

- 90% of students between fourth and eighth grade have been victims.

- 59% of girls have cyber bullied and 41% of boys have cyber bullied.

- 61% of students said that abuse at home often leads to shootings at school.

- 67% of students believe schools are ineffective in addressing bullying, and one in four teachers don't see the harm in bullying.

- 10% of students drop out of school due to constant bullying.

- 87% of students say that school shootings are driven most frequently by a desire for revenge by a victim of bullying (75% of school shootings have been linked to bullying).

- Teens who spend extended periods of time on social media sites are 110% more likely to experience cyber bullying.

- 88% of teens who use social media say that they have seen students belittling other students online.

Effects of bullying

Bullying takes a major toll on a growing mind and can hinder a teen from achieving his or her full potential. Since bullies choose easy targets that stand out, victims may feel as if their "differences" are curses. Of course, this leads to a massive drop in self-esteem (see Chapter 14) and may prompt a downward spiral into anxiety and depression. It's critical that adults and peers get involved in the situation as soon as possible to deter the situation from becoming worse.

Long-term and short-term effects may result from bullying. Bruises and scars heal as time passes, but leave behind memories of the harassment. The good news is that emotional scars heal over time as well. Individuals are able to avoid the occasional hate comment with the support of friends and family and keep the harassment from causing long-term trauma.

Sometimes bullying isn't as simple to recover from as just healing over time. Emotional trauma can lead to fear, suffering, pain, anxiety, and depression. All of these impact how a victim approaches the future and can have detrimental effects on interactions with the others. Contained resentment over being unprotected and harassed can potentially grow into hatred that leads a victim to seek revenge and shut their friends and family out.

Signs of a victim

Although teenagers might be opposed to opening up about their harassment, there are some signs that indicate whether they are victims of bullying ("Effects of Bullying," n.d.).

A victim of bullying may:
- flinch when touched,
- have mood swings and stay in isolation,
- experience a sudden academic deterioration,
- avoid family and friends,
- bully others,
- have mental breakdowns and complain about headaches and stomachaches,
- be frequently picked on or teased in underhanded ways,
- have unexplained bruises and cuts,
- be unable to sleep,
- have items stolen or "lost" without any explanation,
- hover around their phone in a distressed manner,
- have a mental disorder,
- talk about running away or dying, and
- undergo diet changes.

TIPS FOR TEENAGERS

Becoming a target isn't in your control. What you do have the power to control is how you react to it. Proactively try to solve the issue at hand.

Tip #1: Ignore the bully

It can be hard to filter out everything a bully may say to or about you, but it's imperative to avoid the most fights as possible. Bullies typically use verbal attacks to incite a person to throw fists or just to bring you down. If you avoid listening, you'll be less likely to allow it to fuel any rash decisions. Avoid eye contact and keep moving. There are times when standing up to a bully is the smart thing to do. If you know you can't win the fight, there's no point in putting yourself in danger.

Tip #2: Stay true to yourself

You are not what they say you are. The words that roll off a bully's tongue do not define you. It's incredibly vital for you to understand that so that you can move on after being bullied. In an attempt to make themselves feel better, bullies will bring you down. It's easy to lose sight and fall into the trap of believing the names that you're being called. Make sure you know who you are and what you stand for.

The less you allow a bully's words to get to you, the less impact bullies will have, and the less fun they'll have. Not reacting is the most efficient way of stopping most bullying, especially cyber bullying.

Tip #3: Find outlets

Being bullied is stressful, and sometimes you have no choice but to put up with it for a little while until action can be taken. If you're in that position, find ways to outlet the anger and bitterness you might be feeling. Instead of screaming "Why me?" while sobbing into a pillow, channel stress into something proactive, such as painting, singing, dancing, playing sports, or just taking a walk. The more you channel negative emotions into external activities, the easier it will be to deal with bullies and brush off the hate.

Feeling powerless can make you feel alone, scared, and furious. Try to empower yourself. Learn self-defense through the art of Taekwondo or boxing. After one of my friends was bullied constantly in middle school, she took up Taekwondo to learn how to defend herself.

Tip #4: Rely on friends and family

Family is critical when going through rough patches. They may not always be able to protect you from bullies at school, but your family members will be able to keep you safe at home and sympathize with your pain. Family members will be able to find a solution to stop bullying in a way that might be beyond what you can do on your own. Share your anguish with your parents; they'll be able to help you the most. If you can't tell your parents, open up to a sibling who might be able to protect you.

Friends are always great to have in times like these. Bullies tend to avoid bullying large groups, so remaining in a herd of friends might deter a bully's attempt to harass you. If your friends are the ones bullying you, find new friends. These new people might not be the people you initially wanted as besties, but after some icebreakers, you'll find it easier to connect with them.

If you are kind to others, most people will be kind in return. Find shelter under the wings of the people who treat you right. It might take some searching, but I guarantee there's at least one peer that appreciates you.

Tip #5: Switch schools

No, this is not running away. There's no shame at all in switching schools if it protects your safety. This is not giving in or caving to a bully. This is simply avoiding unnecessary physical and emotional harm. Sometimes, absolutely nothing can be done to appease a bully, and in that case, the best route is to take the road out.

Tip #6: Never be a bystander

You've heard it a million times, yet still people don't seem to understand the concept about never being a bystander. I see it happening consistently. When we're reflecting on it, we tell ourselves that we'll stand up for anyone being bullied; we'll stand up for anyone being maliciously teased or tripped into lockers. But when it actually happens, we ignore it, thinking someone else will stop it. We ignore it, thinking that it's not a big deal. We ignore it because we don't want to be the next target.

Stand up for the people being bullied next time, and they'll stand up for you.

Tip #7: Get adult help

We all think we can handle it on our own. We think involving our parents won't do anything and will just get us into a worse situation. Parents make rash decisions, after all, right? But that's where you're wrong. I know it's risky, and I know you're scared, but your parents will be able to help. If you can't talk to your parents, talk to a teacher. Talk to a counselor. Even if it's small acts of aggression, tell an adult and keep providing updates as the situation progresses so that someone is by your side through all of it in case harsher actions are required.

You're not tattling; you're protecting yourself. Turn someone in without feeling ashamed if they're bullying you. They'll get what they deserve. The important thing is your safety.

TIPS FOR PARENTS

Watching your teenager get hurt in any way by anyone can be tough, especially since you're relatively helpless in the situation. Really try to set your child up for success by teaching them how to respond to bullying.

Tip #1: Educate beforehand

Prepare your teenager to face whatever's coming. It's likely they will be teased at some point, so really try to solidify their belief that being different is okay, and that they should ignore anyone who picks on them for it. By strengthening resolve from a young age, your child will be less likely to take to heart what a bully says or does.

Build an escape route to show your child the best way to flee from a bully situation. Warn them about the dangers of social media, and ask them to stay in a group as much as possible.

Tip #2: Know when it's not just roughhousing

Especially from a third person perspective, it can be difficult to determine whether teasing is just playing around or actual bullying. If some teasing is making you uncomfortable or you can see that it's making your teen uncomfortable, keep an eye on what's happening. Ask your child about it. It's better to catch bullying before it gets too out of hand.

Tip #3: Think through all options

After you find out about a bully, going straight to the principal's office might not always be the best idea. Weigh all options and figure out which would be the most effective. Perhaps it's talking to the bully's parents; maybe it's talking to the bully, or even the police. Collect the information relevant to the case such as screenshots of social media hate comments, videos, and pictures of the bullying and record the dates and places. The more documentation, the more compelling your case will be. Check in with the school's bullying policy and cyber-bullying policy to see what action can be taken. Cover all bases and educate yourself on all the options to figure out which one will result in the safety of your child. You can even file a Notice of Harassment and speak with the authorities if nothing is being done.

Occasionally, when there's not enough evidence to support a bullying claim, you might have to just wait for another situation to come up. If you don't feel comfortable doing that, have your teen switch schools.

Tip #4: Safety comes first

It's always beneficial for teenagers to build character and face tormenters confidently. However, sometimes, this idea can be dangerous. Don't write off any bullying as something that your teen should fix. Expecting your teen to resolve the occasional mutual fight with a friend or peer is not a problem. However, talking to a bully who is instigating a one-sided fight most likely isn't going to appease the situation. Safety is a higher priority than learning life skills.

Tip #5: Regular check-ins

If your teen is being bullied, it's unlikely that it'll stop after initial action is taken. Have regular check-ins about what's going on at school and keep the avenue of communication wide open. If the state of the situation has worsened, construct a new game plan and take the issue higher up the chain of authority at the school.

We've all watched, or at least heard about, movies where the cheerleaders and the jocks bully the nerds and the freaks. We've integrated it into our culture and admitted it as a norm, yet it shouldn't be. We shouldn't be condoning pretty popular girls with short skirts and tight shirts harassing geeks with oversized glasses just because of a social hierarchy.

The song goes: "Sticks and stones may break my bones. But words will never hurt me."

Yet some words can hurt and leave deep scars that go beyond physical wounds, that no amount of stitches or bandages will ever heal.

So avoid fitting into the box the bullies want you to fit in. You're not ugly. You're not worthless. You're not unwanted.

You are talented.

You are loved.

You are beautiful.

You are a perfect version of you, and no one can ever take that away from you.

4

Depression

I watched the numbers dance on the pages of my math homework. Flashes of my computer highlighted the words of my English essay with a misty glow. Rap music from my brother's room drifted into my room along with his voice, creating a cloud of happiness above my head. The scent of teriyaki sauce with fried vegetables wafted up to my nose, creating an exciting image of the dinner that my mom would soon set on the table. Finishing my math homework, I turned my head to my computer and the friends that awaited my chat responses. I grinned as they told me jokes and stories, and my mind became carefree and easy. I wanted this life. Little did I know that this life was about to turn into a nightmare.

Everyone slowly began to drag themselves away from their computers, saying a quick goodbye and leaving for dinner. Waiting for one of my only online friends to respond, I began to start on science. Small beeps of urgency emerged from my computer, but I ignored them, determined to finish at least one question of the physics that lay before me. As the beeps became consistently peskier, I turned to my computer. Seeing the sentence, my eyes stopped cold. My heart began to beat louder and louder along with the bass of the tune playing in my ears as I scanned the words before me. My breath came in shallow gasps, and I stopped my hands above the keyboard. Blood pounded in my ears and my fingers quivered as I brought them down to the keyboard, pressing each letter as if pushing too hard might cause the computer to explode. Words became blurry as I stared at the screen and phrases melted into one another, as I attempted to understand the impossible meaning of the sentences that remained scripted before me. My mother's voice blew into my room, loud and angry, yet I heard nothing but a simple faraway screech.

It couldn't be true. After all these weeks, how could I not have noticed? On the screen, two words popped out at me.

"Suicide. Midnight."

Head swimming, my eyes hot and stinging, I typed my simple response in the computer with slow urgency:

"Why?"

As my eyes skimmed over the words that she typed, my mind began to produce unanswerable questions. What could I do to help her? When had she planned this? What was the reason? Could she even be serious about ending her life?

Without even thinking over it, I ran to the phone with shaking hands after finding her home phone number. Eerie shadows danced across my wall behind me as I sprinted, the darkness swallowing the sun's brilliance and casting a sheet over the world. The phone clicked with the three rings before going straight to voicemail. She would not pick up.

The words she had typed to me were short but clear: "I'm sick of my life. I'm ending this pain at midnight." I held the phone, my knuckles white from gripping so tightly. I went back to my laptop and searched Google for a suicide hotline. Fingers stumbling over the keypad, I quickly dialed the number, and a lady picked up, answering with a kind, gentle voice. "What can we do for you?" She listened carefully, asking quick questions with a calm demeanor. Finally, she finished, told me not to worry, and hung up.

That night still remains one of the scariest events that have ever occurred in my life. I felt completely helpless, as if nothing I could ever say would be good enough to save a life. The most logical explanation that I could come up with that night was that my friend was depressed, and a few weeks later, she was diagnosed with exactly that. Depression is a sense of persistent hopelessness and an overwhelming desire to do nothing. Suddenly, activities that a person used to love are no longer appealing. For some, it changes the entire dynamic of their personality and deters them from moving forward with life.

Depression is one of the most common mental disorders in the United States. According to the Anxiety and Depression Association of America (ADAA), in 2014, around 15.7 million adults age 18 years or older in the United States experienced at least one major depressive episode in the last year, which represented 6.7% of all American adults. At any one time, 3–5% of adults suffer from depression. As many as two out of 100 young children and eight out of 100 teens may have serious depression ("Depression," 2016).

Every year, more and more people are diagnosed with depression. As new reports suggest, the cause might be extra stress from school or the media and technology that have taken over the world.

We've all been culprit of throwing out the phrase "I'm so depressed. I can't believe this actually happened to me." But that's really not what depression is. What you may have experienced is a sense of sadness or loss, feelings that everyone experiences. Depression is a constant feeling. It's not a phase. It's not temporary. It's not for attention. It's always there. Even on a good day, depression will creep in, expanding into empty corners of the mind, infecting the joy around a person until suddenly, the happiness no longer exists and dark thoughts cloud their mind.

Most of us know that depression can take many forms. One of the most common forms is bipolar disorder (or manic-depression) in which a person switches between intense feelings of happiness (euphoria) and sadness (depression). Depression brings a variety of emotions. It can make you feel guilty, ashamed, stressed, worthless, disgusting, dejected, and angry. It causes a person to feel irritable and restless or sluggish and grim and amplifies problems and emotions that accompany and result from those problems.

A person doesn't just "get over" depression. You don't wake up one morning, all better, as if it were nothing more than a bad dream. Depression is something that requires ongoing treatment and requires a painstaking battle every single day. When psychological therapy is not enough, medication is required to fix the imbalance of chemicals in the brain.

Depression statistics

Depression is often the driving force behind suicide; it multiplies the chances of a suicide attempt by twelve times. Approximately 20% of teens will experience depression before they reach adulthood. Between 10% and 15% of teenagers have some symptoms of depression ("Teen Depression," n.d.).

According to research done by the Centers for Disease Control and Prevention (CDC), the percentage of teenagers who have seriously contemplated suicide each year has risen to a shocking 20%, and almost one in twelve teenagers attempts suicide. The same percentage of teens who have contemplated suicide have experienced depression before they hit eighteen. Depression is such an underestimated issue, despite the fact that suicide is the third leading cause of death in teens (*Suicide: Facts,* 2015).

The following are some of the statistics published by the National Institute of Mental Health, Pysch Central, and the Anxiety and Depression Association of America ("Suicide," n.d.; Medlar, 2012; "Depression," 2016):

- The average age depression begins to appear is around the age of 14, or the beginning of high school.

- 80% of teens don't receive treatment for their depression. However, of those that do receive treatment, 70% will improve.

- Depression isn't defined by a singular root cause but rather a buildup of various issues and psychological and environmental risk factors.

- 50% of kids with depression will fall back into it at least once after passing adolescence.

Depression can often lead to a variety of other mental illnesses. As a way of coping, many teens with untreated and undiagnosed depression resort to substance abuse, leading to academic fallout, bullying, eating disorders, self-harm, social exclusion, and suicide.

Teenage girls are more than two times as susceptible to depression as teenage boys, although depression in teenage boys tends to be overlooked more often.

According to facts published by CDC, among students in grades nine through twelve in the United States during 2013 (Suicide: Facts, 2015):

- 7.0% of students seriously considered attempting suicide in the previous 12 months (22.4% of females and 11.6% of males).

- 13.6% of students made a plan about how they would attempt suicide in the previous 12 months (16.9% of females and 10.3% of males).

- 8.0% of students attempted suicide one or more times in the previous 12 months (10.6% of females and 5.4% of males).

- 2.7% of students made a suicide attempt that resulted in an injury, poisoning, or an overdose that required medical attention (3.6% of females and 1.8% of males).

Why do teenagers get depression?

Depression cannot be traced back to a root cause. It is not something as simple as food poisoning, where the source can be pinpointed to what could have been the exact reason. Teenagers' social lives and experiences play a large role in determining the way they feel about themselves, and in turn, their chances of developing depression. A variety of factors, including friends and family, contribute, but this mental illness can also be triggered by excessive scarring events. Depression is caused, as Jay Asher refers to it in the book *Thirteen Reasons Why*, by "the snowball effect." The events in life continue to add to a snowball until it grows to an impossible size and speeds up and crushes you with its weight. That is the breaking point. It's an interesting concept that accurately describes the truth of how our experiences shape our lives.

Although researchers still cannot implicitly identify and understand how depression unfolds, there are a few key features associated ("Teen Depression", n.d.). Some of them are:

Genetics is an aspect of the science behind depression that remains unclear, but it is evident that people with depression have chemical imbalances in their brains that affect how they perceive themselves and their surroundings. It has been discovered that 20% to 50% of teens who have been diagnosed with depression have family or relatives with a mental disorder or illness.

Hormones are a well known source of teenager mood fluctuations, causing a teen to be loving one second and aggressive the next. Hormone imbalances and mood swings can also aggravate depression. This is why adolescent girls are at a higher risk for depression; when going through puberty, hormones play a more active role in the development of a female's body, which can then adversely affect her brain.

Lifestyle choices, such as getting less than recommended amounts of sleep, not exercising, and eating unhealthy foods can increase the chances of depression. Healthy lifestyle choices are not only important for physical health but mental health as well.

Friendship circles consisting of people who have negative outlooks on life can often be detrimental and influence a teen's thoughts in a pessimistic way. For example, when associating with others who have depression, if they are constantly negative, you will be more inclined to be as well. It may be nice to have someone to relate to, but it can also be harmful to your recovery if they are not on the same page as you.

Family life that is chaotic or broken can lead to a sense of unhappiness and lack of fulfillment. Divorce, abuse, and certain methods of parenting can be particularly harmful. Family is supposed to be a safety net and support, and when that foundation is not there, it starts off a teenager's life in a precarious position.

Trauma from life events plays a particularly important role in depression. Sometimes, a teenager will endure the death of a loved one, a move, or parents' divorce that stays with them forever and prompts the advent of depression.

Neglect and feelings of being unloved, whether it is by family or friends, causes a teen to doubt their worth. This can then lead to a downward spiral into depression.

Sexual orientation plays a role in depression. Particularly recently, as more individuals have been coming out, there has been a lot of hate being directed toward the LGBTQ+ community, and some of the hatred can be reflected in a teenager's own self perception. They may wonder why they are being targeted and be hesitant about talking to their parents about their sexual orientation, leading to a feeling of seclusion and depression.

Chronic illnesses, such as eating disorders, anxiety disorders, ADHD, insomnia, and other disorders and mental illnesses also contribute to depression. Many times one triggers others, and sometimes, depression can be a side effect of the medications used to treat other disorders. Two-thirds of teens with depression also battle another mental illness or mood disorder.

Low self-esteem and low self-confidence are common precursors to depression. The more insecure an individual is, the more prone that person is to depression, as both can be prompted through a feeling of unworthiness and lack of self-love. For some girls, just one facial pimple can lead to a drop in self-esteem and an increase in the chances of developing depression.

Romance troubleshooting and arguments with a significant other can cause doubt of self-worth, which then traces back to a drop of self-esteem. Another possible scenario is unrequited love, which causes an individual to hold back true feelings and question self-worth.

Societal expectations, whether imposed by parents, friends, or simply society, dictate how teenagers live their lives. Inability to perform to that standard results in a feeling of failure, and teens attach that label to themselves. If they don't please the people around them, they feel as if they are good for nothing, and withdraw into seclusion. Teenagers are people pleasers and simply seek acceptance, so when they are shunned or reprimanded for not reaching a certain level of excellence, whether it is grades, popularity, or sports, they are even harsher on themselves.

Helplessness and feelings of lack of control happen. However, when these things happen repetitively, a teen may feel helpless and find other ways to feel in control like self-harm or dieting. This can prompt depression as well.

Signs of depression

It's probably easy to simply jump to the conclusion that a teen is being moody when he or she exhibits some of the telltale signs of depression. So the real question is how to discern whether it's just a phase or truly depression. Although it can be difficult to tell, it's important to catch depression as soon as possible to prevent future complications.

Most of these symptoms can be a cause of temporary anger or sadness, but usually if they persist for more than two weeks, you may be looking at a case of depression. The following are some symptom or signs taken from Mayo Clinic ("Teen Depression," 2016).

Behavioral symptoms include poor academic performance, substance abuse, hopelessness, school absences, jitters and restlessness, decreased motivation, loss of interest in once-loved activities, irritation, aggression, seclusion or isolation, withdrawal from friends and family, reckless and disruptive behavior, and the development of an argumentative nature.

Physical symptoms include insomnia (inability to sleep), disrupted sleep patterns, sudden changes in weight, appetite changes, neglected appearance or obsession over appearance, fatigue, vague aches and pains (such as headaches, stomach aches, and muscle aches), feebleness, and slowed body movement.

Mental symptoms include slowed thinking or speaking, hazy thinking, indecision, short-term memory loss, and a shortened attention span.

Emotional symptoms include fixation on failures, drop in self-esteem, feeling of worthlessness, feelings of hopelessness toward the future, lack of belief in abilities, sensitivity to dismissal or neglect, self-harm, suicidal action or thoughts, giving away belongings, outbursts of extreme emotion through yelling or crying, need for external validation and reassurance, emptiness, and a desire to flee from home.

It is important to realize that these symptoms are also exhibited in normal teenage behavior, so the only person who can truly diagnose a teenager with depression is a trained health professional like a psychiatrist.

So, is depression treatable?

Definitely! Luckily, there are plenty of steps that can be taken after a diagnosis. Through repetitive treatment and possible medication, it is entirely possible for your child to make a complete recovery. However, it is more than likely that there will be at least one relapse, and it is important for parents to be aware of this and watch for any recurring signs in order to prevent this mental illness from consuming their teen once again.

Therapy can involve one-on-one sessions, group sessions, or family counseling, depending on the severity. Although seeing a therapist is not always easy, it helps teens understand the importance of self-acceptance and comprehend what depression is, how it has affected them, and the best way to battle it. When teenagers don't receive treatment for their depression, it continues to grow and more often than not, they are not able to overcome it without aid. If left untreated, it can lead to life-threatening consequences such as suicide or other mental or emotional disorders. If a teenager refuses to be diagnosed or be put into therapy, a professional should be consulted about the way in which to proceed. Medication is also an integral part of the recovery process if therapy alone is not enough.

The following are some of the most common ways to treat depression, as suggested by Mental Health America and the Mayo Clinic ("Depression in Teens," n.d.; "Teen Depression," 2016):

Psychotherapy is treatment in which a therapist prompts the exploration of the why and how of the self-perception an individual may feel about himself or herself. It allows the person to explore events and feelings that are troubling and painful to recall and dives into the depths of personality in an attempt to unravel the truth and unearth some key factors that have played a role in the fostering of the depression. It focuses on the past and the present and various unconscious propellants for certain behavioral choices.

Cognitive-behavioral therapy is much more focused on the construction of coping methods and changing the structure of negative thoughts many teens may be experiencing. It is geared toward addressing the present and future and ways in which to alleviate suffering and pain by altering behavioral patterns and emotions.

Medication, such as anti-depressants can be prescribed along with therapy to help with chemical imbalances in the brain. The Food and Drug Administration specifically has approved two medications for depression, Fluoxetine (Prozac) and Escitalopram (Lexapro). Talk to your teen's doctor to weigh both the benefits and risks of these medicines and whether medication is the right option.

The first step to recovery is realizing that therapy is required and making an effort to contact a counselor. In a perfect world, those who are aware they have depression would seek out therapy immediately, but most teenagers are not ready to accept their situation and reach out for help. Support is a key factor to ensuring that a teenager feels prepared to face depression head on. In some cases, it may be necessary for a teen to stay in a care facility in a hospital or outside clinic if they have severe depression or are in danger of harming themselves or others.

The most effective methods to treatment encompass both therapy and medicine. It is not a wise idea to use alternative medicine to pursue recovery with your teen, as there may be unknown side effects. Do not replace conventional, proven medical techniques in favor of alternative medicine. Exercise, meditation, yoga, music, or art therapy can also serve as a viable form of therapy and may aid in dealing with depression.

TIPS FOR TEENAGERS

I think middle school and high school are the hardest years of a maturing teenager's life because it can be overwhelming. Obstacles are a normal part of life and feeling down or disheartened after facing an obstacle is also normal. However, if these emotions persist, it is important to be aware of the possible necessary steps to help yourself or to get help. It can be hard to seek help and admit you may have depression, but it will benefit you in the long run.

Tip #1: Be vulnerable

It's hard for many of us to be vulnerable with the people around us, especially when we feel as if society is watching our every move. It feels as if we must always be "posing for life's camera" and displaying our best side. However, it is important to have an outlet or someone who you can talk to about how you feel and ask for advice and guidance.

Many teens feel as if they cannot rely on or talk to their parents about these kinds of things, and I was definitely in the same boat. Having come from India a few decades ago, my parents were not able to grasp the concept of depression and other mental illnesses, since they had never been exposed to diagnoses of depression until arriving in America. Often times, I felt a separation from my parents due, not only to the generation gap, but also to the differences in environments between how they were raised and I was raised. Although it was difficult at first, our family continues to work hard to understand each other, and we have definitely become more aware and sympathetic toward one another. Sometimes, it just takes a little work to educate your parents about the facts, but ultimately it will help you.

If you still feel as if you are unable to connect with your parents, and fear their reactions, find another adult to rely on. This can be a teacher, a relative, or a sibling; it is important to have an older individual to assist you through obstacles and help you make the right decisions regarding how to approach the conversation of depression with friends and family. For me, my guardian angel was my brother, and to this day, he remains one of my most trusted advisors.

Although you may feel alone, you have to keep in mind that you are not. Many people in your life care about you and love you whether you realize it or not. It's easy to shut off and push people away, especially when you're scared of what they will say, but I am here to tell you that the only way you'll recover is to muster up the courage to voice your struggle, so you can get the proper treatment and start the road to recovery. Someone is out there who you can trust; you may have to dig a little deeper and look a little harder, but plenty of people are willing to listen and help. So even though they may not be able to save you from depression, they can at least help you deal with it. They aren't there to "fix you," but simply just to be there for you. Only you can fix yourself.

It can be hard to be vulnerable. I was never the kind of person to make it about me, and kept most of my insecurities and weaknesses to myself, always choosing to conceal them, pretend I was fine, and instead focus my attention on consoling my friends. I realize now how unhealthy that was, and that I should have had an adult I could confide in, because once I found one, I felt as if a weight had been lifted off my shoulders. Find someone you can unburden yourself to. We all need someone to help us lift our baggage.

Tip #2: Try not to wallow

It's easy to get caught up in our own misery and wallow in it, bathing in sadness and rinsing off with our anxieties. When you're depressed, you may shut people out and decide to avoid social interactions because it's too much effort to interact. Even getting out of bed can be difficult, so actually communicating with other human beings is a tall order. But the more secluded you are, the worse your symptoms of depression are likely to get. It is not a good idea to pretend to be happy. Remind yourself of the things you love to do and try to engage in those activities to build a sense of normality and bring some joy back, even if it's temporary. As you reengage with the world, you may feel better, even if that comes bit by bit.

Cut back on social media, the Internet, and other technology that makes you tired and sluggish, because more often than not, you're likely to be more easily aggravated after spending hours online. In addition, it is possible for you to stumble upon something that will be triggering for you, which will detract from the hard work that you may have been doing to recover.

Get support from your support system, which is one of the most crucial things during recovery. Avoid people who are judgmental and mock you for your mental illness. Instead, spend time with people who appreciate you for who you are and offer you reassurance and unconditional love. Our friends know us best and are experts at cheering us up.

Give back; helping others is frequently the best way to help yourself. Making others happy is a powerful anti-depressant and makes you feel as if you're making a difference, reminding you that your presence makes an impact in the world. It's similar to giving presents. I don't know about you, but I know I always like giving presents more than receiving them.

Get active again in activities that you used to love. Don't push yourself, but pick up that paint brush occasionally or write some music. Do some reading by the windowsill, or go shoot some basketballs. If you can't get into the groove again immediately, try not to get frustrated. Simply leave it, and try again later. There's no time limit for doing what you love.

Tip #3: Stay healthy

Healthy lifestyle choices are a must, especially when you're struggling with mental health issues and challenges. Almost everything you do that is healthy will boost your mood somehow, whether it's through an increase in confidence, body acceptance, or just the endorphin rush.

Eat healthy. That's right: no more midnight McDonalds or fast-food runs so you can drown your pain in fifteen cheeseburgers. The healthier you eat, the less sluggish and tired you'll feel, which is especially important when combating something like depression that already makes you want to lie in bed in the dark all day. Junk food might give you a quick high for an hour, but once that sugar rush passes, you'll crash and be even more tired than when you started. Make sure to eat a balanced diet and keep a lot of fruits, vegetables, and protein on hand.

Avoid Alcohol and Drugs. It's always a tempting option to use drugs and alcohol as an escape from the pain of depression, but once the fog passes, you'll be left where you started: empty, hungry, and miserable. Substance abuse aggravates depression immensely and can increase suicidal feelings. If you're addicted, seek help immediately. It's not worth it; getting high and drunk provides a false perception of reality and is incredibly detrimental to your health.

Exercise. Working out gives a rush of endorphins, which is essentially what powers a good mood and offers the same effect as drugs, alcohol, and other pleasure-inducing substances like chocolate. It's the science behind "a runner's high." So, get involved in sports, dance, or biking, or if that's not your speed, then go for daily walks and build on from there. It's guaranteed to help.

Tip #4: Get physical

I'm not talking about exercise this time, and I'm definitely not talking about aggression. What I'm referring to here are hugs. When you hug someone, oxytocin ("the love drug") is released, and it not only lowers blood pressure and stress, but also increases sense of belonging and increases social connections. So when appropriate, go in for a hug, and make it good! As long as it's a consensual hug, both parties will leave the hug just a little bit happier.

Tip #5: Never resort to self-harm or suicide

This is something very near and dear to me, as I've watched people self-harm, and I've lost a friend to suicide. Yes, self-harm releases endorphins and makes you feel temporarily relieved, but it's not the answer. When you feel the need to self-harm, take a pencil and go to your safe haven. Wherever that may be: outside the house, in the bathroom, on your bed, wherever. Play your favorite songs that make you relax and remind you of beautiful memories. Keep those memories close. Now write. Write about all the amazing things that have happened to you. Write about all the memories that make you smile, and about all the people who make you happy. Write until your hand cramps. Now look at this list and remember you could still have pages left of happy memories that you haven't written and books and books left to be written about the memories to come. Stay. Wait for those memories. Experience them so you can write about them one day.

TIPS FOR PARENTS

It can be hard to see your teenager going through something like depression. It can hurt you immensely to see your kid being despondent, and your teen doesn't realize how much it may affect you. Teenagers face a plethora of pressures and spend a lot of time trying to fit into the constraints of society, which can take a staggering emotional toll.

Making sure that your teen has a stable support system and early diagnosis is crucial to a successful recovery. Treatment for depression will teach your teen how to overcome and battle ongoing depression, and prevent relapse, some of which is already being taught in schools. Unlike many adults, teenagers don't have the means to seek help on their own, so it is crucial for you to recognize the symptoms of depression and get help for your teen when you think it's required.

Tip #1: Treat it

Early diagnosis is something that goes a long way in all medical procedures. Just like finding cancer early can be enough to save a patient's life, so can identifying depression. In order to avoid dealing with the truth, I've seen parents reject the idea of their kid "not being perfect." One of our family friends very evidently had a serious case of depression and tried to self-harm numerous times, and even threatened to kill herself. My family finally decided to take action and gathered a group of her friends so they could address the problem head on with her parents. Within minutes of entering the house and discussing this girl's mental illnesses with her parents, our help was rejected.

Her father said, "How dare you come into our home and accuse her of being depressed. We know her better than any of you. She is normal. She is not suicidal. Never come back here."

It took two years and one suicide attempt before her parents finally opened their eyes to the truth and put her into therapy.

Don't wait and hope that the symptoms of depression will fade because they will not. If you have an inkling that your teen is depressed, you should have an open discussion about what he/she may be going through and be ready to listen. Communication is a key.

Here are some tips for communicating readily with your teen:

Acknowledge that depression is real. I've heard one too many times that depression is just "made up for attention." Never invalidate your teen's problems, especially when it's something as serious as depression. Even if their concerns seem irrational and silly, make sure to be entirely supportive and encouraging to show them that you're going to be with them every step of the way. Attempting to explain why "things aren't that bad" or why "people have it worse so they shouldn't feel bad" will just marginalize their problems and make them feel as if you don't take them seriously. This will make them unlikely to open up again in the future.

Listen without lecturing and hold your questions until the end. Listen to what your teen has to say without judgment. Don't retaliate with snarky comments or anxious words. If you listen to your teen, your teen will listen to you. More than anything, teens just need someone to be there for them.

Trust your instinct about what your teen means when they say "everything is fine." Do not dismiss the issue if things don't seem fine. Teenagers are incredibly skilled at hiding their true emotions, so if you feel like they are not being open or honest with you, look into it further with a third party, such as their favorite teacher, counselor, or friend.

Your teenager will likely not be vulnerable on the first try, especially if you've never had a strong relationship. It is normal for them to try to shut you out and isolate themselves. Be persistent about asking them to express how they're feeling while expressing your concern, but remember to be gentle and respectful of your child's comfort level.

Tip #2: Encourage social connection

Depressed teenagers must maintain social contact with friends and continue to do activities that they enjoy. As a parent, it is your responsibility to ensure that they are given opportunities to socialize and reconnect with their surroundings.

Face-to-face interactions each day can do wonders for the comfort level of your teen and may make them feel as if they are not alone. Don't talk to them while you're talking on the phone. Rather, spend time focused only on your teen. If they do not want to talk, then opt for other bonding activities like bowling, board games, and word games.

Encourage your teen to be involved with sports, clubs, theater, music, and other activities, and offer some suggestions of your own that play to your teen's strengths.

Allow for extra social interaction. Let your teen hang out with friends and attend social gatherings, as long as drugs and alcohol are not a major concern. Sometimes, parents can only do so much, which is where friends come in handy. If you don't feel comfortable with your teen going out just yet, ask them to invite friends over for a sleepover or other gathering so that both you and your teen feel safer.

Tip #3: Keep them healthy

Physical health and mental health go hand in hand. Teenagers will often model themselves after what their family members do, and that includes eating and exercising habits. It is more important than ever to put healthy lifestyle choices in place when a family is going through something as taxing as a mental illness.

Exercise programs make a difference. Exercise can be through sports, a gym membership, or even simply walking the dog. Teens should be getting at least an hour of activity every day. If your teen has never been one to exercise, offer other alternatives like swimming, skateboarding, hiking, and biking. Try getting active with them to offer some motivation.

Nutrition is a very big issue in light of depression. I cannot stress enough the importance of getting the right nutrients. Since teens usually don't control their own meals, this responsibility falls frequently on the parents. If your teen is malnourished, they are more likely to develop mental and physical disabilities. Ensure that your teen is actually eating the balanced foods you provide and check how many servings of each food group they need to stay healthy.

Healthy friends are an asset to your teen's health, so make sure your teen's friends are healthy for them. If they are negative influences, start the conversation about how you feel uncomfortable with your teen's current friend group and explain why.

Screen time should be limited. Your teen might hate you a little bit for taking away their electronics, but in the end, it'll be beneficial for them. Excessive technology time can be harmful to maturing minds and can also cause them to become even more secluded.

Encourage sleep because teens need more sleep than adults. Although enforcing a "bed time" may anger your teen, as they'll feel like a child, it might initially be necessary to guarantee that they follow this procedure. Realistically, with school, even seven hours of sleep a night can be a stretch, but advocate for extra sleep whenever possible. Your teen will realize how rested they feel once they begin, and they'll start wanting to get more sleep without you even asking.

Tip #4: Know when to seek professional help

This step is often the hardest. It takes a lot of courage from everyone in the family to accept reality and find a therapist. Parents think that they can fix the problem with support and healthy choices, but it's usually not enough, and professionals are required.

Many options of therapists will exist. Get some feedback. Ask around to see if friends or family members have recommendations. My friend found her therapist through a family friend who worked at a Kaiser Hospital. Her doctor was able to point her in the direction of a very spunky therapist who she clicked with instantly. Weigh various options before you commit to any one treatment.

When a teen gets to offer input as to what treatment options they think would work the best for them or pick the therapist they prefer, they are more involved in the process of treatment, and it will set them up for success. Not every therapist is going to be "a perfect fit," so it's crucial that you find someone that your teenager connects with.

Another thing to point out is that there are risks to medications, so make sure to keep that in mind as you look into treatment plans. Anti-depressants can sometimes have an adverse effect and make depression worse, so have a discussion with your teen's doctor about the safest plan.

Therapy is not easy. As my school counselor often says, "It has to get worse before it can get better." It requires you to dig deep within yourself and revisit painful experiences that you've spent your entire life trying to forget. To say the least, I've gone through boxes and boxes of tissues and spent a lot of time at night rethinking my experiences. I can honestly say that although the road has been long, I've made some serious headway with my self-esteem issues.

It takes a lot to admit to yourself, let alone to others, your feelings. It can be scary sometimes to think about all the repercussions and all the things that might change from taking action to treat your depression. Even after treatment, people hide their stories and hide what they've been through in fear that others will view and judge them differently. If someone runs away because of your past, they don't deserve to be in your future. People will talk, spread rumors, and gossip because that is what human nature inclines them to do. Families will talk. Students will talk. Teachers will talk. But what you may not realize is that the support you will receive is going to be overwhelming, and treatment will do wonders for you, as long as you're open to it.

Treating depression is not a one-sided endeavor. Your therapist or counselor cannot do everything for you. It's going to take commitment from you and support from your family. But I believe that you are strong enough to push through it.

Treatment will be scary.

Treatment will be demanding.

Treatment will be frustrating.

Treatment will be challenging.

But in the end? Treatment will be rewarding.

So take those first few steps and get driving on that road to loving yourself. I think anyone has the power to overcome depression with the right environment, people, and therapy. So go out there and smile a little, compliment some people, and deal out some hugs.

You never know who's feeling the same exact thing as you are. For all you know, they might need that hug just as much as you do.

5

Discrimination

"I'm stuck between two worlds."

I heard these words from a boy from Europe at a leadership program I attended during the summer. My group huddled, gripping hands and sharing comforting gazes as we disclosed our struggles and fears at midnight in a small, cozy room. The boy who spoke seemed lighthearted and easygoing. He was our group's jokester. We never failed to turn around and see him talking to a new girl as he pretended to scope her out and decide whether she was worthy of his attention. Yet despite all of this, he was one of the sweetest, most genuine guys I've ever had the pleasure of meeting. Hearing him talk about his challenges in his home even with racism was an eye-opening experience.

"My father sacrificed everything to make enough money for me to get a good education. I go to a private school that's full of rich, white kids, and I live in a ghetto neighborhood full of poor black kids like me. My neighborhood calls me a 'sell-out,' and my school tells me to crawl back to the gutters in Nigeria. So what the hell do I do?" he said, and I watched the light-heartedness dim in his eyes, as the reality of his situation overtook him.

He was exiled from both of his identities simply because of the environments he was put into due to his skin color. The people with whom he identified ethnically shunned him because of his opportunities while those with whom he shared the same opportunities shunned him because he was black. It left him in a heart-wrenching battle that made him question where he belonged. What was his identity?

Here in America, we pride ourselves on being a "melting pot of cultures" that welcomes a plethora of ethnicities and races. But discrimination happens here much more often than we think or want to think. Racial and ethnic stereotypes play a big role in the prejudice that some of us face.

Typically, races are categorized as follows: "American Indian or Alaska Native," "Asian," "Black or African American," "Native Hawaiian or Other Pacific Islander," and "White." Race pertains to color and physical features, while ethnicity refers to subgroups based on cultural factors. For example, someone who identifies racially as white may be German in ethnicity. The lines between these two have blurred over the years, yet there remains a very big distinction when examined carefully.

Many immigrants and minority groups stay grouped together after making the journey to America. Many people living in Silicon Valley in California call Fremont city, a city in East Bay, as "Fremonistan" due to the mass majority of Indians and Pakistanis who live here. It's often easier for these minorities to live together as it develops a sense of understanding among each family and provides a nostalgic reminder of safety and home. "Ghettos" like these were established in the later part of the nineteenth century, such as the Jewish community on the Lower East Side in New York. These types of communities can prompt the development of certain stereotypes.

Stereotypes play a particularly dominant role in schools. Blonde Caucasians are classified as "airheads." Asians are assumed to excel in mathematics and science. African Americans are known as sports stars with musical abilities. Even when students of these specific races don't fit the idea of their stereotype, the classification still persists.

History and prior experiences can also lead to false generalizations. I went to a seminar hosted by a man named James, who taught me that we are all inherently a little bit racist. He explained to his audience how, when walking on the streets of China, he was warned that natives often attempted to pickpocket foreigners. Yet when he passed by a harmless African American man, he instinctively held his wallet tighter in his jacket. He was cautioned that it was the Chinese who would attempt to rob him, yet he only paid heed when a black man strolled past.

All of us are racist, maybe in ways that we don't even know. You might see a robbery on the news and unconsciously be unsurprised when the culprit is black. Simple innuendos like that fuel the racism and discrimination in our country.

In *Their Eyes Were Watching God*, the author, Zora Neale Hurston, writes about an interesting idea regarding race. The main character, Jamie, grows up surrounded by white children, and having never seen a picture of herself or looked in a mirror she is unaware that her skin color differs in the sense that it is darker. The realization that she is different hits her when she is six as she looks at a picture of the family. Jamie had never prior identified herself by the color of her skin, but rather the community she grew up, which in this case, was a Caucasian family.

Children are very easily swayed and shaped by the influential adults in their lives. Parents usually play the biggest role in their perception of the world and the people around them. Racial attitudes are typically passed down from generation to generation. If your parents have had negative interactions with a certain race, it is likely you will also adopt a similar attitude.

It's in our nature to want to affiliate with those who are similar to us, as shown through preschoolers. Even at such a young age, children notice racial differences and group themselves according to color cliques. Racism takes on a lot of forms. It can be in direct ways like name-calling, slandering, or exclusion, but "micro-aggressions" are much more common in today's era. Micro-aggressions are a form of hostility that may not be recognized at first, but over time, especially for people of color, become painful and offensive to hear. Acts such as asking a black woman if her hair is real or associating a Muslim with terrorist attacks are examples of forms of micro-aggression. Often unintentional, these types of actions and words further perpetuate stereotypes and build a wall of hatred between people.

Discrimination has plagued the world for a long time. Everywhere you look, and in every time period, there are instances of discrimination, whether it is because of race, skin color, or economic situations. The powerful often mistreat the powerless, which is exemplified throughout history.

In Mesoamerica, when Spanish conquistadors came, the indigenous people there, such as the Aztecs, were slaughtered. Once the slave trade started, Africans were automatically regarded as inferior. After the 9/11 attacks, people have been more wary of Muslims than ever, and Middle Easterners have an increased probability of being pulled over for a security check at airports.

Stereotypes are enforced even further through media. In TV shows, Indians are portrayed as the geeky dorks with high IQs, such as Ranjeet in *Phineas and Ferb* and Raj in *The Big Bang Theory*. This can be particularly harmful in schools as students are the audience for these shows. Some studies have shown that between 15% and 20% of students in the United States are frequently bullied (Cohn & Canter, 2003). This statistic will continue to rise if there is ongoing ignorance about racism. When talking about discrimination, it's important to recognize the difference between the concepts of racism, bigotry, and prejudice. Although used interchangeably, it can be useful to be aware of what defines each word.

"Racism" means a system of oppression as a result of a difference in skin color, race, or ethnicity.

"Bigotry" means hatred of an entire group. It is an assumption that your group is superior and the rest are inferior, based off of categories including race, religion, and sexual orientation. An example of this is the Holocaust.

"Prejudice" means a stereotype or idea that you automatically associate with a person or a group of people due to prior knowledge. Prejudice is similar to bigotry in the sense that it is not limited to race, but differs in the fact that while bigotry is negative, prejudice can be negative or positive.

"Reverse racism" means an instance of a member of a minority group mistreating a member of a majority group, which actually falls into the category "bigotry" or "prejudice" rather than "racism."

Too often, racist comments are allowed to slide by. Ignoring the problem of discrimination won't make it go away, which is a message that still needs broadcasting to a wider audience.

Race and ethnicity statistics

Below are some of the statistics published related to racial discrimination ("11 Facts," n.d.):

- African Americans comprise only 13% of the United States population and 14% of the monthly drug users, but are 37% of the people arrested for drug-related offenses in America.

- Studies show that police are more likely to pull over and frisk blacks or Latinos than whites. In New York City, 80% of the stops made were blacks and Latinos, and 85% of those people were frisked, compared to a mere 8% of white people stopped.

- In 2010, the US Sentencing Commission reported that African Americans receive 10% longer sentences than whites through the federal system for the same crimes.

- In 2009 it was reported that African Americans are 21% more likely than whites to receive mandatory minimum sentences and 20% more likely to be sentenced to prison than white drug defendants.

- In a 2009 report, two-thirds of the criminals receiving life sentences were nonwhites.

- African Americans make up 57% of the people in state prisons for drug offenses.

- The US Bureau of Justice Statistics concluded that an African-American male born in 2001 has a 32% chance of going to jail in his lifetime, while a Latino male has a 17% chance, and a white male only has a 6% chance.

- In 2012, 51% of Americans expressed anti-black sentiments in a poll, a 3% increase from 2008. A survey in 2011 revealed that 52% of non-Hispanic whites expressed anti-Hispanic attitudes.

- Reports show that nearly 50% of Americans under 18 are minorities. The trend projects a reversal in the population where by 2030, the majority of people younger than 18 will be of color, and by 2042 nonwhites will be the majority of the United States population.

A survey was done involving over 97,000 public schools and 49 million students by the United States Department of Education ("Expansive Survey," 2014). Some of the most important discoveries are listed below. In the 2011–2012 school year:

- Black students were expelled three times as often as white students.

- Although they only made up 18% of the country's student enrollment, they made up 48% of those with multiple suspensions.

- Black girls were suspended at higher rates than the rest of the girls and the majority of the boys.

- American Indian and Native-Alaskan students made up 3% of expulsions, despite the fact that they only constitute 1% of the student population.

- Although constituting 40% of enrollment at schools with gifted programs, black and Latino students only accounted for 26% of students who were actually accepted.

- Black students were three times as likely and Latino students were twice as likely to attend schools with teachers who did not meet all the license requirements to teach.

Race related stress

Racism can happen a lot more behind the scenes than we might think. However, the dangers with racism don't just stop within teenagers' social or economic lives. Racism damages physical and psychological health. Being discriminated against is stressful, and the emotions that result from being victimized by racist treatment are hard to manage. Some of the possible effects may be depression, anxiety, frustration, low self-esteem, and other health problems.

To deal with these reactions and symptoms, many teens may shut out their family and friends, resort to substance abuse, over or under eat, or change their physical appearance. When people think of racism, they often fail to recognize that racism plays a psychological role in the lives of teenagers. Minority students are bullied, police brutality and profiling exist, and psychological damage occurs on a wide spread scale. Experiencing racism changes the way teenagers perceive and interact with the world. They may become withdrawn or avoid making associations with teens of other races in sports, clubs, and classroom discussions, which may hinder them from moving forward and fulfilling their potential.

Another interesting concept is the "stereotype threat," which is best explained as someone's fear of reaffirming certain racial or ethnic stereotypes through actions. For example, an Asian might fear excelling in a certain subject in school to avoid being grouped as a nerd.

TIPS FOR TEENS

Without realizing it, a teenager might use an offensive racial slur in a joking manner. In unintentional situations like that, it can be hard to step up and point out another's mistake. People might call out the person identifying the racial slur, say they are no fun or that they "take things so seriously."

However, if you want to make a difference and decrease others' ignorance, it's important to stand up against racism in every instance. It's important to make a differentiation between racist people and racist actions. Racist people are fueled by hatred and commit racist actions with intention and purpose. They are aware of their prejudice and bigotry and believe firmly in the justification of their actions. More often than not, racists will not change and the time you spend attempting to educate them on their error will be wasted on deaf ears. Racist actions, particularly in teens, might be a byproduct of their home environment and can be corrected when brought to his/her attention (*Coping With*, n.d.; Hendriksen, n.d.).

Tip #1: Walk away

There's absolutely no shame in turning your back on individuals who are being racist. If you don't have the mental capacity in that moment to put up with them, then you have no obligation to talk to them. It is not your responsibility to correct their false views or educate them simply because you're being targeted. If what someone says gets to you, tell that person to back off, and then do your best to extract yourself from the situation.

Tip #2: Be patient

You are going to run into a lot of ignorant people in your life. Accept that you are going to encounter uneducated teens and adults and do your best to brush off racist comments, especially if the comments don't seem intended to be malicious. Allow the person some leeway and explain why their statement was incorrect.

I remember walking into a store in the mall, and being asked what race I was as I checked out a shirt at the counter. "Indian," I stated, smiling at the two girls working there, one Asian and the other Caucasian.

"Oh, that's so cool! There are like tribes right?" the Asian drawled back, eyes wide as she folded clothes over by the rack.

I sighed slightly as I responded, "No, not American Indian. I mean, like, from the subcontinent of India."

"Oh… are you sure?" the Caucasian worker there piped up.

It took a lot of patience for me to step past their complete lack of awareness, but I did it with a smile on my face. Something like that was such a simple mistake, yet it induced this bitter feeling of disappointment about their lack of information. Sometimes, the best thing you can do for yourself is to stay calm, accept that people will be ignorant, and do your best to correct their misinformation whenever possible.

Tip #3: Respond intelligently

When someone says or does something racist, don't be aggressively defensive. When people respond to an attack with an attack, a war breaks out. Don't point your finger at that person with the statement "you are racist." The better option is to point out that the phrase itself is racist. Change the conversation so it's not about each individual but rather about what's being said. Don't act with rage or be defensive. Just explain why what has been said is racist.

Replying with an intelligent response will foster a sense of respect in the person you're talking to and empower you to stand up for what you believe in more often. Keep it casual and lighthearted if the words are coming from a place of ignorance. Throw out a "hey, dude, that wasn't cool. Lay off next time, okay?" and see how they react. It might take just one person pointing out the racism behind certain words or actions for perpetrators to realize the underlying message behind those words or actions.

Humor is also a great way to let someone know that they've crossed a line with something. A few people in school or in parties throw out the racist "n-word" in a way that can often be offensive. I've found that the only way to get through to them is to push them playfully, make a face, and say "hey c'mon that's rude." Although it took some time, they've definitely cut back on using it.

Encourage dialogue and talk about it maturely, rather than making it a hostile exchange.

Tip #4: Stand up

Staying in the shadows as a bystander rather than getting involved and exposing yourself is safer, but that choice leaves your peers unprotected. If we keep saying "someone else will step up," then we won't learn to step forward and call out unfairness or injustice. Be the one to back up a fellow classmate. There's no need to get physical or use rude comments to respond to racism. Just ensure that the racism stops and that the perpetrator is aware of the mistake.

Opposing a bully might inspire someone else to do the same. In the moment, standing up for yourself or someone else will be difficult, but you'll feel good about advocating for what you believe, for love and acceptance, rather than exclusion.

If teachers are making inappropriate comments, ask a parent to talk to them. They may not realize that they have made an insensitive remark, so explaining why it is offensive can go a long way in improving the classroom environment. Communicating in a direct and rational fashion will aid in making this conversation proceed as smoothly as possible.

Be an ally. If you're in the majority, empower those who are in the minority. Distribute love and protect each other. Students of color can be allies to white students and to each other, and vice versa. If we want to beat racism, we have to stand as a united front.

Tip #5: Join clubs

Finding other people in your same situation may make you feel less alone and allow you to feel heard. Likely other minority students at your school feel the same way as you. A club may give you the perfect outlet to discuss your experiences with racism and how they have affected you. It may also help you create a group identity and ensure that you are integrated into the school's culture.

Tip #6: Develop a cultural identity

Putting up with discrimination can be incredibly traumatizing and take an emotional toll. Everyone has been or knows someone who has been a victim of racism so take solace in family members and share your burden with them. I spent a lot of time running away from my identity because my closest friends were not of my race. I began to suffer from internalized racism, an attitude of racism toward myself and my ethnic group. I got colored contacts, stayed indoors to lighten my skin, and resisted learning anything related to Indian culture. It wasn't until I began to accept myself that I began to accept my cultural identity. Finding myself was important, and the more I accepted my ethnicity and my background, the easier it was to brush past racist comments without letting them get inside my head and affect me on a deeper level. Accepting my cultural inheritance aided in combating the stress I felt and the bigotry that was directed my way.

Celebrate your culture and its themes. Every race is beautiful.

Tip #7: Report it

When a situation has gotten out of hand, it's important to approach an adult, your parents, a teacher, an authority at school, or a police officer, people who are resources of protection. You cannot and should not try to "fix" every uneducated person. If you're making things worse, it's necessary to talk to a third party and inform them about what's happening. This is the only way to prevent racism and provide immediate safety for the victim.

Tip #8: Learn about other cultures

Read about different ethnicities and races. Be careful not to generalize populations and accidently stereotype. It's important to try to get the correct foundation of background information to build knowledge of other cultures and cultural identity.

Befriend minority students and ask them questions about their culture. You'll be surprised what you can learn. You might find out about some crazy traditions or festivals and be invited to attend one with the new friend that you made. Your perception of the world might change based on what you learn. If someone tells you about an unusual custom, don't reject it. Each culture is unique, and a norm of your culture may be considered unusual by others.

It's natural to want to gravitate toward people who are similar to you, but you'll never know who or what you're missing out on if you don't step out of your comfort zone. You might discover a new favorite food or a new favorite activity. Before meeting students from China, I had never realized how delicious Calpis was. I'd always avoided it because of its name, but after some encouragement from my Chinese friends, I took that first sip. Now I can't stop drinking it. Sounds like a miniscule change, but I think it's a perfect example.

TIPS FOR TEACHERS AND SCHOOLS

Sculpting a safe environment in schools is especially essential in making students aware of racism and stopping racist speech and actions in the current generation.

Tip #1: Establish strict guidelines

Establishing rules and regulations about how students are required to treat each other may prevent racism from getting out of hand. In order to combat racism, raise the stakes. This will deter bullies from proceeding with their abuse whether because of a longer suspension or even expulsion. The Race Relations Amendment Act states that all schools must work toward eradicating racial discrimination and ensuring equal opportunities for all races. Be sure to take quick disciplinary action against anyone who is being intolerant toward other students because of race, gender, or sexual orientation. Being lenient will only convey to students that it is okay to be racist.

Tip #2: Have the conversation

Some teachers are uncomfortable talking about race since it can develop into a heated dialogue and debate and treat it as a nonexistent issue. However, it's necessary to face these problems head on and ask questions to invoke thoughtful insight. Talking about discrimination helps teens understand peers and prompts more tolerance.

Encourage students to talk about their experiences and backgrounds and open up the floor for questions that might not otherwise be asked. Throw the hard questions at them. Why does racism develop in the first place? What is the first time they experienced racism? How has their ethnicity changed the way they view identity? Build in segments about racism into curriculums, especially in history and English classes.

Tip #3: Celebrate diversity

A multicultural day will encourage students to open up and talk about their cultures. At my lower school, we celebrated a variety of holidays, from the typical Saint Patrick's Day to Chinese New Year to Indian events like Diwali. It prompted students to embrace different cultures from a young age and even come dressed in cultural clothing. Along the same lines, it's important to discuss events all over the world that have been particularly impactful. We discuss the 9/11 attacks in schools, but we should also discuss events like the Syrian refugee crisis and the terrorist attacks in Paris.

One of my high school history teachers was especially adamant about exploring current events and the problems that plague the world. Even though the class was about past world history, he made sure that we understood what was going on in the present. He would push off lesson plans just so we could express our views on the latest shooting or the latest global crisis, making all of us a little bit more aware. Some teachers may say that this hinders learning and that there isn't enough time, since there's a very formulaic pattern that must be followed to get through the curriculum, but I can confidently say that no harm was done in our class. If anything, we walked away from that class with high AP scores and an even higher understanding of the world around us.

TIPS FOR PARENTS

Tip# 1: Talk about racism

Families are where racist preconceptions originate. Even if you don't realize it, your comments might insinuate a certain message about a race, which then affects your teen's perception of that race.

Even when they are toddlers, be sure to make sure your children notice and accept differences in skin color and hair textures. It's vital that from a young age children tolerate and love every race and ethnicity. Talk to them about culture and spark their curiosity about it by introducing them to fun activities that reflect cultural background. Discuss the origins of racism, and why it may have come about in the first place. The earlier you expose your child to the issues plaguing the world and how to approach them, the earlier you're setting them up for a successful future.

Set a good example, and make sure you do not make racial slurs or overgeneralizations. Encourage your child to make diverse friendships.

Tip #2: Donate

Try to donate money to charities and human rights organizations that fight racism in the United States. Examples are the Southern Poverty Law Center, the Anti-Defamation League, and the Human Rights Campaign. Even if you don't experience racism directly, donating to these organizations helps fight racism.

Tip #3: Use the law

The Civil Rights Act of 1964 protects against racial discrimination, and you have every right to use it to your advantage. If you or your children are discriminated against and deprived of certain freedoms, hire a lawyer to fight against that discrimination. If you do not have the money to hire a lawyer and file a lawsuit, look to organizations that can aid your fight for human rights. Some examples in the United States are the Southern Poverty Law Center or the Anti-Defamation League. Do not be afraid of approaching the racial perpetrator head on and making it evident to them that you will take action if they continue to be biased.

Racism is something that's engrained into the roots of this country and continues to affect us every day. We're making progress but there's still a lot left to do. Discrimination will not just "go away." We have to take active steps to disassemble stereotypes and promote tolerance and acceptance of all races and ethnicities and cultures.

I spent a lot of time running from my identity as a brown person, an Indian. From the moment I stepped into preschool, I wanted to be Caucasian and became best friends with a young Caucasian girl. As I grew up, and my face matured, people guessed less and less that I was Indian. I went to new areas and was called Hispanic, Latino, Persian, Greek, mixed, and so many other races. When I revealed my true identity, I was sometimes discriminated against. My school is more accepting than other areas, so discrimination was never a major issue. When I stepped outside of my school bubble, I realized that people treated me differently once they were aware of my race. That fostered self-loathing and sparked a dialogue of internal racism that I've carried with me throughout my teenage years.

I wanted to see how Indian I was, so I got a DNA test. Turns out I'm 99% Indian. Accepting my cultural identity has been a process. After all, there's no way I can change it, so I might as well be confident in it. We're all different. Besides, where's the fun in all being the same color, race, or culture? Our differences create a picture full of depth and beauty. Without even one color, the picture would be incomplete.

Maybe people will throw me glances as I walk into stores meant for "pretty white girls." But there will also be people who find me "exotic" and find me beautiful for my skin color. And if other people accept me, I should be able to accept myself too. I should love my tan skin and big brown eyes.

We can bridge the gap of ignorance with just a little less racism and a little more love.

It starts with communication.

It starts with love. It starts with us.

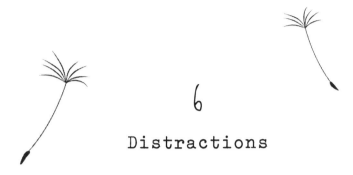

6

Distractions

Social media and technology

The trees melted in a blur of colors as we sped by the other cars that rolled lazily across the freeway in the misty gloom that enveloped the sky. I glanced at the essay on the bright screen of the laptop in front me and hastily finished the paragraph I had been writing, releasing a sigh of relief. We were on our way to school, cruising along with the rest of the morning commuters.

I glanced over at the car next to us and spotted a girl driving a Honda, one hand on the steering wheel, the other on the phone by her thigh. Her face dropped as she fixated on something glinting on the tiny screen beside her, and she began to type, her nails clicking against the glass with a hurried exasperation. I leaned my head against the door, trying to guess what she could possibly be this stressed about in the morning: boyfriend issues, friend squabbles, or a family problem. Judging by the way she was biting her lip and pouting, and involuntarily batting her eyelashes, I decided that she was talking to her boyfriend.

Taking my eyes off the window, I bent down, scooped up my bag, and prepared to get out at my school. Within seconds, I heard tires squeal and a small crunch resonate through the freeway. That same girl had swerved across a lane and crashed into another car, her front bumper smashed into bits. The traffic froze. Within a few minutes, I heard the sirens. As we started moving down slowly in sync with the other cars, I eyed the flashing red and blue lights flooding the morning sky.

Stop and look up from your own phone and begin to realize how much technology has taken over. I've noticed cell phones at restaurant tables, during lunch at school, and even on first dates. It's crazy how much you notice when you take a break from your own screen. Our generation has made some serious strides with technology, and the innovation in this world has led to safer medical treatments, accessibility that allows us to stay connected to loved ones who live far distances from us, and puts information just a tap away. But, technology also interferes in family relationships and decreases interactions with others. We've become slaves to technology.

Not everyone is going to agree with me, but I've recently just put it into perspective. Most of us freak out if we don't have our phones with us every instant of the day. I know I wouldn't be able to survive if I didn't have the opportunity to put my headphones in and listen to music at some point in the day. I can't even wake up in the morning without immediately checking the phone. We depend on social media, which has taken over the majority of our interactions. Seriously, when's the last time you knew someone who got to know his or her boyfriend or girlfriend without texting?

To teenagers, the idea of giving up technology even for one day is a frightening proposition. My friends have gone as far as to say "I'd rather give up my kidney than my phone." We require a means to respond when we know someone is reaching out to us. Flirting, gossiping, and teasing all happen through technology face to face or through crumpled notes smeared with blue pen. Social media is easier because we can ignore people we don't want to talk to and reach out to those we do. There's time to think between each interaction, giving you the greatest chances of saying the right thing. When you have no idea what a word means, you can look it up without looking stupid. Technology saves time.

Many people from older generation like to call phones "family dividers," but in my opinion, although they take away from family connections, they add to social connections. So the ultimate goal is to find a middle ground between both. Teens with low self-esteem especially benefit from social media interactions, as it allows them to venture out and make more friends without direct face-to-face contact until they're ready and comfortable with someone. They often feel as if they will be rejected or shunned, and so social media offers them another venue of communication and expression.

We call it a "cell phone" yet the reality is that teenagers rarely call each other. My own calling history is 90% my parents and 10% my best friend. Once upon a time, teenagers called each other on their landlines, twisting the chord nervously as they sprawled across their beds and asked about each other's days. Rumors took weeks to spread, and secrets were whispered from ear to ear. Now, we text each other within seconds, and gossip spreads like wildfire. I can't count the number of times my friends and I have started a group chat simply to send each other screenshots of texts of the latest drama to collectively come up with a response. We've entertained each other with funny stories and pictures, commenting on the latest fashion mishap or the newest couple. Most of us would not dream of using our phones for anything else.

The most popular times to use Instagram, Facebook, and Snapchat are typically after school and in the evening after homework. Glowing screens full of bright blue alerts and tiny black text, full of tidbits of the juiciest events, fill teenage life and deprive the bustling community of teenagers of proper amounts of sleep. Chats are going on every second, and if you miss one night, you come to school the next day out of the loop and very confused. Being sick for a week meant that I would miss all the drama that occurred, so my friends and I stayed connected by sending each other emails with school updates when one of our crew was absent.

Sure, it helped us all stay connected, but there were so many instances of foul play as well. I saw memes of our classmates being ridiculed and hate messages sent under anonymous names. I grew up fairly sheltered from social media, simply because I didn't have a phone until 8th grade, but as much as I knew the consequences of using social media sites, I knew their value too. I missed out on a lot without a Facebook. I would be asked the day after a party why I didn't show up, and often it was because the invitation was sent out on Facebook, and people would forget to invite me separately. People would approach me and question my decision to not audition for the talent show, and my only response would be "What audition?" School had become so Facebook oriented that being aware of everything that was happening was impossible without it. And without a phone, I didn't even have a means of talking to my friends. Although I'm glad I have a phone now, looking back on it, I'm also glad I didn't have one when I was younger because I had time to devote to developing my app "Aura" and my advice blog, and even this book.

Social media statistics

As I'm sure most of us can guess, Facebook comes in the lead as the most utilized platform with a percentage as high as 71% of all teens per Pew Research Center's Teen Relationship Survey from September 25 through October 9, 2014, and February 10 through March 16, 2015. Instagram and Snapchat follow closely (Lenhart, Anderson, & Smith, 2015). While ancient social networking sites like MySpace and Friendster have fallen out of style, there are still more and more social media sites popping up every day. Apps like musical.ly and periscope are starting to take over as well, becoming even more integrated into daily life. Another Pew Research Center study indicated that 92% of teens go online daily, and over 24% go online "constantly" so clearly there's a market for these types of apps (Lenhart & Page, 2015).

Women use social media more than men, and people 18 to 29 years of age are the most common users. However, while women are more inclined to use social media, men more commonly play video games. Growing up, when someone said "Call of Duty," a dozen heads would turn, none of them female. The stigma surrounding gamers is also primarily male based.

Teenagers receive up to 30 texts per day, and that's the minimal amount. When a conversation begins, hundreds of texts may be passed back and forth, and that's only using the messages app. There are countless other ways of communicating, including through DMs on Instagram, Snaptexting, Facebook Messenger, Kik, and Whatsapp. We spend our lives constantly communicating with those around us. Cyber bullying becomes much more accessible when more social media platforms are used, and other students and peers are able to hide behind the wall of anonymity to send hate to one another. Unhappy teenagers take that unhappiness out on others. It becomes a lot easier to hate on others behind a screen.

"Sexting" is a new word that recently was integrated into the English language because of how common it is in today's society. Apps like Snapchat have made it incredibly easy to send nude pictures or messages because the message or picture disappears after being seen. Innocent phone calls can turn into sexually explicit texts and pictures.

Third party influences are impacting the way teens view themselves. Due to the mass amounts of media encompassing daily lives, teens are exposed constantly to trends. Whether it is about fashion, makeup, or relationships, what teens see on their Facebook and Instagram plays into how they choose to live their lives.

A countless number of my friends hang out with each other and scroll through Instagram together during sleepovers. Others bring their phones to restaurants and interact with the users on their screen rather than the people around them. Based on my own research visiting various restaurants throughout my sophomore year, I realized that over 50% of people having dinner are more attached to their phones than their fellow diners. I've seen couples awkwardly opt to use their phones on first dates rather than talk to each other. Especially in my generation, face-to-face has been traded for screen-to-screen. Repercussions of this depersonalization of communication are already showing up, so now the question is how much more it'll change ("Influence of Mass," 2005).

Why do we use social media?

It's definitely interesting to explore the reasons behind why we use social media in the first place (Hess, 2014):

Staying connected. A lot of teenagers use social media to connect with people and reach out to those who they never would otherwise. We all seek some sort of acceptance, which can be achieved through social media. Just commenting on a peer's picture or chatting with them via messenger about a math test can be the start of a blossoming friendship. You can keep friendships fueled by texting or interacting through social media, something that's especially important when everyone is busy in high school. Instead of hanging out, texting can be a less time consuming option and makes for easy communication, even when thousands of miles apart.

Sense of community is provided by social media, which has integrated a community of people who are easy to talk to and offer support. When you have questions or need to share something, social media provides both anonymous and not anonymous means of talking with others and finding those who can relate.

It's funny that we're not able to find solace in those around us but instead turn to strangers on the Internet. I know so many people who share all of their issues online, but when approached in person, refuse to mention or talk about them. Typically, however, social media communities can be encouraging. When faced with a rude comment, there is a possibility that someone else will stand up for those being attacked. When you have no idea what a certain slang word means, you can search it up quickly to find the answers. It's so useful to be able to learn from people who have asked the same exact questions that you have online.

Identity. Social media can also aid in developing an identity. Following certain blogs, seeing certain posts, and developing ideals and aspirations play a big role in this, and the most exposure usually comes from seeing models or high achieving individuals. Fashionistas follow fashion blogs, nerds follow scientists and math geniuses, and theater geeks follow Broadway stars.

Popularity comes in two types: peer popularity and viewer popularity. Social media helps both of these. Typically, you can gain peer popularity through posts and tweets and texting. By portraying a comedic or sweet persona on social media, other students will be more inclined to want to befriend or get to know you better.

Another type of popularity is viewer popularity. If they are unable to make friends through school, many teens will try to build up a fan following on media, such as YouTube, Vine, or SoundCloud, so that they can earn money and fame. If they begin to get popular, peer popularity will also usually surface along with it.

Selfies were the biggest craze a few years ago. When I got my new iPhone, I distinctly recall running home and taking a selfie. A lot of people take pictures of themselves and use social media to display their face and body in hopes that others will find them attractive. Posting pictures of themselves often also elicits responses and comments from other peers and solidifies self-esteem. Usually, comments on social media especially from other students will be fairly sweet, which can then boost a teenager's self-esteem and body image perception.

Cameras on phones give control to document life and have changed the entire dynamic of being online. Filters, Photoshop, and many other photo editing tools are being used and will continue to be used.

Because everyone else is online, teens want to be online. The majority of the reason that I created my social media sites was because everyone else was on social media. I was missing out on too much, and it had gotten to a point where I was no longer able to keep up with the things my friends were talking about until they explained it to me. I had no idea who Kim Kardashian was, I had no idea which party so and so had gone to, and I had no idea what our grade's plans were for spirit week at school. I was missing out on a lot.

So clearly, we use social media for many reasons. I've heard older generations complain that the world before the Internet was better, but the younger generations advocate for more social media. It's a double-edged sword that has both harmed and benefitted society.

Cons of social media

Just like every other thing that has perks, there are also drawbacks to using social media. Larry Rosen, the professor of psychology at California State University, presented some of the findings he'd discovered through his research:

- 80% of students reported that they switch between studying and technology, such as checking email, Facebook, texting, or watching TV.

- Rosen explains, "Young people's technology use is really about quelling anxiety . . . they don't want to miss out or to be the last person to hear some news (or like or comment about a post online)."

- Facebook is a major distraction to many teens and can result in a lower academic performance. Students who used Facebook during the 15-minute observation period had lower grade-point averages than those who didn't go on the site.

- There are more narcissistic tendencies that form when teens use Facebook, and often anti-social behaviors will also become more concrete with extended periods of use of Facebook.

Although Professor Rosen believes that the advantages, such as "virtual empathy" and learning tools, are starting to outweigh the disadvantages, there are still a lot of strides that need to be made to establish a safe social media environment ("Social Networking's," 2011).

TIPS FOR TEENAGERS

Many of the tips listed below helped me. We are all different, but these tips may be useful.

Tip #1: Monitor yourself

It's so incredibly easy to get caught up in the online world. I will often tell myself "just till I get to the end of my feed" or "just till I check these Snapchat stories," but then I lose track of time. Staying focused is an impossible feat for most of us, especially when there's an essay waiting to be finished on the desk. However, in order to truly stay focused, check in with yourself periodically. If you are being honest with yourself and you realize that you're spending too much time using your phone or computer, find a solution.

During finals, my tactic is usually to stick my phone in a vase. It takes me at least a solid five minutes to be able to get it out, since my hand is too large for the neck of the vase, so I'm usually too lazy to get it out until after I'm done studying. Sometimes, just putting my phone in a different room can be enough to deter me from checking social media, since gaining access to my phone requires standing up and walking.

Another option is also to install a website blocker on your computer. I tried this in middle school. Essentially, input the websites you don't want to be able to access and until what time you don't want to be able to access them. Then set the timer, and the website blocker will not let you enter those websites under any condition until the time is up. This app is a good starting point for those who have no self-control.

Parents can also be good assets. If you need your parents to help keep you focused, ask them to take your phone and only return it when you've finished the task, or ask them to turn off the wifi until you finish. Having others willing to help you accomplish goals is important.

Tip #2: Take breaks

Put your phone away for a while. Your social life will not go down the drain if you drop your phone for a few hours. I was off my phone for a week when I went to a summer camp, and I realized how free and unburdened I felt. I didn't feel an inherent urge to go through all the posts I'd missed on Instagram; I could just go to bed and sleep peacefully. I'm still often too lazy to scroll through my feed nowadays, and so my social media usage has gone down. And I mean, come on, even Google employees have technology breaks during the day. Clearly, there's a reason to take a break.

Tip #3: Multitasking?

Some people work better when they're multitasking, such as listening to music while doing work. However, most studies show that wholly focusing attention onto one activity speeds up the process with less stress. For the most part, try not to multitask. It's usually not more efficient.

Tip #4: Keep the same identity

Don't change who you are online and create an identity completely contrary to your actual identity in real life. People do not appreciate when you act one way on the Internet and another when having face-to-face interactions. I used to try to talk with more maturity online so people would take me seriously, but I realized that the language I was using was completely contrary to the language I used in my daily life. Really try to embrace who you are both in the virtual world and the physical world, and it'll make your life easier.

Tip #5: Be aware

Have a private profile and be aware of who follows or friends you. There are plenty of people who will attempt to send you porn or viruses. It's important that you stay aware to avoid being in unpleasant situations. If someone you don't know tries to follow you, block that person. Do not assume that they have a connection with you. I receive Facebook friend requests from creepy people on a daily basis, and I immediately delete and block all of them.

If peers are being rude or bullying you or others online, call them out on it and then report it. Understand what's happening and try to create a more positive environment.

Tip #6: Find the right idols

It's not at all bad to follow models for fashion tips or makeup tips, or follow basketball players for highlight tapes and trick shots. However, recognize the distinction between your life and the online personas of celebrities. Everything that they do is not necessarily moral or correct. You should not set their activities or fashion choices as the only standards. Use online advice to aid in your endeavors, but do not fall prey to unrealistic ideals and self-deprecate because you haven't reached them. A person can spend an entire life striving for an impossible perfection. Models are photo-shopped, and athletes spend hours and hours practicing their craft every day. Keep that in mind as you scroll through your Instagram feed.

Tip #7: Be comfortable

Make sure you feel comfortable with what you're posting online. If you are not okay with the idea of your parents or future employers seeing what you are posting or sending, then chances are that you shouldn't be broadcasting it all over Facebook or Instagram.

TIPS FOR PARENTS

Tip #1: Recognize the generation gap

Your teen's generation is much more tech savvy. Be aware that your grand-children will probably know how to use a phone better at the age of four than you do right now. You may not understand why your teen is spending so much time online, but to them, it's crucial for a social life. Keep that in mind as you set rules and timelines for technology usage.

Tip #2: Be reasonable

Allow your teen a reasonable amount of time online. They don't have to always have access to their phones, but also remember to be reasonable. If you try to take away their electronics, chances are that they'll simply find another way to get online. They'll sneak their phones into their bedrooms at night or make fake Facebook accounts behind your back.

Set a certain number of hours for technology use initially and explain at what age they can get certain profiles, like Facebook profiles or Instagram accounts. If your teen complies, slowly take away some of the rules and give more freedom. It'll make them feel motivated to continue following your requests and foster a sense of responsibility.

Tip #3: Communicate

Explain why extended use of technology can be bad for teens and try to appeal to them using logic. You may not understand the reasons why they need social media, so if you're open with them, they'll be open with you, and a compromise can be made about technology usage. Ask them to inform you if anything inappropriate is posted or if anyone is bullying them on their profiles.

Tip #4: Monitor your teen online

Create your own account or profile and friend your teen. This way you can monitor what they're posting and make sure that they're being safe online. If your teen is completely against this, it's likely they're hiding something that they don't want you to find. Give them 24 hours to clean up their account and then ask them to friend you.

However, at the same time, it's important that you give them space and privacy. You shouldn't be investigating everything that they post or prying into personal affairs. If something is a concern to their safety, then bring it up, otherwise let your teen come to you and bring up topics, rather than you starting a conversation based off of a picture or drama on their account. Don't dig through their history unless absolutely necessary, and if you are going to, let your teen know why you are doing that. If you become a helicopter parent, your teenager will be more likely to rebel.

Tip #5: Give some leeway

Although it's important to enforce rules, sometimes they will be broken, especially when it comes to technology. Your teen may have extra homework that forces them to stay up past a certain hour with their laptop or may be dealing with drama that warrants extra phone usage. Be ready to allow some rules to bend, but also know which ones are mandatory and come up with appropriate consequences for when they're broken.

Tip #6: Promote cyber safety

Before your teen is swallowed into the community of the online world, make sure they know how to stay safe. Be aware of what sites your teen is planning to visit before going online. Remind your teen to keep personal information off the Internet and not to share passwords. Tell them that you will not tolerate bullying under any circumstance and that if something is happening online that needs outside attention, a parent or adult should be told immediately. Ask them not to interact with people who they don't know and to be wary of what they post or send to others. Also, encourage them to avoid texting or calling when driving.

Social media and technology have been integrated into our society whether we like it or not, and it will continue to change the way in which we go about our daily lives. I still remember receiving a first generation iPod Touch in third grade and finding it the most beautiful creation ever. I remember seeing my parents' flip phones and wanting nothing more than to touch them so I could play a game of solitaire. Now, I go about, cracking the screen of my Apple laptop and wondering when the newest iPhone is going to come out. It's crazy how far we've come in just one generation.

My dad always says that evolution is a necessary aspect of human existence. As we experiment with new things and make headway in a variety of fields, there will always be something that is detrimental, but as we figure out how to properly use advancements, all of our technology will ultimately be for the betterment of society. I guess the only thing we can do is to wait and see.

Maybe I'll catch you on a suspended highway in a flying car one day.

Or maybe Apple will come up with a phone that's both waterproof and has a headphone jack.

Yikes, too soon? Don't tell them I said that.

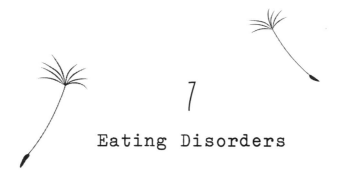

7

Eating Disorders

"Mmf," I grunted as I stumbled past the table I had just hit with my knee. The sun glared into my bare skin, and the hungry buzz of teenagers swallowed the school as a sea of blue and white students weaved in and out of lunch lines. I bowed my head and rushed forward, taking large strides, each bringing me a step closer to the choir room I was aiming for. I was unprotected and vulnerable, unflanked by my girlfriends.

"Sameep!"

My head jerked up as I tried to locate whose voice said my name. Finally, I made eye contact with a football player, who grinned at me sheepishly and bit his lip with hesitant anxiety. Beside him sat a girl, the corners of her mouth curled up in a cruel smirk. She leaned in and nudged him quickly as the entire table of people with whom they were eating giggled in hushed tones. He cleared his throat and almost immediately, all uncertainty was gone. He continued, "Where are you going? To the bathroom to throw up your food?" His group hooted in laughter, as the girl next to him leered at me in amusement.

I felt heat seep into my cheeks as I scurried past, hoping desperately to escape their mocking gazes. Glancing up one last time, I met the jock's eyes. His face fell in apology as he glanced at the pain on my face, and for a second, I saw a flicker of shame, before it was replaced once more with the mask of scorn that he used to maintain his popularity. He sat back down, posture slouched, receiving fist bumps and a kiss from the girl beside him, forgetting me just as quickly as they had noticed me.

The boy who ridiculed me that day was someone that I had considered kind. I'd seen him during class, and he had never failed to offer me the occasional smile or hold the door open for me when my hands were full of textbooks. And no matter how much he apologized to me a year later, I was never able to forget that feeling of utter humiliation and betrayal I felt walking down that lonely pathway to choir.

In schools, eating disorders are mocked. Teens with eating disorders are singled out. Even those without eating disorders are called out when the rumors start. A person just too skinny, too fat, or too focused on diet gets thrown into the mix and labeled.

Growing up, I ate like a bird, simply because I didn't get hungry. Of course I was aware of my image and the way I looked, but it wasn't until people called me out on my weight that I paid attention. Being a 70-pound eighth grader, I was called "attention seeker," "skinny-ass," and "anorexic" by people who assumed that I had an eating disorder.

Teens sit through assemblies on eating disorders each year, but no one seems to put in the effort to respect the issue. Yet it's a serious condition that affects the way many teenagers approach food, and it continues to impact many lifestyles.

In America, 20 million women and 10 million men will suffer from a clinically significant eating disorder at some time in their life (*What Are Eating*, 2012). Eating disorders are more common in households where environmental or cultural stress places focus on appearance and weight. These mental illnesses do not discriminate; they impact people of all genders, races, and ethnicities. They typically surface in the teenage years, more often in girls than boys, but they can also appear at a younger or at an older age. Eating disorders may start as something small like dieting, but can develop into severe life-threatening cases where physical health becomes a major concern. As with many other mental disorders, eating disorders can be accompanied by a variety of other issues such as self-esteem issues and depression.

Many people have heard about anorexia and bulimia, but fail to recognize binge eating and disordered eating as problematic. The four types of eating disorders are as follows (*What Are Eating*, 2012):

Anorexia is a fixation upon weight and calorie intake. Those with anorexia nervosa diet excessively and eat minimally or not at all as to ensure that they eat the least amount of calories possible and lose the maximum amount of weight.

Bulimia is throwing up food. Bulimics may also have a binging disorder, yet the difference is that after they eat, they "purge" all their food by inducing vomiting.

Binge eating is excessive overeating. Many people who binge eat are unable to stop themselves and end up gorging themselves on food they do not wish to intake.

Disordered eating is a lack of control with eating patterns. This condition is pertinent when a patient does not exhibit all the signs of an eating disorder but is at risk for developing one. This includes those who embark on extreme diets, which can lead to anorexia, or those who lose control of their diet, which can then lead to binge eating or bulimia.

Eating disorders are conditions that often overlap and merge into each other over time. For example, it's very possible for a teenager to fall in and out of bulimia and anorexia, simply depending on the circumstances. Adolescents have the highest probability of developing an eating disorder due in part to the circumstances that middle school and high school offer. During this time, both males and females are going through a spectrum of changes, from social to physical to emotional. It can be a very confusing time as teenagers explore their bodies' developments and become more comfortable with who they are. Particularly for females, as their bodies mature, they may feel an increasing amount of insecurity, which is reflected in sky rocketing numbers of girls with eating disorders. Of individuals with anorexia or bulimia, about 5% to 15% are male, while of individuals with binge eating disorders, the number jumps to 35% male (*What Are Eating*, 2012). However, these statistics must be taken with a grain of salt, as likely many cases of male eating disorders go unreported due to the stigma around eating disorders being a problem of girls and women.

Many physical and hormonal changes happen during adolescence that play a role in eating disorder development. Research has pointed out that once teenagers hit puberty, their socio-emotional system begins to adjust and fuels the need to feel societal acceptance and approval. Some theories have surfaced about puberty increasing the production of the hormone estradiol and ovarian hormones, which then in turn activates genes that increase the pervasiveness of eating disorders.

During this coming-of-age journey, a lot of things happen. Friend groups change, romantic interests come to light, physical appearances alter, and a tremendous amount of pressure is introduced. Eating disorders offer a coping method; many people who feel like they have no control in their life find control in their weight, thereby worsening the condition.

Eating disorder statistics

Eating disorders are a widespread problem. Due to the widespread number of people who suffer or have suffered from a clinically critical eating disorder, it's likely that you know someone with an eating disorder, whether you are aware of it or not.

The following are some surprising facts published by National Eating Disorders Association (*What Are Eating*, 2012):

- The rate of development of new cases of eating disorders has been increasing since 1950.

- There has been a rise in incidence of anorexia in young women, ages fifteen to nineteen years in each decade since 1930.

- The incidence of bulimia in girls and women ages ten to thirty-nine years tripled between 1988 and 1993.

The prevalence of eating disorders is similar among non-Hispanic whites, Hispanics, African Americans, and Asians in the United States, with the exception that anorexia nervosa is more common among non-Hispanic whites.

It is common for eating disorders to occur with one or more other psychiatric disorders, which can complicate treatment and make recovery more difficult. Among those who suffer from eating disorders, alcohol and other substance abuse disorders are four times more common than in the general populations; depression and other mood disorders co-occur quite frequently; and a markedly elevated risk for obsessive-compulsive disorder exists.

Four researchers (Dr. Swanson, Dr. Crow, Dr. LeGrange, and Dr. Merikangas) analyzed data from the National Comorbidity Survey Replication Adolescent Supplement, a survey that includes 10,123 face-to-face responses from adolescents between the ages of 13 and 18 years. Five eating disorders were measured in the survey: anorexia nervosa (AN), bulimia nervosa (BN), binge eating disorder (BED), sub-threshold AN (SAN), and sub-threshold BED (SBED), and the rates of each were, respectively, 0.3%, 0.9%, 1.6%, 0.8%, and 2.5%. These eating disorders also sprouted most commonly during the ages of 12 and 13 years old, and while BN and SAN were linked to suicide plans, BN and BED involved suicide attempts (Swanson, Crow, & Grange, 2011).

The following is some data surrounding eating disorders from SAMSHA ("Eating Disorders," n.d.):

- Individuals between ages 12 and 25 years make up 95% of people who have eating disorders.

- 50% of individuals with eating disorders also have depression.

- One-half of all teenage girls and one-third of all teenage boys attempt to control their weight through dieting, fasting, vomiting, smoking, laxatives, and diet pills.

- 47% of girls in fifth through twelfth grade wanted to be thinner due to the standard set by the media.

- Anorexia is the third most frequent chronic illness among teens.

- Eating disorders cause more deaths than any other mental illness.

- 86% of those with eating disorders say that it developed before the age of 20 years.

- 22% of females in college diet "always" or "often" and 25% binge and purge as a weight loss technique.

Common eating disorders

The common eating disorders are classified as below (*What Are Eating*, 2012; "Understanding Eating," n.d.):

1. Anorexia. Anorexics avoid food at all cost. Anything that involves calories is feared. In order to remain the optimal weight, they will starve themselves for extended periods of time, exercise excessively, and take a variety of diet pills and laxatives. Even after losing their initial set amount of pounds, anorexics will feel as if it is not enough and continue to perceive themselves as overweight. When they look in the mirror, a reflection that is not their own stares back at them. We may see skin and bones, but to them, there are layers of fat coating their thighs, draping onto their stomachs, and falling from their cheeks. To an anorexic, this is never thin enough. There is always more weight to lose.

On pro-ana websites, girls and boys promote anorexia and motivate each other to keep losing weight. Many have bios that state their starting weight (SW); their current weight (CW), their first, second, and third weight goals (WG#); and finally their ultimate weight goal (UWG).

The extent to which anorexics will go to ensure that they keep losing weight is terrifying when viewed externally. I've talked to teens who only have a rice cracker and a cup of grapefruit juice every day. I've talked to teens who work out for three hours every day to lose weight. I've talked to teens who have swallowed up to fifteen laxatives at a time on an empty stomach and have lost up to 120 pounds. Anorexia is not something to be taken lightly. It takes over lives and kills teens every single day. This illness becomes an unhealthy obsession that individuals suffering from it cannot escape. It beckons with open arms into a life of falsely promised beauty and love, when in reality, the more weight lost, the greater the desire to shed off even more.

This mental illness affects an incredible number of people, yet many fail to realize the extent to which it has harmed both young girls and boys. Many teens who embark on the horrendous journey of anorexia don't know about the following consequences ("Eating Disorders," n.d.):

Anemia is a lack of blood that occurs due to malnutrition. Individuals with this condition feel dizzy and weak and experience a drop in blood pressure.

Brain shrinkage occurs when an individual goes through a period of starvation. A person's brain can shrink and their intelligence may drop.

Chills result when body temperature drops below 98 degrees because a body does not have enough energy to keep itself warm, which means that someone with anorexia may feel cold often and have bluish fingertips. Lanugo, fine fuzzy hair, will develop on the body in an effort to keep it warm.

Decreased cognitive function occurs in individuals with anorexia because they are incapable of thinking quickly or nearly at the same speed as others. This is known as the psycho-motor delay.

Dry skin and hair loss is caused by dehydration, and when malnutrition occurs, the scalp will become dry and cause hair to fall out. Nails will also become very brittle.

Amenorrhea occurs from starvation for extended periods of time; menstrual cycles will become irregular or stop altogether.

Infertility results from malnutrition. Once the menstrual cycle stops, it is possible for permanent infertility to occur.

Heart damage results from the body being in starvation mode. The body will start to eat away at its own muscle for energy, which puts stress on the heart. In some cases, the heart may simply cease to function.

Osteoporosis, which is loss of bone calcium, due to malnourishment can lead to an increased risk for breaking and fracturing bones.

2. Bulimia. Teenagers with bulimia gorge themselves on large quantities of food and then proceed to vomit up (or purge) whatever consumed. This condition can be incredibly taxing on the body because the body begins the process of mass digesting and then forces it all out again. Bulimia or bulimic patterns are very common, affecting two to three percent of women around the world. Almost half of anorexics also supplement their eating disorder with bulimia or bulimic patterns. In a very similar way to anorexics, bulimics are looking to be skinnier and have more control over their lives.

I've stumbled upon girls throwing up in bathrooms, hearing the retching sounds echo across the marbled bathrooms. I've seen them use their fingers, toothbrushes, and who knows what else to induce vomiting. Tears streaming down their faces, bodies bent over empty toilets, they force their bodies to reject the food they gave it, without realizing the effects.

The following are consequences of bulimia (*What Are Eating*, 2012; "Understanding Eating," n.d.):

Tooth decay results from the stomach acid that comes up with the food and damages the enamel of teeth, stains teeth, and damages gums.

Stomach and intestine damage, such as gastritis, which is an inflammation of the stomach lining, due to the acidic buildup occurs. Laxatives used for bulimic purposes can also damage the digestive tract. Sometimes, the colon may even have to be removed.

Esophagus deterioration from the acid from vomiting to the lining of the esophagus can cause a life-threatening tear in the lining.

Kidney complications from constant dehydration and low potassium levels can contribute to kidney failure and an irregular heart rate or sudden death.

3. Binge Eating Disorder (BED). BED is similar to bulimia in the sense that both involve consuming large quantities of food without control. The difference is, however, that binge eating does not involve purging. There may be sporadic fasting or dieting in response to the guilt of binging. This is unhealthy for the body and can result in obesity.

Some of the long-term consequences include high blood pressure, high cholesterol levels, type II diabetes, and gall bladder disease.

What causes eating disorders?

In a similar fashion to depression, it's impossible to pinpoint one specific reason or cause for the development of an eating disorder. Especially with societal and peer standards being imposed on them from day to day, teenagers are particularly susceptible to feeling unhappy in their bodies. Many teens model themselves off of what is considered attractive in the media, and in this day and age, that happens to be muscular men and toned women. Those involved in activities that are especially critical of body image, such as sports or theater, can be more likely to develop an eating disorder. Personality traits like perfectionism, low self-esteem, and anxiety can also contribute.

When I was nine years old, I heard the phrase "no thanks, too many carbs" too often from my cousins, as they rejected food left and right. My older cousins were over ten years older than me, and to me, they were beautiful role models who I wanted to replicate. When I was 13, I tried out the "no carb" diet too, simply because I thought it was cool. I thought if I avoided carbohydrates, I would become important and slim like them. Simply a phrase heard too often can change the way teenagers approach life. Those same routines in which they watch other people engage, teens will mirror, and diet too hard, too fast. Certain factors, many of which parallel other mental illnesses, are as follows (*What Are Eating*, 2012; "Understanding Eating," n.d.):

Trauma. Going through traumatic events can spur a teenager to need a sense of control, which they may find through an eating disorder. These events can be anything from sexual assault to the death of a family member.

Media focuses on physical beauty in a very big way in American culture. Pictures of models are everywhere; they follow us in grocery stores on magazines and on the sides of buses as we drive on the road. The subtle message in almost all of them is that you must be thin to be beautiful.

Fat talk, meaning comments from peers about appearance, can lead to an eating disorder. Particularly in junior high and high school, it's impossible to avoid discussions about appearance. At almost every sleepover, we had some talk about who had gained the most weight, and how our latest weight loss endeavors were going. We even went as far to rate each other on physical appearance "for fun." Many females bond over "fat talk" which can further aggravate an oncoming eating disorder.

Bullying, which social media has taken to a whole new level, continues to affect people in more ways than initially thought was possible. Anonymity plays a factor in this as well, as students can now get anonymous submissions and messages containing body-shaming comments. In addition, social media sites like Facebook and Instagram have contributed to widespread body dissatisfaction, due to the comments that posted photos receive.

Perfectionism. Many teenagers are driven by the belief that in order to be "worth it," they must be perfect, and this contributes to the sense that the thinner they are, the better they are.

Compensation. Many individuals feel like if they lack talent, beauty, or popularity, they can try to make up for it through a smaller number on a scale.

Popularity is a constant concern for teenagers, and individuals feel as if the only way to gain popularity is to be skinny.

Athletic achievement through competitive sports can lead to eating disorders not only because of the high standard that athletes' bodies are held to, but also because specific uniforms can be form fitting and very exposing for certain individuals. In dance and gymnastics for example, participation can depend on an individual's body type.

Signs of eating disorders

Eating disorders can be incredibly hard to spot, as teenagers are often in denial or do not wish to fess up to what has been consuming them and their lives. Teenagers with eating disorders become skilled at concealing the toll it is taking on them and make up excuses to not eat at the dinner table or hide food in their pockets to then flush down the toilet. Many people assume that in order to have an eating disorder like anorexia or bulimia, a person must be skinny; this is a false statement. Overweight girls with anorexia are often overlooked, as it is assumed that if they were truly anorexic, weight loss would be much more dramatic and make more of an impact on their appearance. The following signs may aid in identifying a teen with an eating disorder (Mayo Clinic Staff, n.d.):

- fasting, coming up with excuses to avoid eating or to eat in secret;
- frequent discussion about body weight and appearance;
- regular trips to the restroom after eating;
- loss of hair, brittle nails, cavities, dry skin;
- irregular eating habits such as not eating for a few meals and then consuming excessive amounts of food;
- use of laxatives or other pills;
- irregular eating habits;
- repeated or periodic dieting or rigidity on foods they can consume;
- food rituals such as moving food around a plate, cutting it up into tiny pieces, or using the same bowl;

- excessive exercise or working out;

- frequently checking in the mirror for flaws;

- continual consumption of foods high in sugars or fat;

- expressing shame or disgust about food habits;

- insomnia; and

- constipation.

Diagnosing eating disorders

The earlier diagnosis takes place, the more likely recovery will happen. Teenagers with eating disorders often conceal their behaviors, making it almost impossible to discern whether a teen actually has an eating disorder. They may appear to eat with regular food habits in front of others, although the real story lies in what happens behind the scenes. Each eating disorder has its own warning signs, and depending on which one it is may impact each body differently. Treatment is incredibly crucial in the recovery process, and although many people with eating disorders will relapse, it is a necessary step for the ultimate well being of that individual. The recommended treatment usually involves a multi-layer action plan that includes therapy of all types, including medical and psychiatric therapy. Nutritional rehabilitation may also be included.

The three types of therapy that a teen may need are: individual, group, and family. Individual therapy is used to correct habits that are unhealthy and focuses on the idea of acceptance and self-love. Meanwhile, group therapy allows for open discussions and a sense of understanding among those who have gone through similar experiences, providing much needed support. Finally, family therapy is geared toward constructing a safe environment for the teen and the rest of the family to ensure that other challenges that arise can be easily navigated and that the family knows how to aid in nutritional habilitation.

Nutritional counseling is focused on education about nutrition, and baby steps toward normal eating habits through meal planning and goal establishment. Coping strategies have to be developed for many teenagers, and distorted thinking patterns and deep-rooted issues are addressed and corrected. These techniques work on solidifying a healthy relationship between the individual and food in the future. When eating disorders are spotted and treated, the individual may be able to make a full recovery, both physically and mentally (Higuera, 2016).

TIPS FOR TEENAGERS

It can be terrifying to go through an eating disorder. I've watched the impact eating disorders have had on some of my friends, and the hauntingly skinny people they've become as a result. Their collarbones protrude underneath their baggy long sleeves as their sunken eyes fill with tears. They smile weakly, their cheekbones casting shadows over their faces as they say, "I'm fine. I'm happy." But the truth is evident.

Tip #1: Remember you are not a number

When a teen is caught up accumulating achievements and always striving to be better, forgetting to appreciate personal strengths is easy. We begin to measure our value through numbers. We correlate a higher worth with a lower number on the scale. It's a process to accept your body and your weight, but self-care begins with a positive internal dialogue. It's okay to have rolls. It's okay to not have a thigh gap. It's okay to not be able to fit your hand around your wrist. Everybody is made differently, and each body has its own proportions. It's about loving your body regardless of its measurements. You don't have to be a size zero to be loved and to love yourself.

Weight fluctuates, and that's something people fail to realize. Muscle weighs more than fat; a fit person weighs more than someone who is unfit. You can gain an entire pound simply from chugging a bottle of water. Weight really doesn't mean anything.

Tip #2: Plan it out

Falling back into old habits is a danger that many people who have struggled with eating disorders face. Try to create a plan and stick to it. Listen to your body's cravings. It's okay to be healthy, just make sure a meal plan doesn't harm your body. Eating well-balanced meals can be more helpful in losing weight than starving. Remember to set aside time to do things you enjoy. Keeping "you time" will help with recovery and get you back in touch with your body.

Tip #3: Redirect your thoughts

Sometimes, redirection is necessary. Try to distract yourself from hating your body and focus on the little moments that offer consolation and remind you of the beauty of life. Maybe it's watching the colors of a sunset meld into each other across the sky, or feeling the sweet taste of a fruit set every taste bud tingling.

When the negative thoughts start invading, reject them. Your mind will repel the idea of body positivity initially because you've trained yourself to be harsh and critical, but it is imperative that you try to redirect these thoughts. It's a habit to look in the mirror and select out body areas that still need to be fixed, still need to be toned, still need to be slimmed, so your responsibility is to actively try to change that thought process. You just have to remind yourself of the things that you love.

Tip #4: Realize your beauty

Sometimes it's important to look around and just realize how lucky you are. Chances are if you're reading this book, you have enough money to spend on books, you have a roof over your head, and you have food on the table. Many people in this world don't get the opportunity for this. On top of that, many teenagers have disabilities and diseases. Show your body some gratitude and realize how lucky you are. Just being aware of all the privileges can be enough to make a positive impact on life.

Tip #5: Don't run away

You may avoid wanting to get better. You might think that recovery will ruin all the work and all the effort you've put into losing pounds. But the truth is that no matter what number you hit, you will never be content with your weight. Eating disorders are a constant demand to be skinnier. We may think that once we hit that goal weight, we'll be happy. We'll feel content, safe, and confident. But each pound lost adds an extra pound of hatred and dissatisfaction.

The only way you'll be happy with your body is to build your body image, slowly and steadily, by getting therapy to recover from an eating disorder. Don't fall prey to the misguided idea that you can handle it on your own; it's likely that it will be too overwhelming. Trust your parents to help you or talk to another adult about getting treatment.

Tip #6: Change your environment

People who are suffering with the same disorder or constantly focusing on appearances will encourage you to fall into a habit of despising your own body, making it even harder to recover. Find body positive friends who support you no matter what and ensure that you always feel like the best version of yourself. Changing the environment in which you spend time goes a long way.

Tip #7: Remember media's deceit

Social media can be the basis for a lot of body shaming comments. Choose to ignore those comments. Not everyone is going to be supportive of you and your recovery, and there will always be someone on the sidelines saying you aren't skinny enough or aren't curvy enough. A constant requirement exists to be the perfect body type: not too skinny, not too fat, but that doesn't exist. Perfection does not exist. Even models require photo manipulation to look like they have bodies adequate enough to make it on the cover of magazines. Magazine photos are not reality.

I fell prey to the same exact thing. I let one comment about my nose affect how I view it. I never considered my nose big until one of my peers commented it on my picture. Since then, I've looked at noses of countless pictures of models and gone as far as to research the amount a nose restructuring job costs. I'm still learning to love my big nose, and I have to constantly remind myself that the perfection I see on magazines does not exist.

Tip #8: Redesign your wardrobe

Wearing the same clothes over and over again can make us feel a little worn and may not be as flattering as they once were. Go through an annual closet cleanout and throw out or donate whatever no longer makes you feel good. Go shopping for new outfits that boost your confidence and make you feel beautiful.

TIPS FOR PARENTS

Parents play an important role in aiding in the recovery of a teenager with an eating disorder. While the battle might be the teen's to fight, parents can provide protection and defense.

Tip #1: Encourage healthy eating habits

Educate your teen about dieting and how malnourishment can adversely affect the body. Eat together as a family to reduce the risk of your teenager skipping meals and to ensure that your teenager eats an adequate amount without overeating. Make sure to set a good example. Teenagers often unknowingly model themselves after whoever is in their life the most, which in many cases are the parents. So if you're dieting, eating irregularly, or fixating on food, they will develop many of the same patterns.

Keep an open discussion about the best options for healthy weight loss such as a balanced diet and an appropriate amount of exercise. Offer to give them occasional cheat days and go out to get ice cream as a family. However, try not to label foods as "good" or "bad." This can set up cravings and feelings of guilt. Rather explain how moderation and balance is important for a healthy lifestyle.

Tip #2: Talk about beauty standards

As with almost every issue, it's important to have healthy conversations with your teen. TV, magazines, movies, and a variety of other media sources paint a picture of what is considered "attractive." Teach your teen to question the images to create a more open conversation about beauty standards.

Tip #3: Promote positivity

Reassurance about beauty when growing up can make a very big impact on a child once they reach adolescence. We've all heard the phrase "my mommy told me I was beautiful," and maybe it's not enough to stop an eating disorder, but it's definitely enough to make the kid feel a little bit better about their physical characteristics.

Ensure that you don't comment on body shapes in a negative way, even if you don't mean it, as your child may pick up on it. In my culture, being light skinned is often considered "attractive," and I often heard Indian mothers pick out Indian girls who were lighter skinned as beautiful. I spent the majority of my middle school years hiding from the sun and getting paler, simply because I'd grown up with the standard that lighter was better ingrained in my mind.

Never criticize your child's appearance or mention their weight. Even saying, "Wow, those jeans have gotten tight, haven't they?" can be enough to trigger self-loathing within a teenager. I can't count the number of times my mom has unknowingly asked me if I needed bigger jeans because they seemed to be a "little tight on the waist." Although I know her intention was pure, it made me examine my weight and pay more attention to it.

Tip #4: Foster self-esteem

Encourage your teens in everything they do. Compliment them when they come downstairs in the morning. Don't use the same compliment every day; change it up and compliment different aspects of them. It'll make the compliment feel more genuine. Throw out a little "those jeans make your legs look bomb" or a "wow that shirt compliments your skin tone," and you're sure to put a smile on your teen's face.

Urge them to express their desires and to make decisions without external help. Encourage them to be assertive and learn how to say no. You can learn all about ways to foster self-esteem in Chapter 14.

Tip #5: Communicate

Once again, communication is key. Talk about eating disorders in a sensitive way that spurs your child to start an ongoing conversation about their challenges and problems. Remind them how much you love them sporadically in different ways. Read up on eating disorders to better understand what your teen is going through and talk to them in private as to not embarrass them. When an issue presents itself, use the word "I" instead of "you." Change the conversation from "you've been avoiding food" to "I've noticed that you've been avoiding food." Be patient; eating disorders are hard to talk about. Remember to be their crutch if they need it; they will have off days, and it's important that you stay strong for them. If your teen doesn't seem to be listening, find other ways to communicate, such as songs or letters. Don't be the "food police"; it's not going to aid them in the long run, because as soon as you're not around, they will resort to their old habits. They have to want to recover. You cannot force it upon them.

It can be very hard to be accepting of your body, and it's something that I think all of us struggle with at some point. I used to count calories with everything I ate, despite the fact that I was underweight for my height. I was glued to a fitness app, constantly entering in the foods that I'd eaten and the exercise I'd completed. It was always a number: the number of calories eaten; the number of pounds lost; the number on the scale. I would weigh myself every day after school in eighth grade, entering in the number with a manic glee as it dropped. Few mornings, a couple of my friends would huddle in a circle during a break, comparing weights, giggling with contempt as we tried to out-compete each other with who could lose the most weight. As I dropped to 70 pounds, my friends would congratulate me, asking me for my secret, begging that I tell them how to do it. It took a lot of work to break the cycle, but now, I haven't weighed myself in a few months.

I heard a story once about a woman who had fat rolls everywhere. She was incredibly obese, yet she happened to be one of the most confident women on the planet. She had come to embrace every single part of herself after a lot of work. Each of her rolls had a name. Her chin fat? Its name was Megan. Her thighs? Jessica and Amy. After hearing that story, I couldn't stop crying. That is what we should all want for ourselves: a love and acceptance so strong that we chose to adopt each flaw as our friend. I asked what her secret was, and her response was as follows:

"If Angelina Jolie can love herself, then why can't I?"

And she's completely right.

You can.

You deserve to just as much as she does.

8

Fashion

"Blue?"

"Nah, not feeling it."

"Black?"

"Too dark."

"White?"

"Too easy to get dirty."

I spotted it, and squeaked. I reached into my suitcase and whipped out my favorite outfit. Within seconds, I had shoved it on and was out the door. Bright green sweatpants with the word "Volleyball" scripted in glittering letters down the side were my trademark. The minute I stepped into camp, I was attacked with a siege of comments.

"This is literally why you don't have a boyfriend," my male friend snorted from behind his computer, as his eyes mocked me with a malevolent glare.

"Yea, honestly, Sameep, what are you wearing?" my best friend said, giggling and tugging at my sweats with her perfectly painted acrylic nails. "You literally look like a leprechaun."

My cheeks flushed with a flurry of pink, and I hid behind my books, burying my feet under the desk.

"Time to shed the Justice outfits, Sameep. Go shop at Brandy."

All I could think about was escaping the classroom once and for all.

"Here, put this on," someone said, and I looked up to find kind eyes looking back at me.

The dancer who sat in the back handed me a pair of leggings, and I nodded in gratitude. She smiled back at me before weaving her way to her seat. For her, that might have been a simple gesture, but to me, it saved me from a day of being mocked and ridiculed. One thing's for sure, I never wore those sweatpants again, in fear of being shamed the way I had been that day when I was twelve.

It's crazy to think how much society's focus has shifted onto appearance and fashion, particularly in this era. I know rich tweens who wear more expensive clothing than their parents and spend more money on one bag of makeup than I have ever spent on my entire wardrobe. Style has become an important part of every high schooler's life, and many are striving to be a fashion icon and set new trends. Once upon a time, fashion was only for the wealthy, but it's transformed into an industry that worms its way into literally everything around us. It's rare to walk down the street and see someone who hasn't developed some sort of fashion, and the media plays a huge role in this trend. TV and social media have influenced the way that we view fashion, and we actively go out and attempt to imitate what we view as stylish or attractive. Dressing in clothes that make you feel "cute" is an automatic confidence booster and enhances your image. It wasn't until I started dressing better and wearing makeup that boys actually started noticing me.

What's interesting is that some foreigners from conservative societies view Western fashion as unstable and orderless, which may to be due to the fact that since America is a melting pot of cultures, there are so many different styles and aspects that go into what we view as "stylish."

Fashion is a not just something that came about as a fabricated idea; it came as a response and an expression. In Roman society, elites would line their togas with purple as a sign of prestige, which then led that clothing to be considered "better." In America, home-stitched clothing came about as a means of expression against Britain. Today, we have goth teens, preppy teens, and hipster teens. I know a guy who dresses only in green every day of the year except for St. Patrick's Day, simply because green is his favorite color. In this day and age, clothing dictates popularity, identity, and power, no matter what the person's age. You want to be taken more seriously? Walk into a location wearing a suit or a professional outfit. I've heard my dad talk about how many times he was offered better service, just because he was dressed in a suit, which made him look important or powerful.

The amount of clothing in the past century alone has skyrocketed, as new techniques and technological aspects to style are being developed. In the 2000s, we've been more focused on comfort. Girls are no longer expected to pin up their hair in tight curls and wear corsets even for a simple trip out to the grocery store. Just take a look around; the majority of us are probably wearing jeans, t-shirts, and sneakers. We've found a style that is both relaxed and timeless. I mean even nonathletes wear athletic clothing, donning soccer sweatpants and Adidas sneakers. However, no matter how much we continue to develop new trends, there will be some aspects that always recycle themselves like chokers from the 1990s and broad shoulders from the 1980s.

What's undeniable is how much more provocative this generation's clothing is. Girls are being defined by their sexuality, and while a hundred years ago, a naked midriff would have been a societal crime, many girls stroll around wearing cropped tank tops and booty shorts during the summer. I'm all for feeling sexy and confident, and if you achieve that by wearing whatever exposes the most skin, who am I to complain? I just know that I'd never truly feel comfortable like that. And so for the people like me who were raised in a conservative culture, there's a spectrum of modest clothing out there too.

As teens, we're taught that beauty is what's important. We see endless racks of magazines, models on the front page with flawless features and perfect bodies. We've come to believe that a level of beauty like that is the truth. We've learned to follow these models and their fashion ideals in hopes of one day achieving that level of perfection, but those magazines are not always an accurate representation of the person in the photo. This doesn't just go for women. Men are taught that in order to be "manly," in order to be "attractive," they must sculpt and tone their body. Boys and girls are more concerned with their appearance than ever before, and this epidemic of "looking cute enough" is sweeping the world. In a typical teen magazine, the Kaiser Family Foundation found that 41% of the articles were about dating or sex, 37% were on beauty and appearance, and only 12% ever mentioned advice about school or careers ("Tweens, Teens," 2004). These tips and tricks about the latest "in" styles make more of an impression than you think and can drive teens to buy more clothes to feel adequate.

A study published on Statistic Brain found that 79% of girls identified shopping as one of their "hobbies and activities." But of course, it is not the actual wandering around the mall that gets them excited; it's the clothes that they get to take home with them. After all, new clothes are the equivalent of waking up on Christmas morning. Forty-one percent of the surveyed teenagers from the same study bought ten or more items of clothing in the past six months ("Teenage Consumer," 2016). Each piece contains memories, whether they're woven into the strands or bunched up in the pockets, like lost coins. Each teenager is different, and the places teens shop differ drastically, but some mainstream stores are very popular with teenage girls.

Teenage girls specifically have been much more invested in the "stereotypical girly look," which essentially comprises tank tops, leggings, boots, and flirty skirts and dresses. Even the average guy is aiming for a laid back, messy, "I look like I didn't try, but I still look hot" kind of look. The problem is that it doesn't just stop at the shirt you're wearing or the pants you've decided to throw on. There are millions of accessories to think about as well. Hats, beanies, headbands, purses, bracelets, watches, socks, and shoes – the list is endless. It's all about the details.

Teen fashion-related statistics

Seventy-five billion dollars: now that's a lot of money. That's also the amount of money that teenagers spend annually, according to Piper Jaffray's 29th semi-annual Take Stock with Teens research survey. About 20% of this money is spent on clothes. We may have started off with fashion as a necessity some 170,000 years ago to keep us warm, but it's turned into an industry that consumes America. Teenagers are the main demographic of all these brands, and it is clear which ones are making the most impact ("Piper Jaffray," 2015).

Teen Vogue partnered with Goldman Sach's Apparel and Accessories Global Investment Research Group to survey trendy, fashion-savvy women to see which brands were their favorites. The survey was based on five criteria: brand awareness, favorability, word of mouth, production ownership, and purchases (Teen Vogue, 2013). The top eighteen brands were as follows:

1. Forever 21	2. Victoria's Secret Pink	3. Victoria's Secret
4. Nike	5. Sephora	6. MAC
7. H&M	8. Converse	9. Urban Outfitters
10. Target	11. EOS	12. Bath and Body Works
13. Sephora Collections	14. Urban Decay	15. Vans
16. Maybelline	17. Luis Vuitton	18. Steve Madden

This doesn't include common stores geared toward teenagers such as Pacsun, Brandy Melville, Hollister, Aeropostale, and Abercrombie. What's interesting to notice is that many of these stores also are makeup stores. Makeup is an integral part of fashion and a girl's womanhood. Girls have begun to wear makeup as early as age eleven, as soon as they enter middle school, and many brands are taking advantage of that demographic.

Piper Jaffray's Taking Stock with Teens survey organizes an average teen's spending in the following way (2015):

- Food: 23%

- Clothes: 20%

- Accessories/personal care/cosmetics: 10%

- Video games/systems: 8%

- Cars: 8%

- Electronics/Gadgets: 8%

- Music/movies: 6%

- Concerts/movies: 6%

TIPS FOR TEENAGERS

In my opinion, there's a lot more to fashion than just covering yourself. Fashion is something that should boost confidence and self-esteem. It should be a form of expression and self-love. There are clothes that are acceptable and clothes that are unacceptable, but the items categorized in each group differ from individual to individual. There will be conservatives who insist that shorts are exposing for women, and there will also be people who walk around in spandex and be okay with it. At the end of the day, it's how you want to portray yourself to other people. Fashion is a big element in life, and always will be. After all, fashion encompasses nearly everything, ranging from sweaters to hairpieces, accessories, bags, and even nails. It's something that is unavoidable. But the way an individual addresses fashion can result in different outcomes. Whether fashion is a curse or a blessing, a poison or an antidote, I don't know. Either way, it starts with understanding and a connection that can only be built through the love of a teenager and a parent.

Tip #1: Be yourself

Too many people will tell you who to be, and how to dress. Don't let that change the person you are. Don't lose yourself by trying to fit into a crowd or by trying to fit in with the latest fads. If the latest styles and trends appeal to you, then go out and buy the clothes that fit into that category, but don't feel required to jump in and follow what peers are doing. For all you know, you could be the one to start the next fashion trend.

Tip #2: Balance a budget

One easy way to reduce the amount you spend is to create a budget. When I was in ninth grade, one of my father's coworkers suggested a plan that he had for his daughter: a budget. So at dinner one night, my father proposed an allowance per se that granted me $2,000 every year. And in reality, that's an enormous sum of money. I'd grown so accustomed to shopping at places that were expensive, I had never realized how much money it really took to satisfy my endless thirst for apparel. It wasn't that we were short of money in any way, but rather it was the learning experience of money management that my parents wanted to teach me. We made a list of the items that I typically bought in a year and estimated the price for each, added it together, and ended up with a sum close to $2,000. After instigating it, I felt both powerful and burdened. Suddenly, I was in charge of my own money. Along the way, I realized the value of money, and now, before I buy even the smallest thing, I ask myself, do I really want this? How many times realistically would I wear this in a year? Could I be spending this money on something better? Even the smallest second of reconsideration usually makes me drop the item off at the next rack, which makes the ones I keep in my hand that much more precious.

Tip #3: Pay no heed to others

There will always be someone to criticize your clothing, so it's important that you are able to look past rude comments and saucy remarks. Women will always be restrained to some extent and have labels ascribed to them. Dress too scantily, and you're called a slut. Dress too conservatively, and you'll be labeled a prude. In this day and age, someone will have a problem with how you dress, and society will encourage that. So dress to please yourself and don't pay heed to the negative comments thrown your way. I know how hard it can be to ignore comments that you get regarding fashion, but if you feel confident, don't let someone take that away from you.

Tip #4: Understand family requirements

Every household has a different standard of what is considered acceptable dress, and it's important that you respect your parents' ideas of what they feel comfortable with you going out of the house wearing. My parents were very conservative with what I wore. Maybe not to the point where I was only allowed to venture out of the house in a long-sleeve shirt and jeans, but it was enough to make me feel self-conscious during the summer. Skirts and dresses could only be worn at parties. Denim shorts and tank tops that didn't cover four inches of my shoulder were off the table. I had to make the choice of either wearing jeans and being asked the question "Aren't you hot?" on various occasions or wearing shorts that went to my knees.

While most teenagers used their Friday night to hang out with their friends or snuggle up in bed to watch the latest movie illegally, I chose my one Friday night to write a six-page essay to my parents containing my arguments as to why I should be allowed to buy clothes that mirrored the societal norm. This work of literature translated into a discussion at the dinner table. After a debate and occasional words of advice thrown at my parents from my brother, we came to the following compromise:

- Skirts, dresses, and shorts can only be worn when the weather is 80 degrees or warmer.

- Shorts must be mid-thigh or longer.

- Sleeveless shirts must cover the entire shoulder.

- No bra or camisole straps can be seen.

- Long shorts must be worn underneath skirts and dresses, and possibly denim shorts.

- At no times can any part of the stomach or cleavage be seen.

- Bikinis are not allowed, and a one-piece bathing suit must be appropriate.

I was grateful my parents were willing to stretch their own norms and what they considered acceptable. In my case, my parents were scared of being too provocative for an unnecessary reason. My parents kept clothing regulations for the sake of gaining respect and staying safe. To them, being the innocent, goody-two-shoes was ideal, and I learned to work with it. You may have to make that sacrifice as well. Be mature and listen to what they have to say. I learned that the reason my parents were terrified of showing too much skin was that they thought it would bring unnecessary attention to me that might lead to harassment or teasing. With a changing society, my parents are learning to work with it, and so am I. Being open to your parents' justifications will show them that you're serious about the discussion and make them more inclined to sympathize with you.

Tip #5: Don't cheat the system

I know plenty of girls who would bring clothes that their parents didn't approve of and change into them at school or at a friend's house. Although it seems like a good idea at the time, you will get caught, and you'll have a lot of explaining to do. In the end, it won't be worth it. Just try to work with your parents and compromise on an acceptable dress code.

Tip #6: Closet cleanouts

If you can afford to, have a summer cleanout every year and donate some clothes to a charity like Goodwill. It's crazy how much clutter you can clean up just by sweeping through your closet and piling up everything you haven't worn recently and don't plan to wear. I get very attached to my clothes and the memories associated with each, but once I get rid of the ones I no longer need, I feel as if a burden has been lifted off my shoulders.

Even if you don't have enough money to mindlessly get rid of old clothes, you can always sell them on a website like Poshmark or Mercari. These both provide virtual closets where users sell clothes they don't want anymore to others. Although the app takes some of the money that you earn, you can still gain a substantial amount as opposed to simply donating them or giving them away.

Tip #7: Don't get obsessed

There's a difference between enjoying a good outfit and being obsessed. Make sure that you're not throwing away other aspects of your life by wasting time to look good. Don't spend all of your time in a mall, when you could be pursuing your passions and connecting with the people you care about. There's no harm in the occasional shopping spree, though.

Tip #8: Keep your age in mind

Especially with makeup, it's important not to overdo it. Makeup can be very detrimental to your skin at an early age, so try using a minimal amount of makeup while you're in junior high. There's no harm in the occasional concealer and mascara, just try not to go overboard and spend hours every morning caking your face in foundation, powder, and perfectly winged eyeliner. You want to make sure you dress age appropriately and apply an appropriate amount of makeup. There's no harm in using makeup to enhance your beauty, but remember you're already beautiful.

TIPS FOR PARENTS

It can be a lot to take in when your teenager skips out the door in tiny shorts and a transparent cotton tank top, but it's important to understand your teen's society and generation (Alexander, 2007).

Tip #1: Develop a common vocabulary

Establish what's acceptable in your household, and explain the justification behind it. The rate at which our society is progressing is astonishing, and clothing that never would have even been considered acceptable is being worn in public. Understand the differences in cultures and eras of the past and present and be open to what your teen has to offer. Sit down and set some guidelines and maybe make a list of what can and can't be worn. That's what my parents and I did, and we renew it every year as I mature.

Tip #2: Remember the age

Your teen is no longer a child. They're going to want to make their own decisions and be responsible for their own fashion choices. Make your teen aware of what it means to wear modest clothing, and how it's important to wear what they feel reflects who they are in the best way possible.

My mom always used the justification that I was not old enough to wear makeup. She believed I was destroying my sensitive skin with chemicals. However, makeup made me confident. It made me feel good. It was a fashion statement for me that allowed me to enhance my beauty, not for others, but for myself. After we talked about it in sophomore year, my mom finally agreed to let me wear some makeup, as long as I didn't overdo it. Realize that your teenager is growing up and grow with them, granting them more freedom for their own style as time passes.

Also keep in mind that this is the age where life is all about being "popular." For me, middle school was a parallel to this idea of perfection: models, makeup tutorials, and "how to get a boy to like you" articles. Suddenly all I cared about was being beautiful. Life was about getting boys to like me and using makeup to achieve that. Life was about being pretty like the popular cliques in movies. Life was about following the newest and cutest fads to be like the girls we seemed to idolize and view as perfect. We conform to society in order to fit in because being different is hard. No one wants to be singled out of a crowd because being singled out means judgment, and teenagers, more than anyone, fear judgment.

Tip #3: Help establish the budget

Set an annual budget and allocate an amount to your teen. Giving teenagers the responsibility of managing their own money and closet will make them feel like you trust them and respect their maturity. Allowing them to experiment with how much they get every year or every month will give them a taste of what adulthood is like and teach the value of money.

Tip #4: Understand and explain

There will be days when your teenager shows up in the car on the way to school wearing an outfit that makes you feel like you have failed as a parent. Take a deep breath, and ask them to go change. Allow your teen to develop an identity using their own fashion choices and be lenient when you need to be. Explain why you feel as if certain garments are unacceptable or inappropriate. While I was growing up, I always craved an explanation that I agreed with and understood. Why did it matter if my legs or my shoulders were shown? I had been raised to respect myself, and I wasn't planning on wearing clothes that would sacrifice my character. That wasn't who I was. Your teen may be wondering the same thing, so when possible, offer reasonable clarifications.

Tip #5: Offer honest opinions

If your teen asks for advice about an outfit, it's because he or she respects and trusts you. Offer honest advice gently. If your teen looks peculiar in a chosen outfit, say that. Your teen wants the truth without feeling bad. It's tricky, but it can be done.

Tip #6: Don't accuse of wasting

It's easy to jump to conclusions and blame your teenager for growing out of clothes that they never wore. My mother chastises me for wasting money on the plethora of clothes that are threatening to break my closet. It seems like a lot, but in truth, it's a collection of my past. It's a collection of my many stages of fashion since first grade. I've worn and cherished every piece of clothing in my closet. Even if you bought something for your teen, and the tag hasn't been taken off, don't be frustrated. Just be aware that this is likely going to happen, and you have to be okay that there will be some outfits that will not be worn.

Tip #7: Go shopping together

Offer to go shopping with your teen sometimes to help them pick out cute, appropriate outfits. My parents and I searched in a multitude of malls all over the city to find articles of clothing that we agreed upon. "The shorts are too short, the shirt is too cropped, and the leggings are too revealing," they would state, simply and firmly. Shopping was a task that resulted in weary legs, a frustrated mother, and a lot of time spent. I remember begging to go to the five-story San Francisco mall in hopes I would find approval worthy clothes for the new school year. It may have taken a lot of time and effort to find clothes that were fair game, but I'm so glad that I did because I no longer had to stress about wondering if I would be reprimanded about the length of my shorts in the morning, since my mom was there to buy them with me in the first place.

Fashion is a way that some demonstrate identity. Fashion creates a community and ties together those belonging to that community. After all, fashion is what some people do for a living. But fashion can be the source of pain, anger, and exclusion like it was for me. I found out society wasn't in agreement with the tomboy outfits I wore growing up that I modeled after my brother. From the minute I stepped into middle school with my baggy neon basketball shorts and Nike t-shirts, I could tell, it would be different. Girls judged me differently because of my fashion. Boys either ran away from me, thinking I was a mistake of nature or rough housed with me like I was one of them. It felt off. I had never known that just the way that I dressed would make me feel like such a stranger.

I remember promising my friends when I was younger that I would never wear skinny jeans or dresses. And then, in less than a blink of an eye, everything I had come to know about myself shifted. So somehow, slowly, but surely, I changed. I may not have noticed it at first, but I began conforming. It began with wearing sweaters on top of my basketball shorts. The month after that, I started wearing skinny jeans. Two months after that, I asked for sleeveless tops. A year later, I began wearing dresses. By eighth grade, I had transformed into a "girl". I had adapted to fit the rules of how a girl should dress, and I no longer stood out, which was my goal: a sense of belonging. I had begun to wear skirts in my school uniform, something I thought I never would have done.

Maybe if I had lived in a different environment, a different world, I would have never changed. Or maybe I still would have ultimately become the clothes-crazed girl I am today. I guess I'll never really know, but I can say one thing for sure: redesigning my closet has made me feel like I fit in and has made me happier. However, that doesn't mean all teenagers should conform. Parents should encourage their teens to express themselves in whatever way they feel comfortable. I had lived too much on the outside, and I finally found a way in through fashion, so I decided to go with the flow.

All I know is I'm still finding myself and who I am and my own style.

Trust me, I thought I was a train wreck, and I like to think I turned out pretty okay.

So if I can do it, you definitely can too.

9

Insomnia Disorder

A flash of light sparkled in my eyes as I blinked away the sleep that still clung to my eyelashes. I glanced at the clock and saw the time "3:24 A.M." and groaned. Who could possibly be texting me at this hour? *Can't sleep. I swear I have insomnia.* I read the blue text message quickly before slumping back into my pillow. I'd deal with this tomorrow. I was too tired to even think about the possibility of my friend not sleeping when all I could think about was sleeping. I talked to her the next day and found that her mind could never be turned off. No matter how much or how long she yawned, closed her eyes, or lay in bed, she could never truly sleep. It took her hours to doze off, and even a tree branch slapping against her window was enough to wake her. It was an on and off disorder that intensified during stressful times and became manageable when everything was going smoothly.

"Do you think I should see a doctor?" another text floated in the next week, a stunning 4:00 A.M. as the send time.

I grunted and typed back: "Yes." In a feeble attempt to make her laugh and dispel her anxiety, I typed back, "I might have to as well if you keep texting me at this hour."

This carried on for a solid month, yet no matter how much she appealed to her parents, they asked her to hold out until the end of the school year.

"It'll go away," they kept telling her.

She spent the next few months tossing and turning, eyes glazing over as she stared at the dust that collected in the lights above her bed. She counted sheep and listened to endless lyrics that flooded through her ears, but nothing was enough to pull her into the sea of sleep. Insomnia is a sleep disorder in which a person has trouble falling asleep or staying asleep. It can rob many adolescents and children of the sleep that their body desperately needs during the crucial period of mental and physical growth and development. It impairs functions and leads to an increase in mood swings and irritability. Insomnia can be an inability to fall asleep, tossing or turning constantly, or waking up and being unable to go back to sleep.

Getting an insufficient amount of sleep is an epidemic that is sweeping the United States according to Sleep Education, which estimates that between 25% and 45% of adolescents fail to obtain enough sleep every night. Lack of sleep also leads to insomnia or exacerbates the problem. About 10% of teens have a chronic insomnia order, which occurs at least three times per week for at least three months. Insomnia interferes with a person's performance at school or work (Heffron, 2014). Based on studies, it is estimated that an employee with insomnia loses about eight days of work performance each year. For the entire US workforce, this adds up to an estimated $63 billion in lost work performance due to insomnia each year.

Insomnia can be temporary, so it is classified into long-term insomnia and short-term insomnia. Typically, short-term insomnia results due to an issue that has recently arisen. Long-term, on the other hand, is a consistent sleep disturbance that can sometimes be traced back to some sort of medical disorder. Although insomnia is a very common problem, it is one of the most under recognized among US teens. Teens with this sleep disorder are more likely to have depression, anxiety, and panic disorders.

Many of these disorders go hand and hand, and each aggravates the other. According to a study published by BBC, teens who go to bed after midnight are 24% more likely to have depression than those who go to bed before 11:00 P.M. Insomnia can begin as early as age eleven and can then continue to harm and impact the adolescent through maturation ("Late-night Teens", 2010).

Teenage insomnia has two primary causes: sleep cycle irregularities and emotional stress. Once insomnia imbeds itself into a teenager's life, many secondary problems arise. Teens may become addicted to coffee, which then further messes up their sleep schedules and results in anxiety that worsens insomnia. It's a cycle of intensity that continues to worsen each problem until, eventually, the individual hits a breaking point.

Signs of sleep disorders

Although the signs may differ for each person, the following are some of the most common, according to Sleep Education ("Insomnia - Symptoms," 2015):

- difficulty in falling or staying asleep;
- consistent sleepiness or fatigue during the day;
- a feeling of exhaustion, even after getting an appropriate amount of sleep;
- memory loss;
- inability to concentrate on daily tasks;
- decreased performance in school;
- other mental illnesses, such as depression, anxiety disorder, or bipolar disorder;
- cravings for sugar;
- dependence on coffee or energy drinks to stay awake;
- decreased motivation;

- waking up very early in the morning and being unable to fall back asleep;

- waking up in the middle of the night; and

- tossing and turning during sleep.

Causes of insomnia

Insomnia usually does not just sprout on its own but is rather an accumulation of psychological, environmental, and physical factors, such as diet, stress, or drastic changes. ("Insomnia - Symptoms," 2015).

Stress is a broad term and is probably one of the most common causes of insomnia. Difficulties in family life, social interactions, and relocation or moving can all contribute to an accumulation of stress and negativity. Sometimes, the body's natural response to cope with this pressure is to, for example, shut down and obstruct sleep. This stress may prompt an individual to overthink everything going on in life as a result, and the activity in the brain may be so loud that sleep is immediately chased away.

Eating habits are often overlooked as a cause of insomnia, but diet plays a very big role in how a person sleeps at night. Drinking coffee or soda or eating sugary foods before bed makes it difficult to obtain a restful sleep. Teens who consume drugs or drink alcohol often experience the same problems. A healthy diet and exercise can positively influence sleep cycles and habits. My parents offer me a glass of warm milk or a soothing tea before bed to ease my body into a peaceful, drowsy lull.

Medications used to treat certain mental disorders can cause insomnia as a side effect.

Environmental conditions can also result in insomnia. Excessive light, heat, or noise in the bedroom prohibit sleep, making it impossible to calm down or get enough peace. Uncomfortable beds may also interfere with sleep, as you'll be too focused on trying to get comfortable. Ensure that electronics and other screens are out of the bedroom, as the artificial lights and radiation can screw with the production of the sleep hormone.

Disorders or physical issues, such as nighttime asthma, allergies, or itchy skin can also get in the way of getting rest. Pulling a muscle can also obstruct sleep, as the pain may distract you from allowing your mind to be at peace. Sometimes, these inconveniences are manageable, but once they flare up, it can be difficult to deal with. Other disorders can also be a cause of insomnia; teens with depression, autism, or Asperger's may also have trouble sleeping.

TIPS FOR TEENS

Tip #1: Develop a sleep cycle

Figure out what bedtime offers you a complete sleep cycle. Use the website sleepyti.me to plan what time to go to bed, so you don't force yourself out of an REM sleep (deep sleep) and wake up feeling tired. Maintain a constant sleep schedule, and put away electronics thirty minutes prior to when you need to head to bed.

Don't watch movies or Skype with your best friend until 2:00 A.M. We've all done it at some point, but this is likely to disrupt sleep patterns and lead to some serious insomnia. One or two nights won't kill you, but if you do it often enough, it'll start to take a toll.

Tip #2: Lifestyle habits

Exercise more often, eat less junk food, and avoid all sugars and caffeine before bed. Caffeine and sugar will hype you up, and what we want is for you to "chill." Avoid the use of drugs and alcohol and try to get enough fresh air in a week. All these factors will help in getting the most restful sleep possible. Drink warm milk before going to bed, or exercise and then take a bubble bath. It's all about what relaxes you the most.

Tip #3: Know when to try again

If you've been lying in bed for more than one hour without being able to sleep, get up and find something else to do until sleepiness hits. Either tire yourself out mentally by doing some work that doesn't involve a lot of brainpower or take a run to tire your muscles. Maybe take a shower to relax before coming back to bed or listen to some soothing music. Set a playlist of music that settles you so you don't have to keep changing the song. That's something that I did almost every night of middle school and high school to distract myself from the drama of my school life. Maybe review some math homework then try to go back to bed. Sometimes, no amount of lying in bed will be enough to carry you off to sleep, but if you relax or tire yourself out before heading to bed, you're more likely to fall asleep easier.

Tip #4: Sleeping environment

Find a bed and a pillow that work for you. Make sure the temperature is right by adding more blankets, turning on the air condition or heater, or sleeping in comfortable clothing. The optimal temperature for a room is usually around 72 degrees; my family likes it to be 68 degrees during winter. Ensure noise in the house is limited, and you're content when going to bed. Try not to think too much about the next day. Put that behind you and come to terms with it, otherwise you'll spend all night thinking about it. Ensure that the aura of your environment is calm, cool, and relaxed. Put shades on the windows to make sure that the room is completely dark. Also, avoid having clocks that are facing you, or just take the clocks out completely. Looking at clocks when you're sleeping can cause anxiety and make it harder to fall asleep. Try curling up with a fuzzy blanket during the winter to create a safer and warmer aura.

Tip #5: Get help

Specialists may need to get involved if you are unable to get an optimal amount of sleep no matter what you try. There are psychological methods that will greatly alleviate stress and make it easier to sleep. Find a sleep specialist and start the conversation. If stress is the reason sleep is impossible, it may be necessary to see a therapist or doctor to get help for these psychological or physical issues and develop a coping plan that will make sleeping a whole lot easier.

TIPS FOR PARENTS

Tip #1: Start early

From an early age, establish good sleeping patterns for your child and make sure to set an example with your own sleeping patterns. It's easy to eliminate childhood insomnia by making sure that your teen is not allowed to stay up all night watching television or playing video games. Those who do are much more likely to suffer from sleep disorders later on.

Tip #2: Reinforce rules

Make sure your teen is following the rules, and make sure that they follow their bedtime ritual and schedule. Allow for some exceptions, especially when time is limited due to extra activities or school, but for the most part, ensure that they are getting seven to eight hours of sleep a night. Talk to your teen and establish a plan together. Set a bedtime, a wake up time, and an electronics usage time. Establish how late into the evening they can eat certain foods, and what to eat after that time. Setting these guidelines may irk your teen initially, but will greatly benefit them in the long run. Offer them incentives to follow these rules and put consequences in place if they don't. I was incredibly frustrated when my parents first imposed these kinds of rules, but when I started sleeping at 11 P.M., I was waking up more refreshed, and I was actually glad to be going to bed earlier.

Tip #3: Communicate

Check in with your teen from time to time about how they're sleeping and monitor their sleeping patterns every couple of months. Make sure that they seem to be having a peaceful sleep, and if they're not, ask them if this is a nightly occurrence. They may be experiencing a lot of stress, so be available if they need to talk. Having someone to communicate with may alleviate some of the stress they're feeling and help them sleep better.

Tip #4: Understand medication risks

Communicate with your doctor completely before getting your teen medication. Some medications will cause insomnia, so it's important to talk to the doctor about other possible alternatives or solutions.

Tip #5: Environment

Set up a good environment for your teen's sleep cycle. Don't watch movies in the middle of the night or make a lot of noise during their sleep periods. Avoid loud conversations or arguments right before bed; instead opt for a peaceful discussion of the day in summary or even just a simple hug and "goodnight." Making your teenage comfortable with the aura of the house, the comfort of the bed, and the temperature of the room will help them. Figure out what works for everyone in the house, establish that as the house standard, and don't change it. Habit is the best, especially in regards to sleep.

Tip #6: Seek a professional

Even if your teenager denies insomnia, it may be better just to take them in for a check up with a doctor. Catching insomnia sooner rather than later before it gets out of hand and impacts your teen's life is the best case scenario.

We've all had nights where we toss and turn, hoping to find the perfect position to no avail and end up just curling up into a ball. We've all had those nights where we lie awake, contemplating the meaning of life and death as memories flood our minds and kick away even the notion of sleep. We've all had those nights where we can't decide about the temperature of our bodies and opt to starfish across the bed, half of our bodies inside the blanket and the other half outside.

What's not normal is experiencing that every night, and it's important to catch that before it's too late. Figure out what works for you; it's different for everyone. Maybe it's sleeping naked, or maybe it's sleeping with a soundtrack of croaking frogs in the background. Experiment and figure out what makes you feel the most rested. I've found that fuzzy socks, onesies, and Disney pillows work the best for me.

So cuddle up with your favorite stuffed animal and get some sleep tonight.

Sweet dreams; don't let the bed buggies bite.

10

Homosexuality

His quivering hands sent me into a frenzy of my own, and the tremors that seemed to rack his soul transposed themselves into his darting green eyes. Barely holding my gaze, he cleared his throat, glancing away once more. I barely knew his name, and I had no idea who he was, save the fact that he was part of my team at the leadership seminar that I attended. One night, we found ourselves sitting cross-legged across from each other, sharing our greatest fears and aspirations as we clutched hands.

"I've never told anyone this," he said, his voice trailed off, and he licked his lips slowly, the artificial light glinting off his braces. I felt the intake of oxygen and felt it rushing through his veins. He squeezed his hands with a gentle fierceness before he continued, "I'm gay."

He blinked quickly, expecting some sort of gasp or blatant words of criticism, but I did nothing but offer him a warm smile and encouraged him to continue. He wove the words together effortlessly, almost as if he'd been practicing the perfect way to say them in the mirror all his life.

"You're one of the only people who know because you seem like the kind of a person who won't judge me. I haven't mentioned it to anyone else. Not my parents, not my siblings, not my friends at school," he said, his jaw clenched. "I'm so scared. They won't accept me. My parents will kick me out. I'll be an outcast. People will call me a fag."

And that's the case for many homosexual teenagers. They're so incredibly terrified of revealing their true identities for fear of being rejected from society. Recently, homosexuality has become a very big deal. We've had former President Obama fight for LGBTQ+ rights in court, particularly marriage. We've made a lot of strides in America, but there's still so much missing because of the generation gap. Homosexuality has been around throughout history and across cultures; it's just always been concealed. Even in ancient Roman times, certain emperors such as Hadrian would have gay lovers who they referred to as "trusted advisors" or "best friends." Recent changes in our attitudes toward gays and lesbians have made individuals more comfortable with their sexual orientations, but there are many actions left to be taken to create the most accepting society possible.

Most homosexual individuals first experience homosexual feelings during adolescence but may brush those feelings off until later on in life. An important thing to remember, however, is that having a sexual experience or relationship with a person of the same sex doesn't necessarily define you as a gay or a bisexual. Experimentation is very common, especially when you're still finding yourself. The origin of homosexuality hasn't been concluded, but one thing is for sure: a person's sexual orientation is not a choice. I know a few gay individuals who wish they could be straight because of the hardships they face once they "come out of the closet," or reveal their sexuality. As a common victim of bullying, I've had one gay friend explain to me, "I love myself, but sometimes I remember how much easier it would be to be straight."

Another gay friend described dealing with sexuality as a war: "It's like a war going on inside you—there's the side that knows who you truly are, and then there's the side that wants to deny it. It's constantly on your mind, you can't get rid of it, and if you are lucky enough to forget about it for a while, it always comes back to you." But that shouldn't be the kind of message we should be sending. Every homosexual individual should be proud of their sexuality and embrace it, not desire to be someone else. That is not what we should stand for.

Types of sexuality

Distinguishing between types of sexuality helps to better understand what homosexuality really is. There are four types of sexualities ("Gay, Lesbian," 2016):

- **Heterosexual**, otherwise called "straight," individuals are attracted to members of the opposite sex.

- **Homosexual** individuals are attracted to members of the same sex. "Gay" is usually used to refer to a homosexual individual of the male sex but can be used colloquially to refer to both sexes. "Lesbian" is used to refer to a homosexual individual of the female sex.

- **Bisexual** individuals are attracted to both sexes.

- **Pansexual** individuals are attracted to any sex, gender, or gender identity.

The acronym "LGBTQ+," a commonly used word in today's era, stands for lesbian, gay, bisexual, transgender, and queer.

Statistics about homosexuality

Youth Risk Behavior Survey (YRBS) survey conducted in the time span of 2001 through 2009 by the Centers of Disease Control and Prevention and data collected from Safe Schools Coalition of Washington yielded the following data reports (*Parent's Influence*, 2013; "LGBT Youth", 2014):

- 91% of responders declared themselves as heterosexual. Three percent to five percent identified as homosexual, and 4.0% to 7.0% were unsure of their sexual identity.

- The percentage of LGB students who were threatened or injured with a weapon on school property in the prior year ranged from 12% to 28%.

- 19% to 29% of gay and lesbian students and 18% to 28% of bisexual students experience dating violence.

- 91.4% of LGBTQ have reported hearing homophobic remarks used to describe them ("faggot," "dyke," etc). Of these individuals, 36.4% have also reported sexual harassment, 46% have reported verbal harassment, and 12.1% have reported physical harassment.

- 6.1% of LGBTQ individuals have reported physical assault in school.

- 21% of self-identified gay men knew they were not straight in junior high, and 17% said they knew in grade school. Women, on the other hand, said that 6.0% knew they were not straight in junior high, and 11% knew in grade school.

- LGB individuals are more likely to engage in drug abuse before the age of thirteen and more likely to have engaged in a physical fight and carried a weapon.

- 38.2% of individuals do not feel comfortable talking to teachers about LGBTQ issues.

- LGB youth are four times as likely to report being threatened with a weapon on school grounds and five times as likely to skip school for fear of their safety.

- LGBTQ youth are also at increased risk for suicidal thoughts and behaviors, suicide attempts, and suicide. A nationally representative study of adolescents in seventh through twelfth grades found that lesbian, gay, and bisexual youth were more than twice as likely to have attempted suicide as their heterosexual peers (*Parent's Influence*, 2013).

What causes homosexuality?

This isn't a question. Nothing "causes" homosexuality. Individuals are born how they are born. Whether it's a genetic trait or something that's related to certain variations in DNA, sexual orientation is not something to be "corrected" or changed. It's encoded into who we are, and each individual has every right to feel the way they do.

Concerns for homosexuality

Many teens try to deny their true sexuality due to reservations about how people will treat them once the news is out. They may feel very isolated and alone, despite the amount of awareness and the growing homosexual community. Other concerns may include (*Parent's Influence*, 2013):

- feeling as if they don't belong in society;

- feeling guilty about who they are;

- being teased, bullied, or harassed by others;

- fearing discrimination when engaging in other activities, joining clubs, or getting a job;

- worrying about AIDS, HIV, and other sexually transmitted diseases; and

- worrying about the response from their family and loved ones.

Due to concerns like these, homosexual teens may withdraw from activities and friends, have very low self-esteem, or have trouble concentrating. These teens are also at a much higher risk of developing depression or finding ways to cope with their emotional battle by abusing drugs or alcohol.

Tips for Homosexual Teens

Whether you're in or out of the closet, there's a lot you can do to get comfortable with who you are and be an inspiration for others. The more we support each other and accept one another, the more love and equality we can spread throughout the world.

Tip #1: Do your research about labels

Many different sexualities and a variety of labels for sexuality are used. I think it's important to research these terms and be sensitive to use them appropriately. Maybe you don't identify with any of them, or you're not sure which label you are, and that's totally okay. You don't have to label yourself. No requirement exists for you to be only one. No time limit exists on you deciding who you are. Don't feel pressured to put a label on yourself. Discover your own sexuality and take as much time as you need to do that. Come out whenever you're ready.

Labels will change over time, and as you experience more, you'll be more in tune with yourself. You might think you're gay right now, but you might later discover you're bisexual. There's no rule against re-identifying yourself when you learn more about your desires and tendencies. Many individuals may also have misconceptions about these labels, so it's important to do your own research so you can educate the people around you. A lot of teenagers and parents don't really understand much beyond the basics of what homosexuality is, so it may be necessary for you to teach them.

Tip #2: Find confidantes

Unfortunately, we still live in a society where it can be dangerous to be anything but straight. You automatically don't fit the societal norm. I can't stress enough how much easier your life will be if you can find a supportive community who will love you no matter what. Start off with one friend or a sibling who you trust. Scope out your parents' views on homosexuality and determine whether they'll be accepting. If you're sure they will be, definitely tell them. If not, wait on it, and find others you can tell first so that you can develop a game plan with them. Really take your time and explore when and to whom you want to come out. You need to find the best possible way and time that will put you in the least amount of danger. A gradual coming out process is usually the most secure, as long as your environment is one that enforces a tolerance policy. I know my school is definitely one of acceptance, and we've had many students openly declare their self-ascribed label.

It's quite honestly appalling that such careful steps have to be taken just to ensure safety for being who you are. Over time, we will not just be tolerant, but rather accepting. One day, homophobia will be destroyed, and people will no longer have to "come out" as gay, because it'll be as easy as declaring you're straight.

Tip #3: Join a community

It can be quite a scary idea to open up to others about an identity that you may have spent your entire life hiding. If your school has it, join the Gay-Straight Alliance Club (GSA) or any other LGBTQ+ positive club. It can be a great way to become more comfortable in your skin and meet peers who are struggling with similar obstacles or facing the same fears that you are ("Gay-Straight Alliances," n.d.).

Tip #4: Give it time

Not everyone is going to be as accepting as you might want when you first reveal your truth. Your family members or friends may need some time to accept the idea. A lot of parents don't understand what it means to be gay. I've heard parents talk about how younger generations have made up the idea of being gay, and I've heard them describe sexual orientation as a "mental disorder." In many regions across the world homosexuality is immediately shunned and shut down. It didn't matter if a boy liked a boy; he would marry a girl and have children to continue the family name. Stay patient. Your news might be a rollercoaster for the entire family. But ultimately, if your parents really do love you, which they likely do, they'll accept you exactly as you are.

Tip #5: Never lose yourself

Look: we're all already aware that society will forever and always be critical. But as you go through the mentally taxing process of coming out, be aware that not everyone will accept you. But that doesn't mean you shouldn't accept yourself.

In the end, it's really about how you view yourself, and not how anyone else views you. Maybe you'll have the best ever coming out story because you grew up in the most nurturing, loving environment, but it might not always be that easy. Society is getting more accepting, but many improvements remain to be made. We'll get there eventually. Our generation is a tolerant, diverse generation, and I know we're going to make strides. But until we get there, don't lose yourself. Never think that you're weird or freakish or strange for being different because you aren't. Many people are fighting the same fight that you are and attempting to embrace their sexuality, so remember that you're never really alone.

Tip #6: Understand the changes

Many aspects of life may change once you come out as gay. People will treat you differently, your relationship with your siblings might change, and the general attitude toward you might be affected, but hopefully all of this will be temporary. Be ready to deal with whatever comes and make sure you have a support system throughout the process.

TIPS FOR PARENTS

I understand that finding out your teen is gay might come as a shock to you. Or maybe you knew all along, and you don't need this chapter. If you don't understand what homosexuality is, you might find yourself wondering how this happened or fearing for your child's future.

"How will my teen have kids when she grows up?"

"Won't my son be bullied and treated differently?"

"What did I do to cause this?"

And although these are valid questions in a sense, take a deep breath and understand that this isn't a choice, and it isn't something you "did." Being straight is just like having brown eyes. But there are other people in the world with blue eyes and green eyes and even violet eyes. Every eye color, every sexuality, and every person is beautiful. You should want the ultimate happiness for your teen. And if that's with someone of the same sex, what's the issue?

Tip #1: Create a safe environment

From a young age, really try to talk about the concept of sexuality with your kids. Find ways to integrate education about sexual identities into your conversations. If children start to question their own sexual identity, they'll feel comfortable with coming to you and asking questions. You'll build a better relationship with your kid and prepare them for the questions they might ask themselves later.

Tip #2: Don't perpetuate gender stereotypes

If your boy wants to be a princess for Halloween, let him. If your girl wants to play football, let her. Don't perpetuate the gender stereotypes molded into society. Especially for transgender individuals, it's important that children are allowed to develop and wear or play or be whatever they want. If you repress identity, children feel an inherent lack of safety and comfort and might be more likely to hide their true sexuality.

Tip #3: Be accepting

It may stretch far from what you're used to, but in America, being homosexual has become common. My parents never really understood the concept of "being gay" until my dad's close friend's son came out as a gay. My parents did their research, listened to the other parents, and then realized that it was nothing to fear. It's a way of life. It's just a different way of life than they were used to. But it's becoming more and more common every single day.

You shouldn't have a problem seeing a man and a man walking down the street holding hands or seeing a woman and a woman caring for a baby together. There is no harmful affect to you. If anything, it teaches these individuals to be more caring and loving, as they understand how it feels to be shunned by society. You are going to be the person that your child needs the most during the coming out process. So really try to be there for them.

If you're shocked, take some time to reflect and do research, but then get back to doing what you do best, which is parenting and loving your child to the best of your ability.

Tip #4: Ask your teen

If you're unsure about your teen's sexuality, don't be afraid to ask him or her. Don't make it a big deal and call a family meeting. Simply remind your teen that it's totally acceptable to be homosexual. The more topics like these are treated casually, the more accepting your teen will be of themselves and of others ("Gay, Lesbian," 2016).

Honestly, it's sad we have to make anything but straight a big deal. We need to start teaching children and parents that being gay isn't a new idea. Homosexual individuals are simply different. And we're all different. Isn't that what makes us beautiful? Love is love, and that will not change. Whether that love is between a man and a man, a woman and a man, or a woman and a woman, it is still love, and that's what is important.

Wear rainbow flags proudly.

Destroy ignorance surrounding homosexuality.

Support our brothers and sisters who are gay and lesbian and bisexual and transgender.

Preach that "gay is okay."

And hopefully, soon people will realize that gay is not just okay; gay is great.

Gay is loved.

Gay is beautiful.

We all are beautiful.

11

Mood Swings

"I can't believe she did that!" a friend said, and her laugh rang out across the cafeteria as we strolled through the line to grab our lunch during one of the summer camps I attended.

We traveled in a pack, daintily picking up our plates and then shuffling to our table as we gossiped. My friend giggled once more and proceeded to take a bite out of her chicken nugget, ripping the top off in one smooth gesture. She clenched the ketchup bottle in her hand, squeezing out dollops with a hunger-driven craze in a feeble attempt to get enough on her plate.

"Hey, can you pass that?" one of my closest friends called out from across the table to another girl.

Within seconds, my friend's smile melted, transforming into a grimace that consumed her. Tears filled her eyes, and before long, she was sobbing, rivers of anguish streaking down her face, leaving mascara stains in the corner of her eyes. "Is that all I'm good for?" she cried, her voice hiccupping into a squeak. "A ketchup passer?"

The girls at my table glanced at each other, gawking at the situation that had just unfolded in front us. We rushed to her side, drowning her in hugs and forehead kisses, promising that everything would be okay.

"Bub, are you okay?" I spoke softly in her ear.

She nodded quickly, a rosy tinge rushing to her cheeks as she dabbed under her eyes. "I have no idea where that came from. I'm so sorry."

I knew that feeling all too well and many women can easily relate to it. Mood swings are expected, especially through puberty and adolescence. Because of this, mood disorders are written off and go undiagnosed. Sometimes, it's important that a professional deal with the underlying psychological issue to appease mood disorders. Teenage hormones contribute to physical growth and sexual development but also are a main reason for mood swings. As these substances take hold, it's evident that the intensity of emotions will increase and become difficult to control.

Emotions and moods dictate our lives, and they can change for a spectrum of reasons. Even individuals with excellent self-control have variations in their mood almost every day, though they don't necessarily display it. When we're happy, our approach to life is different than when we're upset. If you're happy, you're more likely to spread joy to those around you, while if you're sad, you're more likely to wallow in sadness and add each negative event that happens as yet another reason to be upset. Mood swings are common among humans and are considered healthy to maintain in a daily routine. However, when rapid mood swings are occurring within a very short time span, it may be a cause for concern.

"It's just teenage moodiness" is something that my parents have used as an excuse for my behavior. And though that's usually true, as it was often for me, it's also important to recognize that there's a difference between teenage moodiness and mood disorders. A very clear line runs between the two and can be distinguished by three factors: length, intensity, and triggers. The normal reaction after an impactful event is to be moody, whether it is because of a breakup, a lost basketball game, or just a bad grade. These things are called triggers, and being moody is a normal response to a trigger. What's not normal is experiencing heightened mood swings without a major trigger in place. Although a hormone THP is usually known to relieve anxiety, researchers at the State University of New York have revealed that this hormone has the reverse effect in teens and can actually increase the likelihood of mood swings. The cause and duration of this switch is unknown, but it helps us better understand why mood swings are aggravated in teenagers (Smith, 2007).

During puberty, teenagers experience a "noisier brain," making it harder to empathize, do the right thing, or read situations. San Diego State University scientists discovered that teens' abilities to read the emotional stance of the people around them even dips as much as 20%. Another contribution to mood swings is the lack of sleep. Due to schoolwork and social drama, it's difficult to always go to bed at an acceptable time, especially since there's so much happening around us in the teen community. While the darkness hormone melatonin is produced in adults at about 10:00 P.M., it's not produced until 1:00 A.M. to 2:00 A.M. in teens ("Mood Swings, n.d.).

Signs of teenage mood swings

The following are some signs of mood swings or possible mood disorders (Lloyd, 2016). Children may show the following behaviors more often than usual:

- being irritable or upset for more than two weeks;
- extreme blows to self-confidence and self-esteem;
- experiencing a variation of emotions from happy to sad within short periods of time (could also be Bipolar Disorder);
- erratic behavior;
- disregard for others' emotions;
- being disrespectful;
- violent and prolonged temper tantrums;
- sleep irregularities;
- high anxiety, particular separation anxiety;
- a decrease in patience and frustration tolerance;
- abandonment of prior hobbies and activities;

- substance abuse;

- a drop in grades and quality of school work;

- problems in social relationships; and

- a constant need to be active.

Causes of mood swings

Professor Steven Wood revealed that the most likely cause for mood swings in adolescents is a combination of the sex hormones testosterone and estrogen. These hormones prompt the desire for social acceptance and change the way many teenagers think. Although these sex hormones do contribute to most physical changes, they also add to many emotional changes and the uncontrollability of these emotions. (Witchalls, n.d.)

Sometimes, stress can pile on to the point where we hit our breaking point, and everything we've spent so long attempting to save comes crashing down. We all deal with a lot, whether it is financial struggles, family fights, or work issues, but we have to train ourselves to deal with these issues in the proper manner. Other possible aggravators of teens' emotions are drugs and alcohol. Although these bring on a euphoric high at first, too much can negatively impact mental health and prompt a steady decline into a world of highs and lows.

Caffeine does the same thing. While most of us can handle one to two cups of coffee a day, an excess of caffeine for some can bring on mood swings, jitters, and heart palpitations. Caffeine may provide a high for a while, but eventually leads to a crash. It is also incredibly addictive, and it can cause those who miss out on it for one day to be incredibly bipolar. Sugar does the same thing. When the sugar wears off, energy stores are depleted, and mood dips. I'm no stranger to coffee cravings and sugar cravings, so it's all about mediations and knowing the time window that's appropriate.

TIPS FOR TEENS

Tip #1: Sleep

When growing, getting at least eight hours of sleep is a necessity, and although it may not always be realistic, it's important to strive to get as much sleep as possible. A well-rested mind leads to a more relaxed mind, which can minimize moods swings and anxiety and help you think more logically. Keep a routine, and avoid eating sugar before bed. Also attempt to put away your electronics at least thirty minutes prior to when you're about to go to bed.

I never realized how much sleeping more would help in every aspect of life, until I tried it for myself. After going from four hours a night to seven hours a night, I learned how to better cope with my emotions and was able to understand class work with less effort. Before, a constant fog covered my mind, and now, I feel more prepared, less irritable, and a whole lot smarter. I know you don't want to, and you'd rather be spending that time watching the latest Netflix movie or video chatting with friends until the wee hours of the night. But you're not Superman, trust me, and before long, it's going to hit you like a truck, and you will realize how utterly tired you are.

Tip #2: Develop good eating habits

Eating an excess of carbohydrates, sugar, or processed foods will result in a higher likelihood of mood swings. Try to eat a balanced diet consisting of protein, fruits, vegetables, and dairy. Avoid alcohol, caffeine, and energy drinks, and drink as much water as possible. Don't skip meals, but rather keep a constant food meal plan and follow it. Have a good breakfast before leaving the house, and you're guaranteed to start the day off in a better mood.

Tip #3: Exercise

Exercise releases endorphins, which is essentially a "feel good" hormone. Try to get in at least thirty minutes of cardiovascular exercise every day, and you'll be in a good mood. Exercising is a great coping mechanism that many people utilize in their daily routines. Even if I can't always go to the gym, I find myself running whenever I'm upset. Running helps me think clearer and puts me in a better mood. When dealing with drama, I make sure to take a lap around my neighborhood before even thinking of responding to the situation.

Tip #4: Relax

Find methods for relaxation. Sometimes, if you extract yourself from a stressful situation, down a glass of cold water, and take a deep breath, you'll find new solutions. Stress and panic can blur understanding of what to do to solve a problem, but taking a step back will provide time to think of the best way to proceed. Try to find a way to relax, whether through music, the spa, or even meditation. Find a hobby that keeps you centered and balanced and wait so that you don't make any rash decisions. I've found that waiting at least an hour before responding to something that irritates me often alleviates the anger I initially felt and helps me to respond without worsening the situation.

Tip #5: Find someone to confide in

Find someone you can talk to about issues. Friends or peers who understand what you're going through will make you feel more comfortable, and they offer perspectives and solutions that might not have occurred to you.

Whenever I'm upset, the first person I call is my best friend. I've had her send me long texts about how much she loves me and that's often enough to make me feel better. Siblings and parents are also great resources. Talk to your parents? Crazy idea, I know. But try it. It may work for you.

Tip #6: Plan for it

You cannot change the fact that adolescent mood swings happen. They will occur, most likely, in any situation. You may not be able to slow it completely, but learn to appreciate what's happening and be aware of when those hormonal shifts are a cause of something that you cannot control.

Tip #7: Get professional help

Never be scared of reaching out to a professional. Professional therapists may help you find a way to cope with mood swings, such as behavioral therapy, cognitive therapy, literary therapy, and supplements. Talk to your doctor and decide what works for best for you.

TIPS FOR PARENTS

Parents often receive the backlash of teenagers' mood swings, so it's just as important for parents to learn how to cope (Bhargava, 2012).

Tip #1: Understand

Try to be aware of what's happening and offer your teenager leeway. If they're being moody and say something you don't appreciate, take a deep breath before responding. Offer ways to cope and tell them that you'll have the conversation later once they calm down. Teenagers are hard to understand sometimes, and when a teen is moody, he or she becomes an absolute monster. You probably experienced many of the same mood swings that your teenager is experiencing, so really try to relate to them and don't be too harsh on them.

Tip #2: Communicate

Ensure that your teen understands that you're always available to talk and that you want to hear what's upsetting them. Check in with them from time to time and offer coping mechanisms. Maybe take them out for their favorite ice cream or buy that video game they've been wanting. A kind act can go a long way.

Tip #3: Distinguish the line

Know when it's time to see a therapist and be able to distinguish between a passing phase of moodiness and an actual mood disorder. If you're unsure, take your teen in to see a doctor anyway, as it's better to be safe than sorry and get them diagnosed before it gets out of hand.

Can you successfully control your moodiness? Likely not. As much as it sucks, it's incredibly difficult to control mood swings. When experiencing mood swings, use coping mechanisms. When nothing else works, try to relax and wait for the phase to pass. Time fixes mood swings, and more often than not, that initial irritability and anger will quell and fade. Give yourself time to recuperate and wallow in your sadness before pointing yourself in the direction of happiness. It's important for everyone to take their time alone to reflect and come to terms with triggers or events.

Dealing with life is already hard and adding mood swings just increases the pressure. Keep in mind that this is just a stage, and you'll be laughing about it in a few years. The only true advice I can offer you is to stock up on ice cream.

Grab some chocolate and a few tissues.

You'll be just fine.

12

Peer Pressure

"Literally, I've never had this much fun," my friend squealed into my ear as we danced together, our waists swaying as we screamed out the words to the newest Drake song.

The air was dripping with the wild hormones of the night, and the ground seemed to reverberate against our every move. Lights flashed this way and that, and the sweat of the people close to us enveloped us in a pocket of heat that was beginning to set fire to our bodies. Out of nowhere, I was whisked out of the crowd with a harsh yank from my friend, and we stumbled out into the night with the hopes that the cold air would cool our necks and breathe softly on our skin.

"Woo, girl, I ain't never been that sweaty in my life," she said and grinned at me, fanning her face with the back of her hand. Her chocolate skin made her nearly invisible in the darkness, but I could catch the glint of her eyes from miles away.

I chucked my heels off as I sank into the bench, groaning at the pain that throbbed through my feet in a steady rhythm. "Sierra, remind me why I wear heels."

She chuckled and collapsed beside me, as she purred, "Because you're a sexy ass mofo, chica."

My laugh echoed across the shadows that were drawn around us like curtains, and I settled back into my seat, wiggling my toes in the draft that passed us. I turned my head slightly to find Sierra stopped cold, her hands frozen as she brought them to her trembling lips. Within seconds, I heard it.

Footsteps.

Her panicked eyes met mine, and we scooted close together, praying that our duo would be enough to fend off whoever was coming to get us.

"Yo, shawty!" We heard a voice call out into the breeze, and a glimmer of recognition flitted across Sierra's face.

He stepped out in the light, and within seconds, Sierra had launched out of her seat, tackling him in a hug that squeezed his eyes out of his sockets and knocked the wind out of his stomach. "Elijah," she squealed, her arms still around him.

His hearty laugh echoed in our ears, and he pulled me in for a group hug as I stepped up to him.

"Hey, Elijah," I chirped, my smile reaching from ear to ear. Sierra stepped down beside me once more, analyzing him slowly.

He grunted and smoothed his hands over his hair, trying to adjust his stance before speaking. He leaned in toward both of us, voice a low growl as he whispered, "Y'all want some molly? I got it in my dorm. We can go crazy tonight."

I felt Sierra tense next to me. "Nah, we good, Elijah. I ain't ever messin' with drugs again. One shitty experience with weed is all I need to stay the hell away from drugs," she sighed out the words carefully, as if she already had an idea of what his next response would be.

"Sierra, c'mon. You know I'll keep you safe, though. Just one night. When we ever gonna get high with Sam, otherwise?" At the mention of my name, my insides dropped. No way in hell was I doing drugs. He glanced at me. "Sammm..." he drawled pleadingly. "It's fun. Don't tell me you're a pussy." He winked at me playfully.

"I'mma have to pass," I tossed back at him, raising an eyebrow in amusement.

"Screw y'all," he sneered. "I knew you were shits. Real girls have fun. You ain't nothing but a couple of dumb chicks."

It's crazy how much peer pressure plays a role in our daily actions. Most teenagers will base a majority of their decisions on what their friends do, and the more time you spend with your friends, the more likely you are to follow their examples. Teenagers especially often feel an internal pressure to engage in activities that their peers are doing in order to fit in. We crave more than anything to be accepted, and that usually means we go with the flow, even if we're pushed to do something we don't want to do. More often than not, peer pressure is the sole reason that teens begin to smoke and drink. It's a serious issue that can mess with development and growth.

Peer pressure can be brought to bear on serious issues, such as sex, drug abuse, shoplifting, or bullying. It can often lead to a loss of individuality, as you are pressured into doing things you wouldn't originally want to do and into acting out of character. Peer pressure may force you to assimilate to what the people around you enjoy. Teens with low self-esteem are typically the most affected by peer pressure, as they have a need to prove themselves to their peers. These individuals feel like they have few friends, and so, in order to retain the ones they do have and make new ones, they'll allow themselves to be pressured into doing something that they think will portray them as likeable.

Everyone experiences pressure to "fit in." The more insecure a person is, the greater the probability that they will be pushed into doing something they don't want to do. What's important in peer pressure situations is identifying that you are being pressured and then training yourself to stand your ground.

I see peer pressure happening everywhere, yet it's something we've learned to accept as part of our daily lives. It happens in schools, at home, and especially at parties. Dealing with peer pressure is something schools mention briefly during one physical education class in middle school, but it's never really touched again. It's crucial that we start the conversation and explore what it means at a deeper level to prepare teenagers for what's heading their way.

So, how do other teens pressure you?

There are a variety of techniques that can be utilized to coerce someone into doing something, but the most common are as listed. Peer pressure often includes elements of bullying, and as a result, many of the methods used on victims are similar ("Peer Pressure," 2015).

Physical or emotional threats to a victim, such as insults or name calling, is common and makes the victim feel insignificant or worthless. By doing what they are being pressured to do, the victim feels as if the insults no longer apply. The victims are sometimes even threatened with the end of a friendship or relationship. Usually the individual who's doing the peer pressuring threatens to leave the victim or threatens to harm the victim in some way.

Coercion into doing something the victim would not originally do is a common form of peer pressure. This reasoning is usually very convincing and appeals to an irrational side of the victim.

Unspoken pressure is applied when a victim is watching all his or her peers engage in an activity or wear a certain type of clothing and can be a form of internal pressure for the victim.

Positive peer pressure

As common as it is for there to be negative peer pressure, there are also many aspects of positive peer pressure that can motivate us to be better individuals in the following ways (Van Petten, n.d.).

Creates a challenge for students or adults by the others around them to do better in school or be motivated to work harder in certain tasks, activities, or subjects.

Develops empathy and a greater awareness for emotions when they spend so much time worrying about what others think, which improves their social skills. They also develop adaptation skills, as they adjust to the environments around them and learn patience, flexibility, and compromise.

Prevents bad habits when friends influence teens to behave. If a teen is surrounded by individuals who have good moral values, he or she will likely develop similar beneficial habits.

Peer pressure statistics

Research proves that most individuals allow themselves to be peer pressured into things they don't want to do because they feel it'll increase their standing in their social group. The things they may be pressured to do include the following (Moffitt, n.d.):

- 41% of teens are pressured to be mean to others.
- 30% of teen girls are pressured to do drugs or drink alcohol (familyfirstaid.org).
- 23% of teen girls are pressured to have sex.
- 67% of teen girls are pressured to dress a certain way.
- 44% of all teens are pressured to lie, cheat, or steal
- 33% of teen boys feel pressure to have sex (familyfirstaid.org).

As suspected, girls feel pressured to dress a certain way, while teen boys are pressured to have sex, as it proves their "manhood" and is something that they celebrate.

TIPS FOR TEENS

The easiest way to avoid peer pressure is to surround yourself with people who ensure that you are always comfortable and respect your decisions. However, that's not always possible, and so in situations beyond your control, it's important to know how to handle peer pressure ("Peer Pressure," n.d.).

Tip #1: Learn to say no

Find ways that you can respectfully say no without angering the other person. If you have to, practice in a mirror, so that if you're thrown into a situation, you have a pre-set plan of what to say and how to say it. You'll come off as cool and collected, which will deter the people who are pressuring you from continuing to be insistent.

Think of various escape plans or excuses. Establish a code with one of your friends, whether it be hand signals or a text, so that they can come and rescue you from the situation if need be. Have a sibling call you when you text them a number or special agreed upon word, letter, or symbol, which gives you a way to get out of the conversation you're having with another individual.

Tip #2: Make your own choices

It's your life, and you need to be responsible for your choices. Don't let others pressure you into doing what you don't want to do, and don't let them convince you that you do want to do things you know you don't. Get to know who you are and what's good for you and use that to compel yourself to make the right decisions no matter what everyone around you is doing. I know it can be difficult. The lines begin to blur when you're confused as to whether you want to actually do something or you just want to be like everyone else so you can fit in. It's hard to be the one sober person at a party. But you have to establish your own rules according to your values and follow them.

Tip #3: Be secure

It's important to feel confident in who you are as an individual and the choices that you make. Strengthen your self-esteem (check out Chapter 14) and be aware of how the choices that you make will affect you in the future. No one controls your life but you; make sure that you're not letting others convince you to do something that will not benefit you. Find the belief in yourself to say no and not cave to the societal pressures that will always surround you. You have to learn to block them out and be your own person.

Tip #4: Support others

If you see another individual suffering from negative peer pressure, do your best to aid them in extracting themselves from that situation. Helping others will likely strengthen your resolve and reassure you about your own abilities to stand up to others.

Tip #5: Talk to a trusted individual

Sometimes just talking about your fears with a trusted adult or friend can be very calming. You may realize that your fears were irrational and that even if you don't smoke that one time or have sex with your boyfriend because he wants you too, you'll still turn out okay and that everything will be fine. We let our fears get the best of us sometimes, and it can cause us to overthink every situation or possibility. Chances are nothing truly terrible will happen if you say "no."

Tip #6: Develop more friendships

Having more friends will make you feel more confident and give you more options. You'll be less likely to do things you don't want to, since you know you have other places to turn, even if you do lose the friends who are pressuring you.

Tip #7: Find role models

Role models who you look up to can be very helpful when you're put into stressful situations. Reminding yourself that there are others before you who have stood up to obstacles in their own lives may motivate you to stand up to the ones in yours.

TIPS FOR PARENTS

It's important to support your teen through the peer pressure they'll face in high school so that they are prepared for what happens when you're not there to protect them. Start the conversation now, so that they're ready for the future ("Peer Pressure," 2015).

Tip #1: Establish open communication

Develop an open relationship with your child and check in with them regularly. Ask them about their values and morals and what they're comfortable doing, and what their plan is if they're pushed outside of their comfort zones. Plan regular and frequent family activities and strengthen the family bond so that your teen feels that no matter what happens, they will always have family by their side. This will make them more likely to stand up to the friends who attempt to peer pressure them into doing things they do not wish to do.

Tip #2: Keep track of your teen's friends

Respect your teen's space, but also be aware of the friends with whom they associate. Teens need to surround themselves with the right kind of people to ensure that they don't fall into the trap of negative peer pressure and go down a road that they'll regret. If possible, urge your teen to associate with peers who have a positive influence and similar values.

Tip #3: Preach confidence

Praise your teen for taking charge in situations and compliment your teen for standing up to you sometimes. Although it may be annoying and pesky when your teens counter you, it's an important step in asserting their opinions. Teach your teen how to be independent and address ways in which they can resist the peer pressure that will always be around them. Encourage them to be comfortable in their own skin and help them develop healthy self-esteem.

Tip #4: Seek help

If the situation has gotten out of hand, and your teen struggles with combating peer pressure, it may be necessary to talk to a teacher, counselor, or family doctor. Discuss methods or moderation tactics that may help your teen avoid sketchy situations.

Saying no can be hard. The word has only two letters but seems to possess the power of an entire alphabet. When you're watching everyone around you get drunk, and you get offered a drink, it takes a lot of willpower to smile and shake your head. It takes a lot of determination to walk around sober and watch the drunken craze consume everyone around you. You'll see their face drop when you reject the drink, or you'll feel their annoying nudge in your side as they try to convince you otherwise.

But you're making the right decision.

Because at the end of the day, it's your life.

Maybe nothing will happen if you say "yes" that one time, but maybe something will and you'll regret it for the rest of your life. Don't sacrifice your identity to please the people around you. If they don't let you say no, then maybe it's time to say no to them.

13

Friendships, Relationships, and Dating

"I'm bored," my friend said and hopped out of her hotel bed and pounced onto mine, nearly shoving me off of the mattress and onto the rugged carpet below.

I forced one eye open and squinted at her face hovering above mine. "What time is it?" I mumbled, my words bumping into each other as I attempted to shed the fog of sleep that enveloped my mind.

"Three in the morning," she said and grinned sheepishly at me, the oceans in her icy blue eyes dancing in excitement.

I groaned and pulled the crème covers back over my head in protest.

Silence. Unusual. Ivy always fought back. However, I paid no heed as sleep pulled me back into its embrace.

"This. Is. Sparta!" she declared and within seconds, I felt the water seep into my clothes, painting my skin with goose bumps. I yelped and rolled out of bed, capering about as I tried to rid of the excess liquid that had just been dumped onto me.

"You're dead meat," I growled, charging her. She giggled and ran out of our hotel room, grabbing a room key as she fled, sprinting for the elevator. I lunged after her, still in flip-flops, barely throwing myself in between the sliding doors as the elevator rang shut.

"Just where I wanted you," she bellowed in a playful, deep voice. She had somehow snagged a blanket in the heat of the moment, and it was now draped around her shoulders as a sort of robe. I stumbled up, casting a look of reproach at her as I shivered in my silk pajama shorts.

"Where are we off to?" I asked.

Her eyebrows quirked up mischievously as she glanced at the array of buttons in front of us and said, "How about the roof?"

I could see the way her face illuminated at the thought, so I reluctantly agreed. She nodded and pressed the button.

"If we get caught, I'm blaming you," I said.

"Deal."

We were 6,000 miles away from home for a week, exploring Japan together as part of an exchange program. We had investigated every crevice, taken on fake identities, and pranced through the streets, grasping every food we could fit into our grubby little hands as we gripped each other tightly. We'd run through the rain, laughing as the drops clung to our eyelashes and pooled into our already soaked rain boots that squeaked with every step. We'd scooped countless Japanese snacks into our pockets and dug through our wallets to find enough yen to pay for it all, breathing a sigh of relief as we scraped by with just enough. We'd posed in front of moldy statues, sharing secret glances as we watched the natives stare at us with wide eyes and disapproving grimaces.

The elevator dinged and the cold air whipped through my hair as the doors opened into the darkness. A blinking billboard beamed at us over the water, scripting a flaming red reflection of the time across the water that rippled evenly in the breeze. The water under us glimmered with lights as the cars whirred by like angry fireflies, illuminating the night with a blurry haze. I ran to the edge of the roof, my breath lost in the beauty of it all. The night rumbled with the silence of untold stories, but in that moment, I heard nothing but my own presence.

I felt fleece cocoon my shoulders, embracing me with warmth, as Ivy wrapped the blanket around both of us. She rested her head in the crook of my neck, and we stood, hand in hand, the world spinning around us. In that moment, we were limitless.

The world stopped, but Ivy stirred next to me. "Happy Birthday," she whispered.

It was 3:35 A.M., the exact time I had been born 13 years earlier.

I had forgotten, months ago, that I had told Ivy my birth date and time. Somehow, she'd remembered. We spent the next hour lying on the floor, gazing at stars, and talking about life. It's a memory that never fails to enchant me and reminds me of her. Ivy might have changed schools, but the moments we shared last eternally in my memory.

As I grew up, I learned more and more about what friendship meant, and how moments like these created and nurtured friendships. True friendship was driving with the windows rolled down, blasting obnoxious rap music that made other people dance in their cars. Friendship was waking up in the middle of a sleepover to try disgusting jellybeans and then spit them out in the trashcan together. Friendship was going hiking together and then pushing each other into the lake. That was what friendship was about: moments that resonate across a lifetime.

Relationships, both platonic and romantic, shape both childhood, and the future. The people we associate with predominantly control the way in which we carry ourselves and the type of activities in which we engage. Friends tend to be more constant than relationships, and various levels of friendship exist.

Friendships

As teens grow up and progress through middle school, their relationships with parents typically loosen as they try to find acceptance within a friend group. Peer approval is the basis behind most decisions, and most adolescents will develop in specific ways according to their group identity. Friendships are vital for any maturing young adult. They teach the value of other individuals, promote conflict resolution, and encourage compromise and effort from both parties involved. Without at least some friends, it's very difficult to make it through high school, as friends provide support, love, and advice that might not have otherwise been obtained. Finding like-minded friends makes most teens feel safe and protected, as they're able to align and relate with many similar experiences.

These friendships and groups often fluctuate and change as a teen becomes more comfortable in their own skin and discovers what they really want to do. Crowds and cliques will emerge that create segregated groups that force teens to identify with certain characteristics. However, now, with the influx of social media platforms, there are even more ways to make friends. Many teens are making friendships online, despite the possible risks. The Pew Research Center did a Teens Relationship Survey and found that 61% of boys and 52% of girls have made online friends, with 29% of teens claiming that they've made more than five new friends online despite the fact that only 20% of teens have ever met an online friend face to face ("Teenage Relationships," 2014). I know I've certainly made multiple friends online through Instagram or Facebook, and although I've never met some of them, I categorize them as close friends.

Our generation is one of digital friendships, where most bonding occurs through a screen. This is evident even in friendships that were formed on school grounds. According to Pew Research, almost 79% of all teens instant message their friends and 59% of teens video chat with their friends, with 7% video chatting daily ("Teenage Relationships," 2014). For boys especially, video games play a large role in maintaining friendships. Compared to 59% of girls, 84% of boys play video games, with 38% of boys sharing their gaming handles when first meeting a potential "bro." Whether it is through social media comments or video games, these interactions help teens feel closer to friends and give platforms of common interests.

A lot of us try to find friends who we believe will help us rise in the social hierarchy of school, creating a clash between who we want to be and who we're told to be. Girls especially struggle with this, trying to figure out whether to follow the "populars" or face social exclusion.

Males, on the other hand, tend to engage in social exclusion much less. Although the jocks might exile the nerds, it's rare that a jock will throw out another jock of the group. However, with girls, due to one-on-one relationships, it can be difficult to maintain an entire group if you're exiled by one. Sides are usually taken, and the less popular girls may be kicked out of the friend group.

Cliques

No matter where you go, it's likely that you'll encounter cliques. Even at my school where most of the students are focused on excelling academically, cliques exist and create a precarious social hierarchy that dominates each grade. Cliques can help bring together people of similar interests or attributes, but also results in segregation. It's hard to be a social butterfly and switch from group to group, but it can be done, which is something that I learned to master throughout high school.

Some groups will use perceived power to assert dominance over the school. The beautiful girl might ask a boy to carry her Michael Kors backpack from class to class as she fixes her makeup in the mirror. The cliques can be rude and isolated, making the others around them feel inadequate or unwanted. "Leaders" of each clique determine who can or cannot join and condemn individuality in each group. These groups tend to stay together at all times, sitting in class together and during lunch.

The idea of a clique can be attractive when a teen wants to fit in and feel wanted. However, cliques can often be restraining and negatively impact growing minds by forcing members to fit into a mold that their clique requires. Studies show that schools that offer more elective courses and have a more diverse selection tend to hold more cliquish groups determined by race, social status, and gender. However, smaller schools have a lot more overlap in classes and courses, which forces each student to interact with other students, creating less harsh divisions.

The following groupings are based on research organized by Michael Thompson PhD and Lawrence Cohen, PhD, and originally reported in "Children's Peer Relations: A Meta-Analytic Review of Popular, Rejected,

Neglected, Controversial and Average Sociometric Status" ("Social Groups," n.d.):

Populars are categorized as students who are the kings and queens of high school. Typically considered very attractive by everyone, and in many occasions, richer, these students have social abilities that draw others in. Experience also plays a role in this, and so girls or boys who have had sex or have gone to parties and gotten drunk are considered "cooler."

Accepted labels students who are not at the top of the social ranking but considered likeable and "chill." They are not usually the targets of bullies and are smart and outgoing.

Unknowns include teens who are not even ranked at all. Although no one might know their names, they will typically not be the topic of any gossip or rumors and won't be harassed unless they choose to get involved with a popular's life.

Neglected includes students who are often shy and reserved. Neglected teens are ignored by peers and avoid intertwining themselves in any drama or school gossip. They will find other shy students to talk to and have no problems in school.

Controversialists are students who are disliked by some and liked by others, due to their controversial characteristics. Some examples could be class clowns, bullies, and rebels.

Exiles are rejected students who are avoided by almost everyone because of certain differences that make them stand out. They may become sad and isolated in order to avoid being bullied and teased and may act in out in rage or violence as a means of revenge or retaliation.

My high school was different from a lot of high schools because it had a unique social hierarchy. Coming back to the idea that the majority of the students were focused on academics, there were no specific cliques for each student. The groups often overlapped, with basketball jocks who also were part of business clubs, and techies who loved Anime.

I preferred to be a floater, simply because I never fit in with any group. I had learned from my own experiences that cliques change and not everything they do is something that you're comfortable doing. For me, it was always better to have multiple groups to hang out with and choose out of depending on my mood. I learned from each group of friends with whom I associated. Although I hate the idea of stereotyping groups, it's a reality that they exist in a lot of schools, and it's important to bring that to light.

Gangs

This past year I partnered with a church to help tutor some teenagers who couldn't afford private aid. I provided algebra hacks about how to find "X" in an equation, and the students I tutored gave me insight into living in neighborhoods where residents faced daily threats to personal safety. Gangs flooded those streets in the middle of the night, and some of these teenagers would go to bed, wondering whose face would be missing the next day at school. Most of these boys had been approached by gangs too and had worried about the repercussions they might face by rejecting the gun that was slipped into their pockets. I got goose bumps just listening to the reality that I had never encountered.

A wide majority of serious teen violence in America spurs from gangs, and according to The National Gang Center and The Office of Juvenile Justice and Delinquency Prevention, 7% of teenagers are involved in gangs, which means over 772,500 individuals. Data taken from the FBI's 2011 National Gang Threat Assessment indicates that there are 1.4 million gang members total in the United States ("Measuring the Extent," n.d.; "Gangs," 2015).

Despite the risk of being in a gang, there are still so many teenagers who join. Now why do they do it? They might seek money, protection, or a sense of belonging. Most individuals who join have already had experiences with drugs and alcohol and might be approached by a gang member with a convincing argument. Sometimes, teens join gangs simply because they fear the consequences of refusing. Being a member changes your clothing, writing, and activities, so indications that a teenager is in a gang aren't usually too hard to spot.

TIPS FOR TEENS REGARDING FRIENDSHIPS

Navigating through the social sea of high school is hard. Here are some tips that might be able to help you push through it easier.

Tip #1: Stay true to yourself

Of course you have to always make sacrifices to appease your friends, but you should never sacrifice identity. You are who you are, and if your friends don't appreciate that, it's time to find new friends. I'm not saying you should be rude and expect your friends to still like you. But if you love to play video games and your friends condemn it, give yourself some distance and find friends who embrace you for your quirky characteristics and traits.

Growing up, I used to be mocked for being a tomboy. Too scared to fall into the crowds of the unknown, I strove to be accepted by the popular crew of my grade. I changed my dress and activities to fit this ideal, hoping that being "popular" and liked by boys would save me from social exclusion. What's ironic is that I ended up feeling even more excluded by doing this. Sure, I made it into the popular group, but I was still the least popular one in it. I took away the value of true friends from that experience and carried it into high school. I try to make it a point to cut out the people who bring me down for their own gain and surround myself with those who love and appreciate me for who I am. Now, I have friends who I can get my nails done with and also have a Nerf gun fight with, and that's important. Our social rankings have all dissolved, and now we are a bunch of friends with a lot of history.

It's scary to take the first leap and distance yourself from the people who you believe are toxic, especially if you've been friends with them for a long time, but know it'll benefit you in the long run. Your friends should be boosting you up, not tearing you down. Never compromise on that.

Tip #2: Reciprocate and nurture

Friendship can never be one sided. You can't put any effort into a relationship and act surprised when your friends are no longer interested in being friends. Friendships can be time consuming, but they should also be enjoyable for both parties. The more you are proactive about texting, hangouts, giving advice, and being a good listener, the more likely it is that your friendships will blossom. Take time to build them. Start with small conversations, then start sharing problems and hanging out more. Before long, you could be besties. Really show that you care, and remember aspects about them that others don't usually.

Understand limits. Especially when a friendship is just starting out, don't be needy. Test the waters and see how this individual reacts to interactions. If they keep the conversations going, feel encouraged to move forward. If they seem uninterested or bored, they may not be interested in being friends. Being too needy or relentless can be a little creepy and turn people off to the idea of being friends.

Tip #3: Be open

The idea of being friends with the gamers or the nerds or the jocks or anyone outside of your friend group may not be initially appealing. But realize that you'll never know what groups you mesh with the best if you don't try getting to know all of them. Because I floated between groups in high school, I realized that there are gems in each group. There are going to be people you don't like and people you do like, but there are some of both in every clique, so it's about finding those people and developing friendships. You might not want to hang out with that group specifically, but you can always hang out with that individual.

Tip #4: Don't lose hope

You can feel isolated and alone when you aren't in the right clique. You might feel that no one understands you and something is wrong with you. Not every clique is for every person. People mature and grow, and you'll be able to find best friends who mean a lot to you. It took me four years to determine my real friends. Find the people you know you'll want to be friends with even after high school so that you have some support when you go off to college. And if you still feel misunderstood, I promise it'll get better in college. Tough it out for now. I believe in you. It gets better.

Tip #5: Protect yourself

Watch out for what you need. Not everyone, unfortunately, is nice, so if you're in a destructive friendship, get out of it as soon as possible. Friendships are supposed to mutually beneficial relationships, where both parties help each other grow. My brother is incredibly good at finding good-hearted people, and that's shown time and time again through his relationships. His friends would rally up troops during Student Council elections and push them toward voting booths, and they would come and deliver soup to him when he wasn't feeling well. These are the kind of friendships you want. Get out of damaging ones.

Tip #6: Get a parent's help

This suggestion might be baffling. Get a parent's help with making friends? Never! But contrary to what you might think, parents actually have a lot of knowledge on friends. My parents saw right through people in my grade and warned me against certain people who turned out just the way my parents expected. When I was in the first grade, I entered a new school for the first time. I, in my bright pink sparkly overalls, would go and sit at the top of the playground, sobbing softly in the corner.

"Can I play with you?" I'd peep out as little girls raced around me playing tag. But every response I got was a "no." Eventually, my parents spotted little me with no friends a few weeks into school. They pleaded with my teacher to find me friends. She brought over two girls to me who became my best friends for the next five years. I was only six years old, but you never know who your parents might know. They might acquaint you to family friends, and you could find a new clique. Never be closed off to the idea.

TIPS FOR PARENTS REGARDING TEEN FRIENDSHIPS

Watching your teen choosing friends of whom you don't approve is difficult. But forming friendships is a part of life, and your teen needs to develop relationship building skills and socialization skills, which is what the bigger picture of friendship is all about.

Tip #1: Keep your distance

Prying into your teen's life is only going to cause them to close them off to you. Avoid comments about who the right friends are. Don't ask everyday about the drama going on between cliques, or with what groups your teen is associating. The more you back off, the more likely your teen will start the conversation.

Tip #2: Avoid stereotyping

Stereotyping will motivate a teen to identify with that specific group. Avoid stereotyping and celebrate all aspects and characteristics of people so that your teen feels comfortable joining any group.

Tip #3: Offer suggestions, avoid demands

It can be hard not to make comments on certain friends or people that your teen hangs out with. Suggest a certain group or certain individuals as friends, but never demand that your teen bond with anyone. My mom used to unintentionally step into my friendships, telling me to befriend certain groups to avoid the drama occurring in my clique. Being told with whom to be friends upset me, as I felt that she was implying that my own selections were wrong. I avoided being friends with those people specifically for that reason. Although I now realize how dumb that choice was, many teenagers go through the same thought process. Just be aware when you make any proposals.

Tip #4: Provide a safe environment

Peers are not always the most forgiving. I've come home on occasion sobbing because of the mean words that girls threw at me or the fights that broke out over who got to date a certain jock. Having a safe and communicative home environment is a necessity for teenagers to get through high school. The safer they feel at home, the less likely they'll be affected by the drama that goes on at school because there is someplace else to turn. Avoid having fights at home, especially when your teen is stressed out about school, and offer family nights to engage in fun activities as a distraction from thoughts of friend stress.

Tip #5: Encourage extracurricular activities

Extracurricular activities like sports, theater, and painting can encourage new friendships. If a parent encourages these types of hobbies, a teen feels less pressured about cliques, as they will meet more people and have more friend options.

Tip #6: Check in

Don't check in too often, but checking in sometimes is never a bad thing. Ask simple questions about how certain friends are doing to see how your teen responds. Your teen might fill you in on what's happening at school, and might not, but the fact that you're interested will resonate. You'll be more informed and be able to act accordingly if anything goes wrong.

If you see that your teenager is starting to associate with negative influences like students who are known to use drugs or be members of a gang, ask what's going on. Try to resolve the issue calmly by informing your teen of your concerns. This is when you have every right to step in and stop your teen from making poor decisions.

Romantic relationships and dating

Everyone's had a first "crush." I had mine in kindergarten. A boy would chase me around the playground shrilling at the top of his lungs, our giggles melding together in the air, as I hid behind trees and smiled my big, tooth-missing grin.

"Ro likes Sameep," my friends would say as they buzzed around me in bright dresses and pigtails.

"Blech," I responded, pretending to gag, all the while blushing profusely.

I specifically remember him asking my mother if he could attend my princess themed birthday party. He came dressed in a smile, a collared shirt, and a combed down hairdo, and sat right next to me as we ate our cake.

After a year of shy glances and wild goose chases outside, it was finally time to graduate kindergarten. With a suave "call me when you're older," he handed me a little blue folded noted scrawled with his home phone number and a tiny, ill-constructed heart. It meant the world to me, and I kept it in my room until one day, we cleaned the house and unknowingly chucked it in the trash.

Human development includes a phase of "ew cooties!" and a dedication to rejecting dating as fast as possible. However, as we mature, a milestone passes where suddenly we start finding other people attractive. Suddenly, dating is all the rage and becomes the topic of every teenager's clique. Suddenly, parties are filled with questions like:

"If you had to choose one guy to date, who would it be?"

"Top five most attractive girls or boys?"

"How many people have you dated?"

Most of these relationships are short term and temporary. The average relationship lasts between a few weeks and few months. My middle school "relationship" was a grand total of twenty-four hours. Relationships increase in length as individuals mature, and suddenly each relationship lasts anywhere from a few months to a few years. This craze for a relationship is a mixture of factors from hormones to identity crises to societal pressures. Some teens feel like being in a relationship determines their worth, and so they go out of their way to find a significant other. Others think that in order to be cool, they have to date.

In the case of a real and genuine crush, there are the "three C's" determined by PsychologyToday.com, that can be used to measure love (Sheck, n.d.).

Chemistry is the first "spark" where you feel a rush of attraction for an individual and their behaviors. You might get butterflies in your stomach, have sweaty palms, or stutter your words.

Compatibility is the getting to know the person and forming a bond. This accounts for the friendship that encompasses any strong relationship.

Commitment is perhaps one of the most important parts of keeping a relationship going. There will always be ups and downs, but commitment ensures that both sides are in it for the long haul. I like to think that love fluctuates, but constant commitment keeps the relationship going.

Especially when starting out, relationships are incredibly idealized. The only experience that teenagers have is from watching the people around them be in relationships or from the media, which doesn't always show the true side of things. Since teens are usually only seeing the positives and outward masks of relationships, they don't understand the necessity of compromise and accepting flaws in others that come along with dating.

Dating depends on generation and social, historical, and cultural contexts. The avenue of communication in our current culture for teenagers has increased, making everyone more accessible to casual conversations. It's no longer a waiting by the phone for a call situation. Direct messaging on Instagram and Facebook and video chatting through FaceTime and Skype have unearthed new ways to stay in touch and get to know a person without once having to meet in person. Most teens text someone they are interested in before interacting in an in-person date situation. Texting disposes of awkward pauses and jumbled words, which is why many teens prefer texting to in-person interactions, until they get comfortable.

However, this easy accessibility also makes it easy to break up. If you're the one breaking up with your dating partner, this makes it a lot easier on you, since you don't have to see that person cry or have to comfort them. But if you're the person being broken up with, you're going to be left angry and confused, especially if you never saw the breakup coming. Breaking up online is frowned upon and criticized, but most teens have experienced it at least once.

Teens feel their emotions passionately, and teens in love spend a lot of their time fantasizing about the other person. Almost every teen has told another that he or she "loves" them and often regret it when they look back on it. The inexperience of dating can leave a lot of people unsure of what love truly means and cause them to throw around the word carelessly.

Positive aspects of dating

As with most things, there is a positive side of dating. Teens learn important life skills, such as communication, respect, unselfishness, and responsibility (Tucker, n.d.).

Dating develops vital life skills. Early dating sets up a lot of teenagers for success in future relationships. Most adolescents are able to learn from mistakes that they make in early relationships, so that they know how to correctly treat someone in the future when they're avidly looking for a significant other to settle down with. Teens are forced to learn how to compromise with each other to keep the relationship functioning, and they learn time management to balance both another person and their own activities. In addition, they have to develop a variety of other skills such as being a good listener and communicating what they want clearly. These all set up teens for a successful future in looking for a mate.

Dating offers happiness. It's no secret that relationships are incredibly heartwarming. It's nice to have someone shower you with attention and care about you intimately. Being in a relationship keeps you from ever being alone and can often boost self-esteem. The feelings of love release oxytocin, estrogen, and dopamine for up to six months, which can be a real stress relief. Your dating partner might even be able to provide you emotional support and strength during tough times. Overall, the good parts of relationships can positively impact a teenager and make high school a little bit easier.

Dating provides memorable experiences. Relationships offer certain experiences and memories that you would have never otherwise had. Many adults look back on childhood relationships fondly and reminisce about the enjoyable impressions each boyfriend or girlfriend had on them. After all, who else is there to talk about life in the middle of the night while eating ice cream and cuddling on a hill?

Dating prepares young people for college. In college, you have to take off the dating training wheels and date in an entirely new fashion. Suddenly, some relationships are much more mature, and others are just for fun. It's important to have those initial basics down from high school so you can use them to your advantage in college. There are no second chances in the real world, so it's important to be prepared for whatever you'll be faced with.

Negative aspects of dating

As with everything, there are negatives to dating as well as positives ("Teenage Relationships, 2014).

Pressure from dating adds to the pressure from peers and parents. Teens want to please their boyfriends or girlfriends, and so they are more likely to comply to anything that they are pressured to do. This can mean changing their personality to fit what their partner wants, or having sex before they're ready. It's very important to consider pressure, as once in a relationship, it's incredibly hard to work against it.

Relationships require a lot of time. Most teens will spend almost all their time with their partners, and if they cannot spend time in person, they'll be texting or video chatting. It can also take time away in an opposing aspect. If a couple constantly fights, they'll spend unnecessary time and energy bashing each other and arguing over meaningless things.

Breakups are hard. Although breakups are a part of life, they can be difficult especially if a teenager isn't in a good headspace. Breakups during teenage years can cause many people to question their self-worth and ask themselves why they weren't good enough. This can result in a drop in self-esteem and can aggravate pre-existing conditions like anxiety and depression.

Abuse is a serious issue that a lot of people may be afraid to speak about openly. Unhealthy relationships can happen at any age and lead to a life-time of trauma and scars. According to Choose Respect's "Get the Facts: Dating Abuse Statistics" and stats published on Do Something ("Dating Abuse," n.d.; "11 Facts," n.d.):

- One in four adolescents report some sort of abuse every year.
- 80% of females continue to date partners after physical abuse.
- 70% of women said that their rapist was a friend, boyfriend, or acquaintance.
- 20% of girls said their boyfriend threatened violence or self-harm in the event of a breakup.
- 72% of thirteen-year-olds and fourteen-year-olds are dating.
- Roughly 1.5 million high school boys and girls in the United States admit to being intentionally hit or physically harmed in the last year by someone with whom they are romantically involved.
- One in three young people will be in an abusive or unhealthy relationship.
- 25% of high school girls are abused physically or sexually. Teen girls who are abused are six times more likely to become pregnant or contract a sexually transmitted disease.
- 50% of young people who experience rape or physical or sexual abuse will attempt to commit suicide.
- 750,000 teen pregnancies occur every year (three in ten teen American girls before age twenty).

It's important to remember that males can be victims of abuse too. The threat is serious, so it's important for teenagers to be ready to date and have the support of family and friends before investing in a relationship.

Rape is an extreme form of sexual harassment and is something of which all women and men have to be aware. Unfortunately, we live in an age where exploitation happens, and both women and men are raped on a daily basis. It's important to establish the right friends and take part in the right relationships to reduce chances of rape.

Teenage pregnancy is a threat looming over every sexually active young girl. According to The American College of Obstetricians and Gynecologists, there are approximately 750,000 pregnancies every year of fifteen to nineteen-year-olds, although the number has dropped significantly due to more means of birth control ("11 Facts," n.d.). Still, two in five young women will become pregnant and four out of five of those pregnancies will be unintended.

Pregnancy can be a touchy subject, especially with parents and peers, if it happens before the intended age. It can cause a lot of turmoil in a young adult's life and drive away family members and friends. These teens may be bullied by other students or even thrown out by furious parents. Many adolescents have sex before they're ready because they feel pressured to please their partner. If these teens are uneducated about methods of birth control and sex in general, their ignorance can result in an unintended pregnancy.

There's also a correlation between drinking and teen pregnancy. Of pregnancies between the ages of fourteen to twenty-one years, 75% occur under the influence of alcohol. Teenagers are unable to control their impulses and make unwise decisions, according to an article published by Manjiri Kochrekar (2016).

TIPS FOR TEENAGERS ON ROMANTIC RELATIONSHIPS AND DATING

Dating is a part of life and a vital life skill. However, there are aspects to consider before engaging in teen dating to ensure that a teen is ready (Enloe, 2013).

Tip #1: Befriend first

The basis of every strong relationship is a very strong friendship. That's why you see so many teens falling in love with their best friends and getting to know each other before even considering dating. Really learn about your prospective partner's interests and see how you fit in with them. Examine certain quirks and differences and see how you react to them. You can't date someone if everything that person does annoys you.

Trust me, if you become friends before becoming a couple, you'll have more to talk to about and more to like about each other as time goes on. If you start dating too soon, it gets awkward quickly, as both sides feel they have to be perfect in order to keep the other person engaged. It might result in fake identities that are adopted in the hopes of being "more attractive."

Tip #2: Engage with parents

Your parents have their own little love stories. Even my parents, the parents who weren't open to the idea of me dating until junior year in high school, have their own secret stories about their teenage love lives. If you hide your relationship from your parents, it'll build a sense of distrust. Rather, when you feel like you and your partner have been dating for long enough, let your parents know and fill them in on how you feel about the relationship.

I asked my parents tons and tons of questions about the right way to approach a relationship in a way that showed that I respected myself and them. I interrogated my brother for pointers about how to communicate with my boyfriend and set a pace for the relationship with which I was comfortable. You might be closed off to the idea of your parents knowing about your dating life, but also understand that they have lots of information that could help you resolve issues or approach the relationship in a new way.

Tip #3: Understand cultural differences

Every culture is different, and certain cultures are much more open to dating than others are. Indian culture, for example, is conservative and oriented around long-term relationships. My parents have often asked me why I would want to be in a relationship, especially if I knew most likely it wasn't going to last past high school. It's a valid point, and reflects the thought processes of Indian culture specifically. Value systems differ for every culture, and so it's important that you understand the cultural expectations of your family.

Tip #4: Establish boundaries

Make sure to set the relationship at a pace with which you're comfortable and establish boundaries so you never feel violated or unready. If your boyfriend or girlfriend is moving too fast, slow it down. Respect and communication is crucial in a relationship, and the more open you are about feelings, the easier the relationship will progress. If your boyfriend or girlfriend doesn't respond positively to your requests, assert your feelings again. If he or she is still unresponsive, consider ending the relationship. You should never have to sacrifice your morals for the sake of the other person. Certain compromises may have to be made in every relationship, but self-respect is not something that should ever be sacrificed.

Tip #5: Avoid social media

We've all seen those annoying couples who post every single day with the caption "Woman Crush Wednesday" or "Best Babe in the World!" with a photo of the couple kissing. There's no shame in posting a few pictures of your partner and publicly appreciating them. However, posting and talking about it constantly can be quite annoying for followers and friends and could cause arguments between you and your dating partner. Not to mention, it'll take a whole lot of effort to clear your Instagram of these photos if you and this partner break up.

Tip #6: Stay aware and safe

Risks are part of dating someone who you don't really know. Dating students who go to your school is usually less dangerous than dating outside of the school, but it's still important that you are cautious and wary of your surroundings. My parents always feared for my safety when they left me alone with my boyfriend when I dated someone who didn't go to my school and who they hadn't met. However, after we developed some safety escape routes, and I promised to keep them constantly updated, I was allowed to go on a date with him, and I returned home safe and sound. Never feel pressured to do anything you don't want to. If you feel that you're being sexually abused or harassed, call the police or an adult and get out of the situation as fast as you can.

Tip #7: Explore your sexuality

The teenage years are your chance to explore your sexuality. Experiment with different people and figure out what is attractive to you. Determining your sexuality early on will make it easier to find the right dating partners later on. With that in mind, take care not to judge people. Just because someone isn't dating, doesn't mean that they're asexual, gay, lesbian, or straight. Each person develops and matures physically and psychologically in his or her own time and way, and sexuality is part of that maturation. Every person should be encouraged to flourish the way they want to without having to face judgmental rumors.

Tip #8: Don't be superficial

We're all inherently a little superficial, and we explore personalities after being attracted to external appearance. However, now is a good time to start focusing on the less superficial qualities of potential dates such as a potential partner's interests, demeanor, and personality. Dating someone who is only physically attractive, and not emotionally or intellectually attractive, is pointless because you won't be happy.

Tip #9: Manage your time

Time is very limited in high school, and dating takes a lot of time. Make sure you're not sacrificing the things that are important to you for the sake of a relationship. Investing a lot of time in a temporary relationship isn't always a good idea, so it's important to fit dating in with your other priorities and figure out what works. However, you also have to make sure you're devoting enough time to your partner. In a similar way to friendships, relationships require nurturing, so ensure that you're reciprocating your partner's effort if the relationship is one of your priorities.

One way to encourage time management is to use "rain-check cards" to avoid carving out time that you don't have. It makes for a good way to keep the relationship functioning without having to devote all of your time into doing activities together.

Tip #10: Let go

No matter how much you might want it to work, some relationships just won't. No matter how much you try, it'll still fail. That's when you know it's time to let go. Don't feel scared; you'll find someone else. Get the support of your friends and family, get any advice you can, and start the process of moving on. You will find someone else in time when you're ready. Focus on yourself and your identity and work on being happy with yourself. The more in tune you are with yourself, the easier it will be to connect with others and build stronger relationships.

Breakups are painful. Time passes, and wounds heal. Feelings will be intense initially, but after some time passes, you'll be happier than ever and hopefully look back on the relationship fondly.

Tip #11: Single isn't bad

If you're single, enjoy it. You have no one to report to, no one to care for, and no one to track what you're doing. This is your time to shine and really love yourself. You don't need anyone to love you: you come first. And that's something that you really get to focus on when you're single. Love is great and all, but being single is a necessary step. Give it some time and be patient. It'll happen when it needs to.

TIPS FOR PARENTS ON TEEN ROMANTIC RELATIONSHIPS AND DATING

Tip #1: Have "the talk"

The talk: every mother's dream and every father's nightmare. When your teen is old enough, communicate openly about relationships and sex. Share your experiences, and talk about the safety measures that need to be taken. Outline possible dangerous scenarios to give your teen an idea of what could happen. The more educated your teen is, the less likely they are to make a dire mistake.

Tip #2: Set boundaries

Teenagers still make mistakes. It's important that you remain supportive while your teen is in a relationship. If you put too many restrictions, you're guaranteeing rebellion. Don't outlaw certain things; explain why those things are currently being disallowed, and maybe even under what circumstance that might change.

To my mother and father, high school relationships were a waste of time. They considered these relationships temporary and stressful, and my family failed to understand why I would want to date someone in the first place. In a classic Sameep style, I wrote an essay about it. I divulged my reasons for wanting to date, and the benefits dating would provide me. For me, relationships weren't about the end result but about creating memories. My parents heard me out, and we compromised. They set boundaries, and I was then allowed to date.

My first relationship may not have worked out the way I wanted, but it was still a learning experience for which I am grateful. Even now, simply because I'm "allowed" to date, I feel less compelled to until I'm ready. I'd always wanted to have a boyfriend because I wasn't given the option. Now, I barely even care.

Tip #3: Empathize and communicate

Develop a strong relationship with your teens so that they open up to you about their dating life. Don't try to involve yourself too much in the relationship, but definitely empathize with the pain your teen might be feeling and offer suggestions on how to cope with roadblocks that come up. Ask casually about the relationship and how your teen's partner is doing and be polite if he or she comes over to visit.

Tip #4: Don't hover

Let your teenager make his or her own mistakes in the relationship. Don't supervise too much, as it could turn off the dating partner and make your teen feel constricted. Again, it's all about the perfect balance between engaging with and maintaining a respectful distance from your teen's life.

I think at the end of the day, friendships and relationships are incredibly important, but they also change and fluctuate often. It's important to invest, but also understand that it's necessary to detach yourself from the toxic people. An Indian movie I once watched called *Dear Zindagi*, or *Dear Life*, introduced the theory that there can be different types of soul mates. There can be romantic soul mates, music soul mates, outdoor activity soul mates, coffee soul mates, movie soul mates, etc. The beautiful thing is that these soul mates don't have to all be the same person. You can fulfill different aspects of your life with different people. There's a time and a place for everyone and everything.

Whether single or one of a couple, popular or not popular, you're special, and that's all that really matters. So don't worry about dating someone or being friends with everyone; be your own best friend, your own dedicated partner.

After all, chocolate is always on sale the day after Valentines.

And that's open for anyone.

14

Self-Confidence and Self-Esteem

"God, please make me beautiful," I would pray, kneeling in front of my mirror with my hands in front of me. It was a nightly ritual for me; it was a request that I whispered with every part of my body.

For me, growing up through middle school was a constant challenge. I was the Bianca to an entire group of Caseys and Jesses. It was no lie that the girlfriends I chose to hang out with were models that boys chased after with hungry smiles and awe-struck eyes, but it led to a constant beauty standard that I could never live up to. I spent my entire middle school experience trying to prove that I was worthy of their friendship and worthy of the spot that I held in the social stratosphere of our school because of them. I was always asked the question, "Why are you in that group?" and it led me to question it also. How did someone like me end up with some of the most attractive and powerful people in school as friends?

"Sameep's a four on a good day," I would hear as I walked by a snickering group of boys sitting by the doorway. Perhaps it was due to my glasses or my fashion sense at the time, but comments like that chipped away at my confidence and left me with a sense of unworthiness and discontent. Before my mom would allow me to get my eyebrows done, I would wrench the tiny hairs using my hands, hoping that I could tame the wild caterpillar beasts by thinning them out.

Puberty was kind to me, and I have bopped up a few attractiveness levels since I was thirteen, but who hasn't? Even now, I can't pass by a mirror without looking at myself carefully. My friends and family may tell me that I'm beautiful, but those words mean nothing to me without my own approval. Over time, I've realized that one comment has made me so self-conscious about my looks.

In this day and age specifically, self-esteem has become a pressing epidemic that continues to impact almost every teenager and changes the way that we view our capabilities and ourselves. Self-confidence is something that many people lack, and that lack of self-confidence is detrimental. Self-confidence and self-esteem are not very different. Self-confidence means to trust in your own capabilities to be successful in the world. Self-esteem is the attribution of self-worth to yourself and belief in the fact that you are good enough. It is possible to be very self-confident and have low self-esteem, such as is the case with many celebrities, who are able to please crowds full of people but then resort to purging to lose weight.

Self-esteem and self-confidence change the way a person tackles obstacles. People with low self-esteem avoid making mistakes. People with high self-esteem are eager to develop as individuals and are unafraid to make mistakes. Whether because of media, friends, or parents, meeting an unrealistic standard undermines self-confidence and erodes self-esteem.

Teenagers with low self-esteem interact with their surroundings in a manner demonstrating lack of social skills and downplay their strengths and abilities. They criticize themselves, and when asked what they wish they could change about themselves, they will list many things off the top of their heads. People with low self-esteem will put on a mask of confidence to protect themselves and keep from being exposed.

In middle school, I would walk through hallways with my head down, headphones in, in fear of attracting attention to myself. For me, eye contact has always been a form of vulnerability, and I avoided it, as I felt that it would be easier for people to examine me thoroughly and point out the flaws.

Characteristics of low self-esteem

Self-esteem can be influenced by a variety of factors, but some of the most common are: a troubled childhood; less-than-satisfactory academic or sports performance; issues with physical appearance, breakups, hormonal changes, and disabilities; and medical and mental issues.

Insecure individuals demonstrate the following ("Signs of Low Self-esteem," 2015):

- criticize themselves excessively;
- avoid eye contact;
- brush off compliments or deny them;
- use self-deprecating words to describe themselves often such as "dumb," "gross," or "ugly";
- always blame themselves when things don't work out like they wanted them to;
- don't take credit for what they deserve;
- display an aura of confidence to compensate for their true feeling of insecurity;
- apologize constantly;
- feel a need to prove their worth and therefore are easily manipulated into doing favors for others;
- spend excessive time obsessing about their appearance;
- gossip often and put others down as a defense mechanism; and
- speak loudly or angrily to get attention.

In order to deal with their self-esteem problems, many individuals will use some of the following coping strategies ("The Issue," n.d.):

Drugs or alcohol create a temporary feeling of bliss; many teens use substance abuse as a way to escape from their lack of confidence and esteem.

Smoking aids teenagers with low self-esteem to cope with stress, anxiety, and depression (Samet).

Binging on food may cause obesity as a result of feeling a constant blanket of hopelessness or diminished control over their lives.

Social isolation results from a fear of judgment; many insecure individuals will avoid social contact and going to social gatherings. Many teenagers who feel like they will not succeed drop out of school completely to avoid any sort of competition.

Self-harm or suicide may happen when self-loathing becomes overwhelming, and an individual feels as if they are no longer equipped to deal with it. Self-harm replaces intangible emotional pain with concrete physical pain, to gain control and to punish oneself. Suicide is an alternative harming method to escape the suffering and emotional pain that one may feel.

Bullying others re-appropriates anger and insecurity to get a sense of authority and power by manipulating other helpless students. Bullies take out hatred for themselves on others. Some may also be seeking attention by creating situations in which they are praised or punished.

Sex at an early age for girls with a lack of self-esteem, may be used as a form of compensation. Some people feel that they have nothing else to offer to a romantic partner, so they offer their body instead.

Statistics pertaining to self-confidence and self-esteem

It's surprising how pressing self-esteem issues are. Dr. Joe Rubino, in *The Self Esteem Book*, states that over 85% of the world's population is impacted by low self-esteem. Girls between the ages of nine and seventeen in particular are shown to have the lowest self-esteem. Due to physical changes and critique, girls are subject to much more body scrutiny, leading to more romanticized ideals of "perfection."

According to the Dove Self Esteem Project (DSEP), six in ten girls opt out of activities they would have otherwise participated in, because they're stressed about how they'll look by doing those activities. Whether it's hindering them from participating in drama, playing a sport, or joining an academic club, self-esteem is slowly taking over these young girls' lives and steering them away from their passions. This negativity impacts women even later on in life, shown by the following statistic: eight percent of women will sometimes skip work when they feel bad about the way they look (*Real Girls*, 2008).

Some of the following statistics still astound me. According to the Real Girls, Real Pressure: National Report on the State of Self Esteem, Dove Self-Esteem Fund:

- 75% of girls who had low self-esteem found means to deal with their confidence issues through drinking, eating disorders, self-harm, or bullying.

- 50% of teenagers have tried some method of dieting such as laxatives, fasting, etc.

- 71% of girls with low self-esteem feel as if their appearance does not meet a necessary beauty standard.

- Girls with confidence issues are four times more likely to engage in sexual activities that they later on regret.

- 38% of middle school and high school boys have used protein supplements to enhance their muscles, and 8% have admitted to using steroids.

- Almost 50% of girls between the ages of fifteen and seventeen need encouragement to join clubs and branch out to various activities.

- 23% of girls between the ages of fifteen and seventeen are too intimidated to raise their hand in class.

TIPS FOR TEENS

"I could never pull that off. I'm not good enough." We've all thought that phrase. Maybe it was about the outfit your friend was wearing. Maybe it was the trick they showed you while playing soccer. Maybe it was just how quickly they computed a math problem. That's when the doubt creeps in, and we begin to believe that we are not enough.

A few months ago, someone asked me what I wanted in life. My answer was "to be good enough."

The next question she asked me I've never forgotten because it made me question what I was striving for: "But what is good enough? Not to your parents, not to your friends, not to your boyfriend, but to you. What is good enough to you?"

I'd spent my entire childhood wishing I was good enough, but I still don't know what that entails. Sometimes we inadvertently make little mantras for ourselves that solidify our beliefs in our flaws, and it becomes a cycle that is impossible to destroy. In order to bury our self-hatred, we resort to other activities and find ways to cover up our insecurities, whether that be through dieting, makeup, or plastic surgery, and we try to compensate through, for example, promiscuous fashion or offering parts of ourselves up to please the people around us. We fear that others will see us the way that we do, and so we run and hide behind masks of confidence and happiness.

So many things occur in our daily lives that can lead to buckets of uncertainty and doubts about who we are as people. There are days when you'll be walking through a hallway full of crowded people, and you'll never have felt more alone than when you weave through them in a desperate attempt to get through to your class waiting at the other end. It's so important to keep in mind self-worth. Too often, we spend time loving others and giving up pieces of ourselves to keep them happy and forget to love ourselves. We spend so much time trying to be perfect to fit in with a group. Yet that's the thing we fail to realize. Our imperfections are what make us perfect. Without flaws, we would be boring, absent of dynamic and intrigue.

When you search up the definition of "imperfection" on Google, you're left with the following words: "defect, fault, flaw, deformity, discoloration, disfigurement." Each of those words possesses such a negative connotation, yet the reality is that defects are what make us beautiful. Each difference leads to something new. Faults led to the evolution of animals, so why can't they also lead to the evolution and development of our personalities?

You are who you are, and the only choice you have is to embrace it. You can run from it, but one day it will catch up with you, and you will have no choice but to accept yourself, flaws and all. You should not feel obligated to fit in with a certain standard of beauty or what's portrayed in the media because as much as you may not believe this now, you are good enough. Here are some tips that have worked for me and some other friends:

Tip #1: Make mistakes

It's okay to make mistakes. We all do. Don't let it hinder you from moving forward, but rather let it empower you to learn and apply what you learned next time. Don't let your fear get the best of you. Sometimes, the fear of judgment or the fear of failure will keep you from doing something that you want. Just take a deep breath and try to find the courage within you. Chances are, no one's going to even notice.

Tip #2: Be authentic

If someone doesn't like the real you, that's not your problem. You'll be a lot less stressed if you stop trying to live up to everyone else's expectations and instead just fulfill your own. What you're feeling is normal. We all go through self-esteem issues at some point, although the strength of it varies from person to person. It's okay to not feel your best all the time. The important thing is that you pick yourself back up and remember that you're enough.

Tip #3: Appreciate yourself

Sometimes just finding one thing you like about yourself every morning is enough to make a positive impact. Look in the mirror in the mornings, and find one feature or one thing that you like about yourself. Start every morning like that, and before long, you might even be complimenting yourself on accident. Another option is to buy a set of inspirational cards and read one when you wake up each morning. An endless list of reasons exists to be thankful for the body you have.

Try not to criticize yourself. We often do it without realizing, so when you do criticize yourself, find a positive as well. You're a piece of art. Not everyone is going to see your beauty and love your beauty. What's important is that you do, and you portray it confidently. Appreciate what makes you special. Those unique skills are what contribute to making you a rare person, so make sure you give them the positive attention that they deserve. Forget about the past. Sometimes we carry baggage with us that weighs us down and reminds us of all the things we've done wrong. Try to drop that baggage and focus on the present.

Tip #4: Meet people

Make connections with people. If you make genuine connections with others and find trusted sources and friends upon whom you can rely, you'll feel much more secure in who you are. A lot of people in the world feel the same way you do, so remember that you're never truly alone.

Tip #5: Control your own happiness

Walk away from negative people and negative comments. When you choose to listen, you're inherently giving someone else the power to control your happiness and your self-esteem. It's all about the little things that'll keep you confident in your own skin.

Tip #6: Have fun and exercise

Step out of your comfort zone and try new things and go to social events. You might end up learning something about the people around you and yourself. Exercise regularly. It'll improve your mood and keep you feeling more fit and content with who you are. Don't overstress yourself. It's easy to get worked up over the smallest things. Take a step back and talk to someone you trust about some of your options.

Tip #7: Get help

Sometimes, you just need someone to remind you of how important you are. It's going to take some work, but you have to realize that you are good enough. Let yourself have bad days, but remember to dust yourself off and keep going. I know what it feels like to gaze into a mirror and cry because you hate what you see. But you have to realize that although you may not see your beauty, the people around you do.

Talk to a therapist, your parent, or a family friend. There are times when it can get rough, but you will come out of therapy more confident and ready to accept yourself.

TIPS FOR PARENTS

A healthy, nurturing environment is crucial for the development of a happy, confident child. When parents are accepting and loving, a teenager is more inclined to accept and love who he or she is. However, if the parents are excessively demanding and set unrealistic goals or are overprotective and overbearing, their child may believe that he or she is incapable and inferior. Developing a safe relationship is one of the most crucial aspects to fostering self-love in your child. Most of the time, it's more important to be a friend than a parent and to provide a stable foundation for your teen's development.

Tip #1: Praise and appreciate

Remind your teenager of the reasons that you love them. Just as you may feel like your child is ungrateful, teenagers often feel unappreciated and alone. The more you encourage and nurture your teen, the higher his or her self-esteem will rise. Give random hugs. Sometimes just coming up to your teen's room to give them a hug will be enough to make them feel a little bit more self-confident.

Tip #2: Ask for opinions and offer responsibility

Ask for your teen's opinions and make sure they feel included in conversations. Neglect can make a teenager feel like the entire world is ignoring them and that their existence doesn't matter. Avoid this by involving them in discussions and treating them like adults. Offer responsibility to them. Bestowing responsibilities proves your confidence in your teen and suggests that they are growing up and maturing into an adult.

Tip #3: Communicate openly

Communicate with your teen. Make sure they know they can rely on you if they need you or need to talk. It's hard enough for teens to open up to parents about friend problems and confidence and body issues, but if the parent is supportive and kind, it'll encourage more vulnerability. Don't compare your teen to siblings. Siblings set high bars for the others in their family, so it's important to remind each of your children of his or her uniqueness.

Tip #4: Provide opportunities to build confidence

Give your child opportunities to try new things. Your teen will discover aptitudes that may boost their self-confidence. Encourage your child to keep trying even after mistakes are made. Everyone makes mistakes, and until your teen becomes comfortable with making them, he or she will be unable to learn and improve.

Tip #5: Have your teen's back

Ensure that you listen to your child without judgment and offer alternative viewpoints without an argumentative demeanor. A lot of the time, hormonal teenagers blow conflicts up internally, and when viewed by a third party, these problems seem trivial. Focus on resolving the issue and avoid commenting on how irrelevant the conflict will be in the future, since what matters most to a teenager is the present moment.

Tip #5: Don't be a helicopter parent

Let your child develop as he or she needs to, and interfere only when absolutely necessary. Don't push for your child to share things with you, as more often than not, it will convince them to keep quiet.

Tip #6: Pay attention to your teen's friends

Don't pick friends out for your teenager, but be aware of the values and the characters with whom they might be associating so that you can offer advice and guidance. If you have an issue with an individual with whom your teen is hanging out, bring it up with them and offer an alternative solution or tell them to be wary.

Tip #7: Be a role model

Be confident and act as a role model. If you're confident in your own abilities, your teen will notice it and model their own stature after you. Practice social skills with your teen. Give them tips on how to engage in social activities to keep conversations going and make new friends

Tip #8: Find a therapist

Sometimes self-esteem issues become unmanageable and can lead to more serious issues. A therapist is simply a gym for the mind. Take advantage of the facilities you have and focus on your child's mental health.

This journey has been hard, and it will continue to be hard, and I'm perfectly aware of that. I've fallen flat on my face, I've shed tears, and I've gotten scrapes and bruises both on the outside and the inside. I've seen the people around me struggle with their self-worth, and I've seen them hate themselves for not reaching their ideal of beauty.

Ultimately, it's how we choose to let our experiences influence us. People deserve happiness, but most of the time we're not offered it on a silver platter. You can view the glass as half empty or half full, sure, but you have to also remember that you can drink from the glass and let it fuel you. We spend so much time focusing on how to view a given situation, but the most important thing is to do something about it.

You are not perfect. I am not perfect. We are all not perfect. But that's what makes us human. It is what distinguishes us from one another. You have talents that I wish I possessed, and I have advantages that you wish you possessed. But until you stop comparing yourself to the people around you, you will never truly be able to be happy. My dad used to say, "If you're not the best in something, then don't do it." But that's the thing. We're all the best in our own way. There is no global "best." There will always be someone better than you, and someone who you're better than at some random skill. And the sooner you learn to embrace that fact, the sooner you will learn to embrace yourself.

It pains me that some of the most beautiful people are the ones who fail to realize it. I can see your beauty. We are all imperfectly perfect. So I hope one day you are able to look into the mirror and say to yourself:

"I love me."

Because you should.

You truly should.

15

Siblings

The bell chimed above us as we embraced one last time before weaving our way through the buzzing students, trying to find our first class of the day. The upper classmen towered above us as they stumbled past, already counting the days until they graduated. I shuffled by, giving out high fives and throwing smiles at my fellow freshman and then skipped into my first class. Settling into the front row seat, I pulled out my notebook and scribbled down the requirements scrawled across the board in front of me. A stout man came from behind the desk, using the back of his hand to push his falling glasses back up the bridge of his nose. He began to call role, his gravelly voice echoing across the poster-clad walls, dark grey eyes darting from one student to the other as he began to put face to name. Finally, he got to my name. "Sameep Mangat?"

I raised my hand as I said, "Here."

He squinted, peering over his glasses to gaze at me. He smiled before responding, "Any relation to Simar Mangat?"

Sighing softly, I plastered a smile on my face and nodded. The next five minutes went by as he reminisced about having my brother in his class, and the positive energy that was carried in with everything my brother did. It was no secret that my brother was a superstar; he'd been class president, a soccer captain, hard-working, dedicated, and most of all, a little ball of positivity and energy that never failed to make people around him smile. He'd made the strongest relationships with all of his teachers, and I never failed to hear about all of his achievements from all of the teachers who had taught him.

My new teacher looked back at me as he finished recalling memories involving Simar and smiled, a warm, light-hearted glint in his eye. He said, "Let's hope you turned out just like him."

I laughed uneasily before sinking back into my seat, knowing perfectly well that the rest of my day would go by just like this. I would be identified as someone's sister, not my own person.

I adore my older brother. He's my role model and my hero. He's the guy I come to for advice on anything and everything, and he's my best friend and my confidant. Yet my entire childhood was spent in his shadow, constantly trying to touch the bar that he'd set just a little too high for me. The pressure to live up to the standard Simar established bore down on me every day. Teachers I ran into could tell me at least one way in which he positively impacted them. I understood why, I mean after all, he infected me with his love and energy, so why wouldn't he do the same for the other people around him?

The problem, however, was that I felt buried under his achievements, and I kept trying to find a way to rise above them. When I was in pre-school, I wanted to be like my brother. We would play Call of Duty together, and more often than not, I ended up the loser. Being the sore loser I was, I would start to cry, accusing my brother of cheating, a crime he had never committed.

After every fight, my parents used to look at us both and laugh quietly as they said, "One day, you'll regret being mean to each other, and you'll wish you had more time together." My mother would take us in her arms and stroke our hair with gentle hands and speak softly. "Soon your brother will be gone to college. You may not realize it now, but you'll miss him. And pretty soon you'll be wondering why you weren't better friends when he was still around. That's the way life is. We all grow up, and after he goes to college, he's going to settle down somewhere and start a family, and he won't have as much time anymore for you. That's just the way it is. So enjoy every second he's around."

Until then, the concept of time had never really hit me. When he got into Stanford and left the house, somehow I was still being compared to him, as if we were side by side, every single day. Why did I feel this constant obligation to fill his shoes? I mean, after all, we both have our own strengths. I can belt out a Beyonce song better than he can, and he can beat me in a tennis match, even on the Wii.

It took a long time to accept that I would never be exactly like him. People's expectations of me reflected back on the expectations I had for myself, and I was left unsatisfied. After years of struggling with who I was, I finally found a leadership program called HOBY where my facilitator shed new light on using the model my brother set to better myself. My brother left behind a legacy for me to slide into, and his relationships with teachers made it easier to make even stronger ones for myself, as most of them already knew who I was. He paved roads for me to travel, and his achievements became motivations for me to work harder. Anything I needed help with, my brother had probably already done, making it easy to navigate my way through school.

I am proud to say that my brother is one of my best friends. When he comes home from college, we binge watch Netflix and the newest Disney movie in theaters together. We talk about relationships, and he gives me college advice, and lie under the stars to talk about the meaning of life. We venture through waterfalls and draw circles in the stream with our feet as we contemplate how we've matured since the last time we were together. Throughout these past two years, I've really valued my friendship with him. It was something that I had never really realized I would depend on so much and hold onto so dearly. Not enough people understand the value of maintaining a healthy relationship with siblings, and the ways in which it affects a person dynamically and unexpectedly.

Sibling statistics

Advantages and disadvantages exist to having a sibling, and more than 80% of Americans understand this struggle (Lyon, 2009). In today's culture researchers say that it's actually more common for a teenager to have a sibling than a father. A relationship with a sibling can be the longest relationship that a person is likely to have in their lives, and so a sibling's influence is just as potent as a parent's ("15 Fascinating," 2011).

Time. It's no secret that siblings spend a lot of time together, particularly when they're younger. Over 33% of time is devoted to sibling interactions once children hit the age of eleven years, and even into adolescence, siblings still spend an average of eleven hours with each other every week, as observed by a Penn State University study. Certain sibling pairs even spend up to seventeen hours a week together (Harrington, 2016).

Fights are unavoidable considering the amount of time siblings spend together as kids growing up. It's been found that on average, siblings between the ages of three and seven fight 3.5 times an hour, and kids who are even younger fight every ten minutes. As they mature, that same hatred blossoms into a friendship. I hated my brother growing up, and I even found old journals that he doodled in, with phrases like "Sameep sux!" and little rockets raining down on a stick figure representation of me. Thankfully, that's no longer the case.

Preferences occur, although most parents outwardly deny that they have a favorite child. Over 65% of mothers and 70% of fathers exhibit a preference for one child, usually the older one, according to a study by Katherine Conger at the University of California, Davis. This can be damaging to the other child's self-esteem and self-confidence in the long run and cause them to feel unwanted. I was the culprit of accusing my parents of favoritism all the time growing up.

Intelligence is usually highest in firstborns, averaging up to three points higher than younger siblings (Carey, 2007). The strongest theory backing up this observation is that younger siblings may ask for help on certain academic tasks, thereby reinforcing the concepts and ideas for the older sibling. However, other studies have also shown that the younger sibling is typically smarter up until age twelve, and then it flips to the older sibling.

Health differences between older siblings and younger siblings include longer life expectancy for the older, perhaps due to the fact that a younger mother means younger eggs, which means healthier babies. However, younger siblings have a decreased probability of developing allergies and eczema, since by the time they are born, the house is already awash with germs brought in by the older sibling, forcing younger siblings' immune systems to become more resistant. In my situation, however, I was the one who ended up with both allergies and eczema, despite being the younger sibling. Unfair, right?

Extroversion in younger siblings in large families occurs primarily because the younger sibling is used to dealing with more people and forced to speak up for attention. Younger siblings are also found to be much more creative, rebellious, and lighthearted when interacting with others.

Gender norms. Although it seems more logical for opposite sex siblings to mimic one another and meld into each other's gender stereotypes, opposite sex siblings can also prompt de-identification, where each child tries to ensure that they have their own place in the family by reinforcing gender norms. Girls may seek traditionally girly things while boys opt for the rough and tough activities labeled as "manly." In my situation, I spent a lot of time doing tomboy things in early childhood, chasing after my brother and wrestling with him. I would sneak into his room and scoop up his old shirts and basketball shorts and then wear them to school. Because of the bullying I received for "acting like a boy" in lower school, I jumped to the opposite extreme and started waxing, buying cute clothes, wearing makeup, and keeping my hair down constantly.

Advantages of having a sibling

Siblings are great friends to have and can prompt a lot of positive experiences and values. Following are some advantages of having a sibling (Lyon, 2009):

Dating is easier if a person is at least used to having a near-age member of the opposite gender to interact with. An older sibling can often also give good advice in regards to how to approach a crush and what to do in relationships, due to increased experience with dating.

Stress buffering in a variety of situations is another thing a sibling can provide. Whether it's parental divorce, friend issues, or self-esteem problems, there's a sense of reliability that can only be found in a sibling. I remember coming home one evening, after one of the worst fights I ever had with my friends. I was in my own bed, crying, when I heard the softest sniffling in another room. I pushed open the door to my brother's room to find him curled up, sobbing against his pillow. Without giving it a second thought, I jumped on the bed, aligning myself against his back with my arms around his waist. For a solid ten minutes, we just lay there, shedding tears, taking comfort in each other's presence. To this day, it remains one of the most intimate moments I've had with my brother and an instance I continue to cherish.

Positive interactions result from healthy discussions about differing opinions, and even arguments, with siblings. These discussions teach teens how to interact with peers. Since sibling love is pretty unconditional, all arguments are forced to be resolved at some point, which trains siblings involved how to interact with peers. My brother and I would usually solve our conflicts by talking about what was upsetting or damaging. I learned a lot about apologizing and being a good friend because of him, and I learned how to deal with arguments and the correct way to ask for forgiveness.

Academics are influenced when an older sibling precedes a younger one in school. "Sibling spillover effect," a phenomenon studied by the University of Essex in the UK occurs when an older sibling is able to provide aid on comprehending concepts, info about certain classes, or insight into certain teachers to a younger sibling, which typically helps them do better in school. I can't count the number of times I looked to my brother to teach me something I didn't understand or asked him for advice on how to study for a certain teacher's tests. His knowledge about our high school made my entire experience much more fulfilling.

Character development is accentuated by having a sibling, whether it's just learning how to resolve arguments or learning how to nurture and care for others in a complimentary fashion.

Standards set by parents can be affected by an older sibling. As children, my brother and I were not allowed to go to sleepovers, but as time passed, my brother fought for the right to go. Once he obtained that freedom, I obtained it as well, which meant that he'd fought the battle for me. The same thing happened with us for phones.

Disadvantages of having a sibling

While many benefits to having a sibling exist, there are also some drawbacks. Sharing is something you're forced to learn very well, and if you're unable to create a positive relationship with your sibling, it can be difficult to endure living with them. Following are some disadvantages of having siblings (Swiger, 2015):

Mental-health vulnerability has been proven by Clare Stocker to exist among siblings with poor relationships. These pairs are more vulnerable to mental health illnesses, such as anxiety, depression, and criminal behavior. One study suggests that by the age of fifty years, men who had defective sibling relations before the age of twenty had an increased likelihood of developing depression.

Parent favoritism is disheartening for children and a blow to a less-loved sibling's self-esteem. Less favored siblings can be associated with anxiety, depression, and a very negative self-perception. Parental love sets the foundation for self-love for many teenagers, and if that foundation is not there, it can make a deadly impact. It has a very similar impact to when parents are divorced or unhappily together.

Early exposure of younger siblings to things that they may not necessarily be ready to know or understand occurs. Since I was the younger sibling, I got a lot more exposure as to what happens at college, parties, and other PG-13 topics. This early information was both a blessing and a curse. I'm definitely glad I'm more educated, but I know for sure that my parents aren't.

Bad habits by an older sibling or actions that are harmful make the younger sibling twice as likely to do the same thing. For example, if an older sibling is an alcoholic, the younger sibling may assume that drinking is okay and will be twice as likely to drink. With smoking, the numbers rise to four times as likely.

TIPS FOR TEENS

Building a relationship with your sibling takes hard work, so it's a constant maturation and growth process that requires a lot effort. The following are tips that worked for me but might also help you.

Tip #1: Set boundaries

This is definitely one of the most important tips. It's so incredibly important for you and your sibling to set boundaries and keep some time for privacy. Let your sibling know which clothes are okay to borrow and when it's okay to borrow them. Set quiet times that allow you to have your privacy. Respect when they want to be alone so that they respect when you want to be alone.

Tip #2: Listen well

You'd be amazed to learn what secrets your sibling is holding back from you. If you take the first step and try to be open with them, you'll make strides in your friendship. Try to understand them and listen to what they have to say. This has worked incredibly well for my brother and me.

Tip #3: Be respectful

Just like with your friends, you have to respect your sibling. You and your sibling may not always get along, and it may not always be fun, but it's important that you respect your sibling as a human being. Be kind and think before you speak, especially when they anger you. I've seen my friends and their siblings call each other names, and to this day, they're still not friends. You could be missing out on something great.

Tip #4: Share everything

You may not always want to, but sharing can be very healthy for your friendship. You can bond with each other by sharing clothes or toys that you both like. Share milkshakes or share a secret location. The more things you find in common with each other and the more you share with each other, the stronger the bond between you will be.

Tip #5: Speak your mind

In a respectful and mature way, of course, let your sibling know why or how he or she is being annoying and do what you can to resolve the issue. The only way to become best friends with your brother or sister is to share with them how you're feeling without escalating into an argument. At the age of twelve, I assumed that ignoring my brother whenever I was angry was the optimal way to fix the problem. It took my brother a lot of hugs to get me to talk, and once I did share my problem with him, we became even closer than before.

Tip #6: Accept mistakes

No one ever wants to admit that they're the one who is wrong, but it's especially important with a sibling that you swallow your pride and apologize, even if you're not the one at fault. One thing I've learned over the years is that if you apologize, it's likely that the other person will follow suit and apologize as well.

Tip #7: Forgive

As important as it is to be able to ask for forgiveness, it's also a necessity to give it willingly. Your sibling is a best friend who you need, and eventually you're going to have to forgive them, so you might as well forgive them sooner than later.

While at Disneyworld Florida one year, my parents told me to hang out with my brother. Simar, of course, wanted to go alone, so he attempted to lose me in the crowd as I tagged at his heels. Within seconds of looking away from the top of his head bobbing through the crowd, I lost him, and, distraught, I found a light-clad picnic table to perch upon. I pulled out my headphones and closed my eyes so I could dissolve into the beat, and my brother jumped out at me, knocking me off the table. Angrily, I stood up and walked away, but he grabbed the jack of the ear-buds and attempted to yank me back. What happened instead was a small "pop" that echoed in our ears and resulted in the wire being ripped. Being as I treated my ear-buds like my baby, my eyes filled with tears, and I screamed at him, my little voice carrying the sharpness of a thousand knives.

In order to apologize, my brother jogged from store to store until he found an acceptable pair of new ear-buds, and then spent the entire night hugging me until I forgave him.

Tip #8: Bonding experiences

Whenever you get the time, go do a fun bonding activity with your sibling. The amount of inside jokes that can sprout as a result of just one outing is incredible. My brother and I make it a routine to hang out whenever he's home from college, and we do a variety of things. We've gone hiking in national parks, played each other in dodge ball, watched the sunrise on a grassy field, and had Disney marathons together. Whether it's shopping sprees or sports, I know having my brother by my side will make it infinitely more exciting.

Tip #9: Unconditional love

You can always count on your family for unconditional love. No matter what they do, we have to find it within ourselves to forgive and love them even more than before. It's one of the most powerful solutions to any problem we may ever face.

Tip #10: You are you

It's easy to get caught up in your sibling's shadow, no matter whether you're the younger one or the older one. It's important that you don't compare yourself to your sibling. Each person has his or her own strengths, and the only thing you can do is use those strengths to your advantage. You don't have to like the same things or be good at the same things as your sibling. Don't let others tell you who to be.

TIPS FOR PARENTS

Sibling wars can be some of the scariest things to be caught in the middle of. So then the question comes, how do you deter sibling rivalries?

Tip #1: Split attention

It's likely when a new baby comes, you'll be spending more time on the little one than your existing child. Be sure to shower the older one with just as much love and explain that sometimes you might have to focus solely on the baby, simply because it's not capable of being independent yet. The same goes for when the older sibling enters high school. You may be much more focused on the older sibling since they are entering a new phase in their life, but it's important that you shower younger children with love as well.

When my brother went to high school, I was in fourth grade. Since my brother was entering a critical point in his life, especially during the junior and senior years before college, my parents were very focused on him, which left me feeling pretty alone and unwanted throughout middle school. Because I was not getting the same amount of attention, I assumed

I was simply not as important in our family, which led me to believe I was unloved. My parents later explained to me why, but it still stays with me.

Ensure that both children feel equally loved and feel as if they're being treated the same. If you give one sibling privileges, but not the other, there is likely to be underlying contempt that will only damage your relationship with your children and their relationship with one another. However, there is a time for everything. Each child has his or her own needs, so the main thing is that you are treating your child individually.

Tip #2: Family cheerleading

Create a sense of love among the entire family through routine vacations and activities like camping and board game night. Build a structure of support for all the children and have them cheer for each other whenever one succeeds. Teach them to take pride in one another's achievements and also their own. This will teach them love, responsibility, and make them more comfortable being themselves.

Tip #3: Empathy

Get your children to think from the other's perspectives. The two golden rules of preschool are treat others how you want to be treated, and if you don't have something nice to say, don't say anything at all. These two rules will not only help them in their sibling relationships but also with school peers.

Tip #4: Know when to get involved

Don't get involved unless totally necessary. Little things like squabbles over toys and food are things that children have to learn how to handle without external help. Teach them about compromise, and then leave it up to them to practice it. If they are unable to sort it out by themselves then make them aware that if they cannot solve the problem within the next few minutes, there will be consequences, and, for example, no one will get to play with the toy.

When bigger problems arise, like name-calling and abuse, call the victimizer out and find a suitable punishment. In the same way that bullying is not tolerated at school, there is no place for it at home.

Sometimes, the best way to deal with younger children who are having a difficult time expressing their feelings is to use a concept called the feeling stick. Give one sibling a stick or an object. Whoever is in possession of that object may speak, but no one else can. When holding the feeling stick, the only phrase that can be said is "I'm feeling [insert feelings here] because [insert reason for feelings here]." This offers a method of communication using a physical representation, which is particularly helpful for children.

Tip #5: Don't compare

This is a must. Never compare your children. When you start comparing them, they'll start comparing themselves to each other. Each sibling has strengths, and you must encourage each one to utilize those strengths as much as possible. Unfortunately, teenagers are compared to their peers on a daily basis. They will be compared by grades, skill in sports, skill in music, and even in attractiveness. Comparing your children is just one more comparison for them to endure. They don't need that. Avoid comments like, "I wish you could do that like your brother," or "at your age, your sister had already done this." It'll stay with them.

Tip #6: Destroy gender norms

Do not perpetuate gender stereotypes. Do not assume that your girl will be into dresses and getting her nails done. Do not assume that your boy will want to play video games or play sports. The more you reinforce these norms, the more likely children feel pressured to become who they are not. Allow your teen to flourish the way they want to and be supportive in everything that they do, even if that way is incredibly different than their sibling.

Tip #7: Help mend

Although sibling relationships typically do get better as they mature and grow, in some cases, they don't. If your children don't get along, intervene and try to mend the relationship. It's not in your power to fix it, but you can definitely help by starting the conversation. Find out the root causes for the hatred between your children and work out the best way in which to promote a healthy, flourishing relationship.

Make sure that both sides feel heard. You can definitely mediate the situation and encourage clear communication from one sibling to the other. Remind them the importance of sibling relationships, and how, in many situations, siblings are the only people to be there for each other. It's okay if they don't take up the idea immediately. Building a healthy relationship is a process.

Being a sibling is both a blessing and a curse. You get a lifelong best friend and worst enemy. As much as sibling relationships may suck in the beginning, they prove to be the most valuable treasures. I don't really know what I would have done without my brother. He's my emotional supporter, night and day. He's the one I trust with my deepest and darkest secrets, and the one who makes me feel safest.

My brother's hugs are to die for, and his smile is contagious. Even with him at college, I feel like our bond has only gotten stronger. We even hold entire conversations using only gifs, something we like to call "engi-flish." When he comes home, we meet up with other siblings and have a "Sibling Olympics," a sort of compilation of various activities such as egg tosses and three-legged races. We go hiking in places we're not supposed to and go adventuring into school to find old teachers we both know. We've created memories to last one, and maybe even two, lifetimes.

Everything Simar accomplishes makes my heart swell with pride, and even his mistakes give me hope. My brother is rare, and I love him so much that my heart weighs more every day because of it. But I'm sure that's something that all siblings say. Having a sibling is like having a favorite chair. It might get old, it might wear down, and it might get dusty, but it will never fail to welcome you back into its arms. It will never fail to give you a hug, no matter how many times you might screw up, and it will always be there to support you.

Your favorite chair will be there to listen to all of your rants and all of the gossip.

The only difference is that your sibling has a voice to respond.

And that is precious.

16

Substance Abuse

Drug and alcohol addiction

"Please, I need water," the patient croaked, as he gazed up with glossy eyes at the relative beside his bed. Feeling helpless, the relative sighed gently before proceeding to get a wet cotton roll to clean the patient's lips with water.

"No. Water. I need water," he repeated in a hoarse voice, using up the last of his energy to appeal to the man beside him.

No one is to give him water. Water will convert to poison. The doctor's instruction rang out in the relative's ears as he watched on with sympathy. It wasn't until later that I'd heard this story and discovered the scary truth that the relative on duty that night was, in fact, my dad, and the patient was his twenty-six-year-old cousin. Dad still remembers it all: his cousin's sallow complexion staring back up at him and the beeping of the heart monitor ringing against his brain.

At 3:35 A.M., the cousin took my dad's hand shakily, gripping it until his knuckles turned white. My father's heart dropped as he felt the pulse fading away, dissolving into the skin. He called out to the nurse and the doctor, but by the time they reached the room, his cousin was already gone, leaving behind his wife and his one-year-old son.

A drug overdose had cost my father's cousin his entire world, a simple repercussion of the choices he had made in high school. One drug had led to another, and by the time his mother had discovered the truth, his fate had already been sealed. Over the next few years after their discovery, my dad's cousin was put through therapy and was slowly weaned off of drugs. His therapy was successful, and he made strides forward in recovery as he started a business, got married, and had a son, until one day, he met up with his school friends. In celebration, they downed shot after shot of hard liquor and smoked joint after joint of marijuana. That night, he passed away because of one mistake. One relapse changed not only his life, but also the lives of his loved ones.

My dad's aunt never fully accepted the death of her son. She withered away in her home, empty thoughts echoing in her ears, as she replayed every opportunity she could have had to save him. But in the end, there was nothing she could have done, for he was his own destroyer. No matter where you live, no matter the environment you grow up in, there is a possibility that there will be drugs and alcohol. They will be first introduced in high school to teenagers and then become even more accessible in college. For some, it's a simple experiment that they abandon soon after, while for others, it becomes a life consuming addiction that haunts their every moment. Even in the Asian academic-oriented private school that I went to, there were cases of drug abuse.

More than anyone else, parents are affected by having a teenager who is hooked on either drugs or alcohol. It leads to hours of fights and hate. I've seen the toll drug and alcohol abuse takes on families as it demolishes the very framework of each relationship. Last year, I heard about a boy, brimming with potential, weighed down by drugs. His parents pulled him out of school, hoping that by spending time with him, they'd be able to wean him off. He was so dependent that he started having seizures, and medical treatment had no effect. He stole money from the house to buy drugs and resorted to violence.

One night, his parents decided that the only alternative was to give him a choice. He could choose the safety of his home, or he could choose drugs. He chose drugs and was thrown out of his own home and onto the streets. After wandering through empty alleyways and bathing in apartment swimming pools for a week, he returned home, promising to try rehab. This continuous cycle of recovery and relapse occurred time and time again, until finally, he had become homeless one too many times. He joined an intensive care rehabilitation program in Los Angeles in early 2016 and is still, to this day, recovering as he faces his own personal war against drugs.

But the problem is that not everyone recovers.

Substance abuse statistics

The United States represents 5% of the world's population and 75% of prescription drugs taken. Of teens who abuse prescription drugs, 60% get them free from friends and relatives (Vogt, 2013). Underage drinking costs the United States more than $58 billion every year. This cost is the equivalent of $216.22 for every man, woman, and child and $577.91 for every household in the United States (Levy, Stewart, & Wilbur, 1999).

Substance abuse has been tracked for more than thirty-five years and continues to be a more pressing concern each and every day. The following statistics are taken from the Monitoring the Future (MTF) survey, which is conducted annually by the National Institute on Drug Abuse (NIDA), a component of the National Institute of Health (NIH) and conducted by the University of Michigan. The good news is that the results show a decline in the use of marijuana, alcohol, tobacco, and other prescription medications, among the nation's teens. In this 2016 report, over 45,473 students participated across 372 private and public schools. Below are some of the statistics ("Monitoring the Future," 2016):

- 55.6% of twelfth graders, 38% of tenth graders, and 17.6% of eighth graders, reported having used alcohol in the past year.

- 37.3% of twelfth graders, 20.5% of tenth graders, and 5.7% of eighth graders reported they have been drunk at least once.

- 3.4% of eighth graders reported binge drinking (five or more drinks in a row in the last two weeks) while 15.5% high school seniors reported binge drinking.

- 38.3% of high school seniors in states with medical marijuana laws reported past year marijuana use, compared to 33.3% in non-medical marijuana states

- Marijuana and ecigarettes are more popular than regular tobacco cigarettes. Within the last twenty-five years, cigarette smoking has dropped from 10.7% to 1.8% in high school seniors.

- 14.3% of twelfth graders say they used an illicit drug other than marijuana.

Prescription drug usage among high school seniors in the past year:

- 2.9% reported misuse of the pain reliever Vicodin, compared to nearly 10% a decade ago.

- 4.8% reported misuse of all opioid pain relievers.

- 6.2% used Adderall.

- 1.2% used Ritalin.

- 4.9% used benzodiazepines, a kind of tranquilizer.

Here are a few other facts and statistics on drug abuse in teens ("Teen Drug," n.d.):

- Over 60% of teens report that drugs of some kind are kept, sold, and used at their school.

- 1.3% of high school seniors have tried bath salts.

- 28% of teens know at least one person who has tried ecstasy.

- More teenagers die from taking prescription drugs than the use of cocaine and heroin combined.

- 64% of teens say they have used prescription painkillers that they got from a friend or family member.

Alcohol is the leading factor in the top three causes of death among individuals 15–20 years of age, which are auto crashes, homicides, and suicides.

It is important to keep in mind that these statistics are collected from the students who were willing to admit to what they had tried and consumed. But there are plenty who refuse to report their drug use. How much is being left unsaid? How many statistics are being exempt? These statistics are alarming, but we also have to give some credit to the fact that teenagers are making strides on being better-educated and making better decisions in regards to smoking and alcohol use. On the other hand, the abuse of marijuana and prescription drugs becomes a greater epidemic day by day.

Marijuana can hinder memory and perception and stunt a teenager's brain development, yet a lot of teenagers are unaware of these known risks. Many private schools offer a required drug education course, but classes like these often go unheeded in public schools. According to National Institute of Drug Abuse (NIDA), there were nearly 4.6 million drug-related emergency hospital visits each year, 45% of which regard drug abuse. Arrested teens often test positive for drug use, and The National Institute of Justices Arrestee and Drug Monitoring System reported that 66% of arrested male adolescents had marijuana in their systems ("Drug-Related Hospital," 2011).

Another epidemic that seemed to sweep the nation a few years ago was the use of codeine in cough syrups to achieve a high. After being rapped about in almost every young rapper's mixtapes, high school and college students picked up on it, and before long, it became more popular than ever. Its easy accessibility and consumption made it common among teenagers, and so, pharmaceutical companies began to put warnings on the back of the containers in hopes of discouraging substance abuse. Abuse of DXM sent almost 5,500 people in 2004 alone to the emergency rooms, including children as young as twelve years old, according to an article published on WebMD (Smith, 2012).

Reasons behind substance abuse

The reasons for drug abuse are complicated and range from curiosity to chemistry (Hudson, n.d.).

Curiosity is a huge motivating factor for teens to try many things. We've all wondered on occasion about the unknown whether it's drugs or any number of other topics. I've heard my friends describe using certain drugs as a feeling of bliss, of flying, as if the constraints of the world have been lifted. In that moment, there is nothing but a blinding sense of satisfaction. Growing up surrounded by drugs in both everyday life and the media can be difficult, and some teenagers who have never tried them feel as if they're missing out. Teenagers have an implicit need to explore and experience the world. Realistically, it's not surprising that so many adolescents feel the need to try alcohol or drugs.

Ironically, sometimes when teens are educated about the dangers of drugs, they feel even more interest in experimentation: "These are what drugs are. You can't have them." The natural teenage response is to then want to try them.

Fitting in is a constant need for teenagers: to be "one of the cool kids" who struts down the hallway at school with an aura of self-confidence. Most teenagers strive for this through sports, fashion, drugs, or all three. It starts with one friend trying a cigarette because someone popular on the sports team did. It spreads, slowly and steadily, infecting the students in every group, in every corner. Suddenly, if you refuse a cigarette, you are labeled for it. Craving to fit in and belong prompts teenagers to start experimenting. It's "just a drink" to them. "Just some weed" at a party. The simple desire to be part of something with the people who matter the most to them at the time spurs on the experimentation.

Media romanticizes drug use, whether through news reporting Justin Bieber's latest DUI, Kanye's newest song, or a movie like *Neighbors*. Drug usage is portrayed as normal: a common representation of how adults smoke and drink for pleasure. These same images reflect upon a teenager's life, and before long, the dangers they're taught about in school are thrown out the window.

As measured by a 2011 study, 47% of teens agreed that movies and TV shows portrayed drugs as a customary thing to do. These adolescents were seven times more likely to smoke, six times more likely to use pot, and five times more likely to drink (Guedea, n.d.).

Attention from disobeying parents is a motivating factor for many things a teen does. Almost every teen has had one instance where they wished nothing more than to piss their parents off. When a parent restrains them, many students feel as if their only option is to lash out in defiance and flaunt independence. Adolescents are stuck between the adult world and a child's world, drastically different. They receive some freedoms but not others, and most can't wait to gain complete control of their lives.

Idleness may prompt drug use. When a teen is left with extra time, more often than not, he or she finds a new activity, which may include substance abuse. It starts with a "Hey dude, you free Friday night?" and leads to much more. A bored teenager with money can do even more damage, as more doors open when cash is introduced into the equation.

Escape from the pressure of school and society is sought after by teens, and many find it in drugs. It's about surviving "now." Coping with the obstacles of life causes stress and pain, whether self-esteem issues, bullying, a romantic heartbreak, or anything else. The teenage years can be a particularly emotional ride that takes a toll on everyone, including the people around the teenager. When there are no other outlets, it can be easy to fall into drugs and alcohol where there is no judgment.

Dopamine feels good. That's something we must address head on; it is not something we can run from. Initially, the use of the drugs and alcohol prompts a buzz, and it's one of the reasons teenagers are motivated to keep trying it. I've heard it explained from tipsy peers as they've stumbled toward me and explained their reasoning in drunken yells.

"It helps me forget."

"It's the buzz."

"I feel safe. And fuzzy. And warm."

It's such a short-term thing, yet we crave this feeling of happiness, this dopamine that is released when we drink or smoke. Dopamine is addictive, and sometimes, when everything else is going south, drugs are the only outlet that some can rely on so they don't completely lose the feeling of hope. What we don't realize is that a high from drugs is temporary and harmful and can change an entire life in an instant. So then that raises the next question.

Where do teenagers get drugs?

Getting drugs has gotten easier because the appetite for them has increased. It's not as simple as a sole "drug dealer" on a sketchy corner that parents tell their children to avoid anymore, since drugs, from bath salts to cough medicine, can literally be found everywhere. Drugs and alcohol can be found in the medicine cabinet at home, at a neighbor's house, at parties, online, with a friend, with a dealer, and at school. When students have cash, buying drugs can be as easy as buying food.

I've been offered drugs despite having a reputation for avoiding them. It was as simple as sitting outside a building on a picnic table and having a guy who was high approach me, shoot a toothy smile my way, and wink as he asked me if I wanted some "molly." I've had my friends at summer camps slip packets of cocaine into my hand as they whispered "shhhh" with darting eyes and pale, shaking hands.

The seniors at some schools even hide marijuana in the couches of school lounges, right in front of teachers' eyes. Drugs are everywhere, and no matter how hard teenagers may try to avoid them, they will be exposed, so ultimately, parents can only hope that the foundation they built will hold up against the peer pressure their teen will be facing. Having a sibling in college gives a younger sibling better access to drugs. Having a friend who smokes weed opens up a plethora of other options. Raiding parents' stashes is another popular source; while everyone is downstairs busy arguing about the latest Trump or Hillary abomination, a teen can sneak up to a bathroom and check the drawers for painkillers, cough medicines, and alcohol.

Fake IDs are common when buying alcohol or cigarettes, and finding a supplier is easier through Facebook connections. Stumbling across dealers on highway intersections is more common than one might think. There are many options everywhere, and it'll never truly be possible to eliminate them all. The methods of drug intake constantly change to suit the needs of the users. A professor in a girls' college in India shared with me the various styles in which teens at the college had begun to consume drugs. One of the most astonishing stories I heard was girls spreading back pain ointment cream on a piece of bread and eating it.

There are so many awful instances of drug abuse that are overlooked for the more favorable and glamorized version of beer pong and dimly lit parties. To teenagers, it's about the ecstasy, the buzz, and the dulling of the world around them.

TIPS FOR TEENAGERS

We've all pledged not to do drugs when we are educated about the side effects and the consequences, but it's hard to uphold our promises when we're put in a situation where it seems like the only option is to resort to substance use. It's likely that you will try alcohol and drugs because that is a reality in our generation, but that doesn't mean you can't learn how to safely drink or avoid drinking whenever you can (NIDA Blog Team, 2015).

Tip # 1: Learn to say "no"

Sometimes, if you say "no" enough times, the people around you will stop asking and respect your decision. Often times, our fear of a negative response and of damage to our popularity keeps us from doing what we know is right. We feel like we should just join in since everyone else is doing it, but the important thing is to remember that no one but you knows what is right for you. Practice in the mirror if you have to, but don't be afraid to say no. If the pressure is still coming on strong, get up and walk out. It takes a lot of courage to do that, especially when the idea of becoming an outsider pops into your mind, but in the end, it truly is worth it. It's hard to make that first step, but it's important that you respect yourself enough to do what is safest and most comfortable for you, even if that means leaving and never looking back. But more often than not, we have some idea of what's coming. If you're not confident enough to refuse drugs and alcohol, avoid going to parties until you are.

Tip # 2: Construct a squad

Pay attention to the types of people with whom you are hanging out. If you're hanging out with teens who do drugs, it's likely that you're going to be exposed to those kinds of scenarios, so just keep that in mind when making friends. It's important to find a group who will support you no matter what decision you make and respect your views. Always make sure that if you're drinking, you have someone to take care of you. You don't want to be that "drunk kid" that is taken advantage of. Ask someone to stay sober and have your back if you choose to drink or do drugs.

Tip # 3: Be the designated driver

One person needs to remain sober so that everyone can get home safely, and if you offer, most people will be grateful you aren't high or drunk. If you're drinking or getting high, ensure that you have a designated driver who can legally drive you home and will vow to stay sober.

Tip # 4: Keep a dupe drink

Sometimes we don't know what's coming, and we're struck by surprise when someone winks and offers us a red cup full of beer. Keep a bottled drink like a soda or iced tea with you to drink at parties. Fill a solo cup up with the liquid, and I guarantee that people will be less likely to pressure you. If someone offers you a drink, just smile and throw back, "got one already." They're not going to check what's in the cup.

Tip # 5: Get out

Make up an excuse about why you must leave a situation. Use a parent or sibling excuse, or say that your friend needs to be picked up from somewhere. Sometimes, blaming your parents is the best thing you can do, and I'm sure they'll appreciate that you're staying out of trouble. Use the sports team excuse. Although it is true that sports teams will often engage in substance abuse together, you can sometimes get out of getting intoxicated by saying that you have to stay away from drugs to maximize your athletic performance.

Unanticipated things happen at parties. Almost every single teen gets drunk at least once. Even if you don't drink, chances are you're going to be in a situation where your ride to the party is drunk. If this does occur, it's important that you take the precautions necessary to ensure your safety. After the party, here are your options.

- Find another ride home. Find a sober friend to give you a lift.

- If you're sober, ask for the keys so you can drive everyone home safely.

- Call someone to pick you up. Although Mom and Dad may not be the happiest campers about getting out of bed late at night, at least they'll be grateful that you didn't put yourself at risk.

- Call an Uber or a Lyft or a taxi. Just keep in mind that if you're a girl, you have to take a few more precautions.

- Crash at the host's house. Ask if you can sleep over in one of the guest rooms, and let someone know where you are.

We struggle a lot with being different, but the important thing to remember is that sometimes different is better. You might hate it now, but being the sober one might be the smart choice. It's hard when you see everyone around you having fun and partying, but the important thing to remember is that the bliss is short term. Your peers may end up doing things they regret because they won't have control over what they're doing. It can feel like you're missing out, but trust me you're not.

TIPS FOR PARENTS

Parents struggle with the fight against their teens falling into substance abuse. One of the most important things parents can do is listen to their child. Build a foundation of trust and love and watch out for changes in behavior. Communication is key in these kinds of situations. When a parent has a discussion with a teenager about getting drunk and high, it is estimated that it can lessen the chance of this occurring by 42% ("Tips for Dads," 2012). Only a quarter of teens actually report ever talking about drugs or alcohol use in their families.

Growing up, I was simply told not to get intoxicated, and I found that I despised it as well as I watched the people around at parties get drunk. I was educated about it in school, and I found that I had my own resentment toward substance use. However, not everyone is like me, and not everyone will be as closed off to the idea of using drugs and alcohol.

Tip # 1: Listen to your child

Set aside some time and ask your teenager their views on drugs and alcohol and watch for body language for cues that indicate what they feel. Check in regularly with them and make them feel safe and comfortable. Establish a strong relationship with them and build upon it every day so that they understand that drugs are not their only escape.

Tip # 2: Share your experience

Share your experiences with drugs and alcohol so that your teens are more open to discussing the topic. Discuss the side effects and consequences of drug and alcohol use and talk about ways that they can resist peer pressure. Play an active role in their lives and make sure they feel comfortable and safe. There's no harm in even telling them about your alcohol and drug adventures if it makes them laugh, just warn them against going too far.

Give them lessons they can take away from your stories and ask them to apply those lessons to their own lives.

Tip # 3: Know your child

Know what your teen is doing and pay attention to their whereabouts. I'm not saying be a helicopter parent, but be aware in case they do end up needing you.

Tip # 4: Establish rules and provide support

Establish rules so your teen knows the laws of your house. Keep an eye on prescription drugs so you are aware if any go missing. Teenagers need someone they can talk to, and many resort to drugs when they fail to find a role model in whom they can confide.

Watch out for telltale signs that your child is hooked on drugs. These include:

- a withdrawal from family and friends;
- medicine containers or packets hidden in their rooms;
- extreme changes in friends, school performance, sleeping patterns, appetite, or moods;
- secrecy about possessions;
- missing items or money from around the house; and
- a change in physical appearance, for example, red eyes, extreme weight gain or loss, or bags under eyes.

If your teen does admit to substance abuse, enforce the consequences you have established and take the necessary steps to ensure that they are not addicted. Rehab or therapy might be in order. It's never too late to start the conversation with your teen and teach them how to make healthy choices.

Tip #5: Set a good example

Make sure the people with whom you associate and your own choices and actions set a good example for your child. Teens take after their role models; in this case that's you.

Tip #6: Be understanding

Yes, your child will most likely get drunk or high at some point. The more you clamp down on them and restrict their actions, the more likely they are to rebel. If they want to try alcohol, ask them to wait until they're of legal age. Be understanding if something happens and allow for some leeway if it was a one-time occurrence. Usually, if teenagers have bad experiences with drugs or alcohol, they'll be more likely to avoid it. So be aware and figure out the best plan for your teenager.

Communities must pull together to fight drug abuse; sometimes that might mean holding the media responsible for the manner in which drugs and alcohol are portrayed. As awareness increases and art and culture reflect the true nature of drug abuse, we must work to take the necessary steps within our own households.

Yes, drinking is common. People get fake IDs and find dealers and buy drugs. It's a reality, but the more we raise awareness about it, the safer we can make each other. Be careful. You're going to do what you want to do. As long as you're safe, that's all that really matters.

So have fun, and cheers to safe drinking!

Family Fundamentals

Family Fundamentals

If you've read this book (or at least more than one chapter), you've probably recognized some common themes throughout the tips provided. Sure, many reasons come to play in the topics the book discusses, and there are diverse tactics and methods to combat these topics. The underlying idea, however, is that these problems are not the responsibility of one individual. It's a group effort, in this case, a family effort, that prompts the character development that leads to healthy and happy young people. Stronger individuals means stronger families, which in turn means a stronger society. The obstacle is that this family effort is getting lost in the daily age of technology, where we're too focused on our phones at the dinner table and engulfed by a sea of text messages and social media posts.

Teens are under a lot of stress, and it's important that they establish core values and structure in their families to help the coping process and make the transition into adulthood slightly easier. We need to use the vast knowledge at our disposal to our advantage instead of allowing it to distract us to a fault.

Parenting is a complex process, and I think even being a "perfect" parent wouldn't be enough to prevent all the issues of adolescence. So in a society where perfection doesn't exist, but teens and parents are told to be "perfect," it's no wonder families feel stressed. Adolescence is a confusing phase of life, and learning how to handle various situations is key to fostering skills to be a successful, happy adult. It's a family's responsibility to provide a teen with an environment in which they will be able to grow as an individual and discover who they are.

Parents, your teen will learn how to behave from you, and it's a necessity that you set a good example. But don't forget, you'll also learn a lot from your teen. Overall, it should be a net positive flow of love, values, attitudes, behaviors, and experiences that make a productive contribution to self, family, community, and even society.

It's kind of crazy how much I've learned about my own issues just from flipping through the research that was required for this book, and it opened my eyes to a common pattern that I saw in taking action toward many of the problems. The four ingredients necessary to develop what we like to call The Family Fundamentals are communication, empathy, love and compassion, and safe judgment.

1) COMMUNICATION

We all know teenagers are not the most skilled at holding engaging conversations with their parents, so communicating with them can be difficult. We hop into cars, turn our faces, and respond with the least amount of words possible.

But as difficult as it is, building an open line of communication is essential to getting through to each other. Build an atmosphere of trust and understanding about what each family member is experiencing. The more comfortable you are with each other, the more likely it is that you'll rely on each other when something really needs to be discussed.

Have routine check-ins

Parents: Explore topics pertaining to your kid's life and do your best to get involved to an extent with which your teen is comfortable. It's all about the baby steps. You might have to start with small conversations about that cute boy she kind of likes or what was for lunch, but eventually you'll work way to the utter roasting Bridgette was forced to endure during English or the drama about Jason and the four girls who like him. It takes time and effort, but be reasonably persistent, and you will succeed.

Teens: I was never one to tell my parents about anything, so I can get how hard it can be to keep them updated about your life. I was always resistant to the idea of filling in my parents about the latest drama because I didn't want them involved in my life. I had the preconceived notion that they would be judgmental and analyze everything I told them. But once you initially bridge that gap, you'll realize how helpful it is to have your parents as allies. I tell my mom about the boys who break my heart or the fights that I'm experiencing with my friends. I've come home and cried about the mean words that my classmates said, or the utter disappointment I felt when I got a grade that was less than satisfactory. Opening up has taught me how to have a relationship with my parents, and it's something that I never knew how to do until this year. Just for once, try it; it might take some time, but it's worth it. Be receptive to your parents and share what's going on in your life.

Use "in" activities to spend more time together and create happy memories

Parents: This might require some stepping out of your comfort zone, but that in and of itself could be worth it, especially if it means some quality time with your teen. Offer some ideas like laser tag or shopping or even bowling and try to make it a family night that can be fun for everyone. Ask your teen to style your hair or give you a makeover, or maybe bring an entire bag of quarters to spend at the crane machine at the arcade. It's all about the moments and conversations that will strengthen the bond between you and your teen. These outings or activities will give your teen time to talk to you and communicate their emotions and ideas to you. Build up positive, memorable experiences that outweigh the negative ones. When shaky moments in your relationship occur, turn it into something positive and recall all the times your teen has been receptive. Keep in mind the happiness fostered by these interactions.

Teens: I know, I know, you probably think I'm crazy. Let your mom come shopping with you? Let your dad play Call of Duty with you? As if! I'm no stranger to putting my headphones in and getting as far as possible from the women's section in Nordstrom or politely declining when my father takes the Xbox controller. But a lot of these activities can be fun and really eye opening for the entire family. Be open to what your parents suggest, and go the extra mile for them. For all you know, you might end up enjoying the activity and want to do it again. Time together is about creating opportunities to communicate. This might also be your one chance to throw out all your mom's wool turtlenecks and your dad's dingy sweatpants or prove to your family that you are the ultimate gaming master.

Try to adapt to the current technology

Parents: You know that emoji keyboard? My mom just discovered it, and she can't get enough of it. Now that's saying something, because I wouldn't describe my mother as the most tech savvy, and she's perfectly aware of that. But she's made strides in using current technology to the best of her ability. Really try to learn about your computers and phones (even get pointers from your kids) so that you learn to communicate with your teen in their "language." You'd be surprised how adorable and "chill" teens think it is for a parent to attempt and sometimes succeed in accurately using emoticons and slang.

Teens: We all know how entertaining it is to see your dad or mom text back "LOL ILY ☺" in the middle of the day. Try to teach your parents all about texting (maybe not all of those special little acronyms, but at least some of them) and be responsive to whatever they're sending your way. Sending adorable dog GIFs to one another in a group text is something my family also likes to do. It's heartwarming and silly, and most importantly it is something we all share.

Communication is the first step in any relationship, especially when it comes to family. Without communication, there is no relationship; if there is no relationship, are we really a "family"? So just make an effort to open communication channels to ensure that everyone's talking, whether it's a matter of extreme significance or just a silly text.

2) EMPATHY

So now that you're actually talking, employ some empathy. Empathy is vital to any relationship. Really make an effort to understand each other's point of views and ask questions when you're unsure. Never attack the other for having views that don't line up with yours, and try to relate to what they're saying.

Teenagers crave independence. We are neither considered adults nor children, and it leaves us feeling very confused. We pull away from parents, and that can lead to distance and gaps in thought processes. However, we are not unreasonable; we will not disregard everything our parents say. Probably listening patiently is something most teenagers have to work on, but trying to look at situations from viewpoints other than your own helps make listening patiently and respectfully easier.

Parents: Take a step back and let your teenager explore who he or she is before you try to step in and guide them toward who you want them to be. Empathize with what they're going through, and be lenient when you need to be. Share your own experiences from growing up with them; it'll remind them that you were once a teenager too. If you have reservations about certain topics or subjects, share the story you have related to the topic so that your teenager understands where you're coming from. If you grew up in a conservative environment, let them know that no matter how much reasoning, you'll never truly be comfortable with suggestive clothing. Maybe one of your friends was sexually assaulted at a party and so you don't want them at parties until a certain age. It's all about sharing the reasoning behind the rules set for them so that they understand you are not trying to restrict their activities because you don't trust them; you are trying to protect them because you understand things about the world they don't. A little conversation goes a long way.

Teens: Oh trust me it makes me angry too. When your parents tell you not to do something that you really want to do. I get it. But try to hear them out. They have a reason. Maybe they don't want you to wear those shorts or go to that party or be friends with those people. And a lot of the times, there's some reason, rational or irrational, that they have for that condition. Try to be understanding and (keyword) empathetic and understand where they're coming from. Listen to their stories and compromise with them. As much as they hear you out, you need to hear them out. Demonstrate maturity and listen patiently and respectfully to what they have to say without retaliating.

Empathy goes hand in hand with communication because in order for communication to continue, you have to understand each other. Otherwise, you'll talk once, get into an argument, and never talk again. It takes a little self-control, but it can be mastered over time.

3) LOVE AND COMPASSION

Love is literally what fuels any relationship. Whether it is platonic, romantic, or familial, love is necessary to keep a relationship alive. In the end, it's not about the gifts, or even the advantages, you give your child, but the amount of affection and attention you provide. It's all about those little words of advice and those hugs on downer days. Unconditional love is quite honestly what is needed in any relationship formula.

This kind of love can be called agapé. Agapé is a universal, limitless love that transcends obstacles and is present no matter what the situation. That is the kind of love we need.

Parents: That doesn't mean you can't reprimand your teen. If they do something wrong, they should be held accountable. But when it's all over and done with, make it clear to them how much you care and love them. Ensure that they're aware of the extent to which your affection stretches and do little things that make them smile. Communicate it through your words and your actions rather than just through material objects. Your teen wants to feel needed and useful, and they'll be much more secure if they're made aware that their family will love them through anything and everything.

Teens: It's not just your parents' responsibility to make you feel wanted. You need to take that extra step and try to relay to your parents how much they mean to you. No matter how much they might upset you, your parents probably mean the world to you, so really try to let them know how you feel. Give them unexpected hugs and kisses, tell them you love them before stepping out of the car, and do the little things like cleaning your room or helping around the house without being asked. Do it out of selflessness, not in the hopes that they'll return the favor. It's as much your responsibility as it is your parents' responsibility to make everyone in your family feel included and appreciated.

4) JUDGMENT OR KNOWING WHEN TO GET HELP

Brushing problems under the rug is easier than facing them sometimes, and to refuse to acknowledge the gravity of the situation at hand can be tempting. Maybe parents don't believe anything is actually wrong. Perhaps the teen won't fess up to anything for fear of treatment. Certain problems can even be overlooked as "normal teenage behavior." That's where judgment comes in. You need to know when lines have been crossed and help from an outside source is necessary.

Parents: Learning that your child is failing at something—especially something like being happy or being healthy—can hurt and be scary, and I know I've seen my parents hurt whenever they see me hurting. But you can't look the other way and pretend everything's fine. Take the initiative and address the problem, even if your teen is resistant. Don't compromise when it comes to your child's health. Come to terms with your teen's problem and figure out a solution, whether it is therapy or rehab or medication. Be aware of what's happening and know the signs. One or two glitches aren't an issue, but when things get out of hand and can no longer simply be confronted at home, you need to get help involved. Don't be scared of counselors and psychiatrists; they're truly helpful.

Teens: Chances are you don't want to talk to a therapist or a counselor about whatever you're going through. You feel like you can deal with it on your own, since you're independent and any sign that you're not okay would freak your parents out. But sometimes getting help from an outside source, whether that is a school counselor or a doctor or therapist, is essential. Be open with your family about what you're facing, so they can support you and establish the best game plan. There's nothing wrong with seeing a doctor for mental disorders that are out of your control or going to rehab to treat addiction. In the long run, you will be a healthier, happier you. So communicate your emotions and share your experiences with your family. They want to help you, but they can't do that if you stay quiet about your struggles. Your safety is your parents' priority. They have your best interests in mind, so don't hold it against them if they do something or get help for you without your permission.

So now you've read what I think are the fundamental ideas of family, aka the core values on which to build a relationship, especially a family relationship. Actively incorporating these into your life is important, whether or not issues exist in your family. Honestly, if you remember nothing else from this book, I hope you remember these four basic ideas. They can be applied to any case and any situation.

A happier family means happier individual family members with individually happier lives, and that's key to a smoother functioning adolescence. So crack out those family recipes and gather around a table and get to know each other. Learn old stories and tell new ones. Help one another reach dreams and avoid pitfalls. Your family is a treasure trove of experiences and support, and there's so much yet to discover. You might spend an entire lifetime learning everything there is to know about your family members.

The clock is ticking.

I suggest you start now.

CONCLUSION
Goodbye for Now

Welcome to the other side.

I hope you found your voyage to be both educational and thought provoking. I never expected for this book to mean as much to me as it does now. When I started writing this, I assumed it would be just my thoughts scrawled down, embellished with fancy words and nostalgic anecdotes. But every page of this book has given me a sense of satisfaction. Every sentence I've written has added to my self-worth. Every paragraph has made me feel as if I'm contributing to the world in a positive way. Every word has made my life clearer.

And now, seventeen chapters later, I feel as if I'm enough.

Maybe you learned nothing from this book except that teenagers are a lot more messed up than you thought. Maybe you learned an entire library worth of information that pertains to you or your family in just one chapter. Whatever it may be, I hope that I somehow helped you be a little more aware and a little more prepared for the world. So I guess this is my last chance to really communicate any straggler pieces of information. If the idea of a little motivation spiel grosses you out, feel free to skip ahead a few paragraphs. So, here goes:

Find your passion, and never stop working toward it. If you had asked me ten years ago if I thought I would ever get the opportunity to write a book, a childhood dream of mine, I would have said no. But guess whose name is on the cover of this very book!

Don't let people tear you down. You are the only person who can determine your value. If you think you're a million bucks, don't let anyone tell you that you belong at the dollar store. You have every right to be confident in your skin. Just make sure you're modest at the same time. Hard balance, but you'll find it. You don't want to come across pompous, but you have every right to be proud of who you are. You are unique; there is literally no one who is just like you, and honestly, that's amazing. Never apologize for being who you are.

Never stop making an impact on the people around you. Go out of your way to touch people and change their lives. Just complimenting a stranger as you pass by them in the mall might be enough to make them smile a little bit and improve their entire day. Leave a positive footprint in the world. You probably already have, but you should never stop leaving more.

Treat yourself once in a while. We all get stressed, and we all deserve a break. Go ahead and take a spa day or buy yourself that new shirt. Life is too short to spend all your attention focusing on other people. Do what makes you happy. Go crazy.

Don't cave to negative peer pressure. Period.

Try to look at the big picture. What matters to you the most will likely change over time. The activities and people who stress you out today may not be there tomorrow or they may be the ones helping you. Take a step back and just breathe. It's going to be okay.

Stop caring so much about the irrelevant things. Stop caring if she'll say no if you ask her out. Stop caring if he'll ever like you back. Stop caring if they'll judge you for wearing that. Stop caring if society will think you're making a fool out of yourself. Life is too short to worry about what other people think. Those who mind don't matter, and those who matter don't mind.

Enjoy the little moments. Don't let people tell you that the small things are a "waste of time." If you enjoy it, go for it. There's beauty in the small things. There's brilliance in taking a detour to drive through your favorite light-adorned street. There's joy in staying up until 4:00 A.M. to watch the glimmering lights of the city cut through the peaceful silence. There's innocence in dancing in the first rain of the season in your pajamas and fuzzy socks until you're soaked to the core. There's tranquility in reading your favorite book as you float in a sea of bubbles in your bathtub. There's no such thing as a waste of time if you're using that time to add value to your life. Life's too short to not seize the moment.

Now, to the actual final closing paragraph:

My future is dependent on me. Your future is dependent on you. But most importantly, our future is dependent on us. It's our responsibility to make the most of it. This is our time. I've given you what I can, and now it's your turn to use it. Make an effort to bridge the gap between yourself and your family. Work to empathize and understand and compromise. For far too long it's been parents telling other parents how to be a "perfect parent," but now it's a teen's turn to change the way the world views the teenager species. It's our chance to tear down the wall between teenagers and parents.

I'm not going to say goodbye, as I know this is not a final farewell. Rather, I would like to say "au revoir," which literally means "goodbye until we meet again."

Thank you for this experience.

Thank you for this journey.

And thank you for being you.

Goodbye for now, my friend.

I hope to see you again, on the other side of the wall.

UNITED STATES HOTLINES

Main Hotlines:

depression: 1-630-482-9696

suicide: 1-800-784-8433

lifeLine: 1-800-273-8255

trevor project: 1-866-488-7386

sexuality support: 1-800-246-7743

eating disorders: 1-847-831-3438

rape and sexual assault: 1-800-656-4673

grief support: 1-650-321-5272

runaway: 1-800-843-5200, 1-800-843-5678, 1-800-621-4000

exhale; after abortion: 1-866-4394253

Depression

Suicide Hotline: *1-800-SUICIDE (2433)* – Can use in US, U.K., Canada and Singapore

Suicide Crisis Line: *1-800-999-9999*

National Suicide Prevention Helpline: *1-800-273-TALK (8245)*

National Adolescent Suicide Helpline: *1-800-621-4000*

Postpartum Depression: *1-800-PPD-MOMS*

NDMDA Depression Hotline – Support Group: *1-800-826-3632*

Veterans: *1-877-VET2VET*

Crisis Help Line – For Any Kind of Crisis: *1-800-233-4357*

Suicide & Depression Crisis Line – Covenant House: *1-800-999-9999*

Domestic Abuse

National Child Abuse Helpline: *1-800-422-4453*

National Domestic Violence Crisis Line: *1-800-799-SAFE (7233)*

National Domestic Violence Hotline (TDD:(*1-800-787-32324*

Center for the Prevention of School Violence: *1-800-299-6504*

Child Abuse Helpline: *1-800-4-A-CHILD (1-800-422-4453)*

Domestic Violence Helpline: *1-800-548-2722*

Healing Woman Foundation (Abuse:(*1-800-477-4111*

Child Abuse Hotline Support & Information: *1-800-792-5200*

Women's Aid National Domestic Violence Helpline: (UK Only) *0345 023 468*

Sexual Abuse Centre: (UK Only) *0117 935 1707*

Sexual Assault Support (24/7, English & Spanish:(*1-800-223-5001*

Domestic & Teen Dating Violence (English & Spanish: *1-800-992-2600*

Alcohol & Drug Abuse

National Association for Children of Alcoholics: *1-888-55-4COAS (1-888-554-2627)*

National Drug Abuse: *1-800-662-HELP (4357)*

Al-Anon/Alateen Hope & Help for young people who are the relatives & friends of a problem drinker:(*1-800-344-2666*

Alcohol/Drug Abuse Hotline: *1-800-662-HELP (4357)*

Be Sober Hotline: *1-800-BE-SOBER (1-800-237-6237)*

Cocaine Help Line: *1-800-COCAINE (1-800-262-2463)*

24 Hour Cocaine Support Line: *1-800-992-9239*

Ecstasy Addiction: *1-800-468-6933*

Marijuana Anonymous: *1-800-766-6779*

Youth & Teen Hotlines

National Youth Crisis Support: *1-800-448-4663*

Youth America Hotline: *1-877-YOUTHLINE (1-877-968-8454)*

Covenant House Nine-Line (Teens:(*1-800-999-9999*

Boys Town National: *1-800-448-3000*

Teen Helpline: *1-800-400-0900*

TeenLine: *1-800-522-8336*

Youth Crisis Support: *1-800-448-4663* or *1-800-422-0009*

Runaway Support (All Calls are Confidential:(*1-800-231-6946*

Child Helpline: (UK Only) *0800 1111*

Kids Helpline (Australia) *1800 55 1800*

Pregnancy Hotlines

AAA Crisis Pregnancy Center: *1-800-560-0717*

Pregnancy Support: *1-800-4-OPTIONS (1-800-467-8466)*

Pregnancy National Helpline: *1-800-356-5761*

Young Pregnant Support: *1-800 550-4900*

Gay and Lesbian Hotlines

The Trevor Helpline (For homosexuality questions or problems:(*1-800-850-8078*

Gay & Lesbian National Support: *1-888-THE-GLNH (1-888-843-4564)*

Gay, Lesbian, Bisexual, and Transgender (GLBT) Youth Support Line: *1-800-850-8078*

Lesbian & Gay Switchboard: (UK Only) *0121 622 6589*

Lothian Gay & Lesbian Switchboard – Scotland: (Scotland Only) *0131 556 4049*

Other Hotlines

Self-Injury Support: *1-800-DONT CUT (1-800-366-8288)* (**www.selfin-jury.com**)

Eating Disorders Awareness and Prevention: *1-800-931-2237* (Hours: 8am-noon daily, PST)

Eating Disorders Center: *1-888-236-1188*

Help Finding a Therapist: *1-800-THERAPIST (1-800-843-7274)*

Panic Disorder Information and Support: *1-800-64-PANIC (1-800-647-2642)*

TalkZone (Peer Counselors:(*1-800-475-TALK (1-800-475-2855)*

Parental Stress Hotline: *1-800-632-8188*

National AIDS Helpline: *(UK Only) 0800 567 123*

REFERENCES

There are many websites, blogs, and non-profit organization helping teenagers going through teenager issues. Below are some of the resources used for my research. Any resources neglected to be mentioned is purely accidental and unintentional.

Chapter 1: Academic Pressure

Academic pressure. (2013, October). Retrieved from Palo Alto Medical Foundation website: http://www.pamf.org/teen/life/stress/academic-pressure.html

Americans want more pressure on students, the Chinese want less. (2011, August 23). Retrieved June 12, 2017, from Pew Research Center website: http://www.pewglobal.org/2011/08/23/americans-want-more-pressure-on-students-the-chinese-want-less/

Jayson, S. (2014, February 11). Teens and stress: Bad habits begin early. Retrieved from USA Today website: http://www.usatoday.com/story/news/nation/2014/02/11/stress-teens-psychological/5266739/

Kelly, M. (2015). Everybody is a genius. In *The rhythm of life: Living every day with passion and purpose* (15th ed., p. 80) [Google Books Preview].

School stress takes a toll on health, teens and parents say. (2013, December 2). Retrieved from NPR website: http://www. npr.org/sections/health-shots/2013/12/02/246599742/ school-stress-takes-a-toll-on-health-teens-and-parents-say

Slobogin, K. (2002, April 5). Survey: Many students say cheating's OK. Retrieved June 12, 2017, from CNN website: http://www.cnn. com/2002/fyi/teachers.ednews/04/05/highschool.cheating/

Stress in America™ 2013 highlights: Are teens adopting adults' Stress habits? (2013). Retrieved from American Psychological Association website: http://www.apa.org/news/press/releases/stress/2013/high-lights.aspx

Teens and sleep. (n.d.). Retrieved December 25, 2016, from National Sleep Foundation website: https://sleepfoundation.org/sleep-topics/ teens-and-sleep

Chapter 2: Anxiety

Anxiety. (n.d.). Retrieved December 2016, from Beyond Blue website: https://www.youthbeyondblue.com/understand-what's-going-on/ anxiety

Anxiety and depression facts and statistics. (2016, August). Retrieved June 13, 2017, from Anxiety and Depression Association of America website: https://www.adaa.org/about-adaa/press-room/facts-statistics

Anxiety disorders. (2016, March). Retrieved June 13, 2017, from National Institute of Mental Health website: https://www.nimh.nih.gov/health/ topics/anxiety-disorders/index.shtml

Anxiety disorders in teenagers. (2016, February 12). Retrieved June 13, 2017, from Raising Children Network website: http://raisingchildren. net.au/articles/anxiety_disorders_teenagers.html

Bailey, E. (2008, December 16). Ten signs your teens may have an anxiety disorder. Retrieved from Health Central website: http://www.health-central.com/anxiety/c/22705/52585/anxiety-disorder/

Causes, symptoms, & effects of anxiety. (n.d.). Retrieved 2016, from Village Behavioral Health website: http://www.villagebh.com/ disorders/anxiety/symptoms-signs-effects#Statistics

Children and teens. (n.d.). Retrieved from Anxiety and Depression Association of America website: https://www.adaa.org/ living-with-anxiety/children

Hurst, M. (n.d.). Anxiety in teens – symptoms & treatment. Retrieved June 13, 2017, from CRC Health website: http://www.crchealth.com/ troubled-teenagers/teenage-anxiety/

Lehman, J. (n.d.). Anxious kids: Are you dealing with an inse-cure teen? Retrieved December 24, 2016, from Empowering Parents website: https://www.empoweringparents.com/article/ anxious-kids-are-you-dealing-with-an-insecure-teen/#

Treating anxiety disorders in children & adolescents. (2013, May 20). Retrieved December 24, 2016, from The Cleveland Clinic website: https://my.clevelandclinic.org/ childrens-hospital/health-info/ages-stages/childhood/ hic_Treating_Anxiety_Disorders_in_Children_and_Adolescents

Understanding the facts about anxiety disorder and depression. (2014, April). Retrieved from Anxiety and Depression Association of America website: https://www.adaa.org/understanding-anxiety

What are anxiety disorders? (n.d.). Retrieved from WebMD
    website: http://www.webmd.com/anxiety-panic/guide/
    mental-health-anxiety-disorders

Chapter 3: Bullying

Boose, G., Segal, R., & Segal, J. (n.d.). Dealing with bullying. Retrieved
    from HelpGuide.org website: http://www.helpguide.org/articles/
    abuse/dealing-with-bullying.htm

A bullying guide for young people. (2016, October 11). Retrieved June 14,
    2017, from The National Autistic Society website: http://www.autism.
    org.uk/about/in-education/bullying/guide-young-people.aspx

Cohn, A., & Canter, A. (2003, October 7). Bullying: Facts for schools and
    parents. Retrieved June 13, 2017, from NASP Center website: http://
    www.naspcenter.org/factsheets/bullying_fs.html

Davis, S., & Nixon, C. (2010). *The youth voice research project:*
    Victimization and strategies. Retrieved June 14, 2017, from http://
    njbullying.org/documents/YVPMarch2010.pdf

Effects of bullying. (n.d.). Retrieved December 25, 2016, from Stop
    Bullying website: https://www.stopbullying.gov/at-risk/effects/

Espelage, D. L., & Holt, M. K. (2013). Suicidal ideation and school bul-
    lying experiences after controlling for depression and delinquency.
    Journal of Adolescent Health, 53. Retrieved from http://www.ncdsv.
    org/images/JAH_Suicidal-ideation-and-school-bullying_7-2013.pdf

Gini, G., & Espelage, D. D. (2014) Peer victimization, cyberbullying, and
    suicide risk in children and adolescents. *JAMA Pediatrics, 312*, 545-
    546. Retrieved from
    http://jamanetwork.com/journals/jama/article-abstract/1892227

GLSEN. (2013). The 2013 National School Climate Survey. Retrieved from https://www.glsen.org/sites/default/files/2013%20National%20 School%20Climate%20Survey%20Full%20Report_0.pdf

Grissom, S. (2012, October 8). Nation's educators continue push for safe, bully-free environments. Retrieved June 14, 2017, from National Education Association website: http://www.nea.org/home/53298.htm

Hatzenbuehler, M. L., & Keyes, K. M. (2012). Inclusive anti-bullying policies and reduced risk of suicide attempts in lesbian and gay youth. *Journal of Adolescent Health*, *53*, 21-26. Retrieved from http://www. ncbi.nlm.nih.gov/pmc/articles/PMC3696185/?tool=pmcentrez

Hawkins, D. L., Pepler, D. J., & Craig, W. M. (2001). Naturalistic obser-vations of peer interventions in bullying. *Social Development*, *10*(4), 512-527. Retrieved from http://bullylab.com/Portals/0/ Naturalistic%20observations%20of%20peer%20interventions%20 in%20bullying.pdf

Juvonen, J. (2012, May 3). Psychologist's studies make sense of bullying. Retrieved June 13, 2017, from UCLA Newsroom website: http://news-room.ucla.edu/stories/bullying-jaana-juvonen-233108

Kann, L., Kinchen, S., & Shanklin, S. (2014). United States 2013 results. *High School Youth Risk Behavior Survey, Center for Disease Control*. Retrieved from http://www.cdc.gov/mmwr/pdf/ss/ss6304.pdf

The link between bullying, depression and suicide. (2016, October 27). Retrieved from No Bullying website: https://nobullying.com/ the-link-between-bullying-depression-and-suicide/

McCallion, G., & Feder, J. (2013). Student bullying: Overview of research, federal initiatives, and legal issues. *Congressional Research Service*. Retrieved from http://www.fas.org/sgp/crs/misc/R43254.pdf

Modecki, K. L., Minchin, J., Harbaugh, A. G., Guerra, N. G., & Runions, K. C. (2014). Bullying prevelance across contexts: A meta-analysis measuring cyber and traditional bullying. *Journal of Adolescent Health, 55*, 602-611. Retrieved from http://www.jahonline.org/article/S1054-139X(14)00254-7/abstract

National Center for Educational Statistics. (2015). Student reports of bullying and cyberbullying: Results from the 2013 school crime supplement to the National Victimization Survey. *US Department of Education.* Retrieved from http://nces.ed.gov/pubsearch/pubsinfo.asp?pubid=2015056

Patchin, J. W., & Hinduja, S. (2016). Summary of our cyberbullying research (2004-2016). *Cyberbullying Research Center.*Retrieved from http://cyberbullying.org/summary-of-our-cyberbullying-research

Peart, K. N. (2008, July 16). Bullying-Suicide link explored in new study by researchers at Yale. Retrieved June 13, 2017, from Yale News website: http://news.yale.edu/2008/07/16/bullying-suicide-link-explored-new-study-researchers-yale

Perren, S., Ettekal, I., & Ladd, G. (2013). The impact of peer victimization on later maladjustment: Mediating and moderating effects of hostile and self-blaming attributions. *Child Psychology and Psychiatry, 54*, 46-55. Retrieved from https://www.ncbi.nlm.nih.gov/pmc/articles/PMC3527635/

Petrosino, A., Guckenburg, S., DeVoe, J., & Hanson, T. (2010). *What characteristics of bullying, bullying victims, and schools are associated with increased reporting of bullying to school officials? National Center for Education Evaluation and Regional Assistance.* Retrieved from http://ies.ed.gov/ncee/edlabs/regions/northeast/pdf/REL_2010092_sum.pdf

Puhl, R. M., Luedicke, J., & Heuer, C. (2011). Weight-based victimization toward overweight adolescents: Observations and reactions of peers.

Journal of School Health, *81*(11), 696-703. Retrieved from http://www.ncbi.nlm.nih.gov/pubmed/21972990

Puhl, R. M., Peterson, J. L., & Luedicke, J. (2012). Strategies to address weight-based victimization: Youths' preferred support interventions from classmates, teachers, and parents. *Journal of Youth and Adolescence*, *42*(3), 315-327. Retrieved from http://www.yaleruddcenter.org/resources/upload/docs/what/bias/Youth_Preferred_Interventions_JYA_11.12.pdf.

Reed, K. P., Nugent, W., & Cooper, R. L. (2015). Testing a path model of relationships between gender, age, and bullying victimization and violent behavior, substance abuse, depression, suicidal ideation, and suicide attempts in adolescents.*Children and Youth Services Review, 55*, 125-137. Retrieved from http://www.sciencedirect.com/science/article/pii/S0190740915001656

Rose, C. A., Monda-Amaya, L. E., & Espelage, D. L. (2011). Bullying perpetration and victimization in special education: A review of the literature. *Remedial and Special Education, 32*, 114-130. Retrieved from http://rse.sagepub.com/content/early/2010/02/18/0741932510361247.abstract

Russell, S. T., Sinclair, K., Poteat, P., & Koenig, B. (2012). Adolescent health and harassment based on discriminatory bias. *American Journal of Public Health*, *102*(3), 493-495. Retrieved from http://www.ncbi.nlm.nih.gov/pubmed/22390513

Strauss, V. (2010, October 20). New data on bullying: 17% report regular abuse. *The Washington Post*. Retrieved from http://voices.washingtonpost.com/answer-sheet/bullying/2010bullyvictimdata.html

Teenage bullying. (n.d.). Retrieved December 25, 2016, from Bullying Statistics website: http://www.bullyingstatistics.org/content/teenage-bullying.html

Thornberg, T., Tenenbaum, L., Varjas, K., Meyers, J., Jungert, T., & Vanegas, G. (2012). Bystander motivation in bullying incidents: To intervene or not to intervene? *Western Journal of Emergency Medicine, 8*(3), 247-252. Retrieved from http://www.ncbi.nlm.nih.gov/pmc/articles/PMC3415829/

Treatment for victims of bullying. (n.d.). Retrieved June 13, 2017, from Village Behavioral Health website: http://www.villagebh.com/disorders/bullying

Understanding bullying. (2016). Retrieved June 14, 2017, from Centers for Disease Control and Prevention website: https://www.cdc.gov/violenceprevention/pdf/bullying_factsheet.pdf

Youth Risk Behavior Survey. (2015). Trends in the prevalence of behaviors that contribute to violence. *Centers for Disease Control.* Retrieved from *http://www.cdc.gov/healthyyouth/data/yrbs/pdf/trends/2015_us_violence_trend_yrbs.pdf*

Chapter 4: Depression

Berger, F. K. (2014, October 31). Recognizing teen depression (D. Zieve, B. Conaway, & A.D.A.M., Ed.). Retrieved November 18, 2016, from Medline Plus website: https://medlineplus.gov/ency/patientinstructions/000648.htm

Causes, symptoms, & effects of depression. (n.d.). Retrieved December 25, 2016, from Village Behavioral Health website: http://www.villagebh.com/depression/symptoms-signs-effects#Effects-of-Teenage-Depression-

Depression. (2016, August). Retrieved June 13, 2017, from Anxiety and Depression Association of America website: https://www.adaa.org/understanding-anxiety/depression

Depression in childhood and adolescence. (2009, April 19). Retrieved June 13, 2017, from Wikipedia website: https://en.wikipedia.org/wiki/Depression_in_childhood_and_adolescence

Depression in teens. (n.d.). Retrieved June 13, 2017, from Mental Health America website: http://www.mentalhealthamerica.net/conditions/depression-teens

Medlar, F. (Ed.). (2012, July 21). A few signs your teenager may be depressed. Retrieved June 13, 2017, from Psych Central website: http://psychcentral.com/blog/archives/2012/07/21/a-few-signs-your-teenager-may-be-depressed/

Suicide. (n.d.). Retrieved June 13, 2017, from National Institute of Mental Health website: https://www.nimh.nih.gov/health/statistics/suicide/index.shtml

Suicide: Facts at a glance. (2015). Retrieved June 13, 2017, from Centers for Disease Control and Prevention website: https://www.cdc.gov/ViolencePrevention/pdf/Suicide-DataSheet-a.pdf

Teen depression. (n.d.). Retrieved June 13, 2017, from I Need a LightHouse website: https://www.ineedalighthouse.org/depression-suicide/teen-depression/

Teen depression. (n.d.). Retrieved June 13, 2017, from WebMD website: http://www.webmd.com/depression/guide/teen-depression#1

Teen depression: Symptoms and causes. (2016, July 6). Retrieved June 13, 2017, from Mayo Clinic website: http://www.mayoclinic.org/diseases-conditions/teen-depression/symptoms-causes/dxc-20164556

Teen depression: Treatment. (2016, July 6). Retrieved June 13, 2017, from Mayo Clinic website: http://www.mayoclinic.org/diseases-conditions/teen-depression/diagnosis-treatment/treatment/txc-20164566

Vidyarthi, K. (2015). Top 10 common causes and reasons for teenage depression. Retrieved June 13, 2017, from Listovative website: http://listovative.com/top-10-common-causes-and-reasons-for-teenage-depression/

Chapter 5: Discrimination

Are zero tolerance policies effective in the schools? (2008, December). Retrieved June 13, 2017, from American Psychologist Association website: https://www.apa.org/pubs/info/reports/zero-tolerance.pdf

Bonczar, T. B., & Beck, A. J. (n.d.). *Lifetime likelihood of going to state or federal prison.* Retrieved June 14, 2017, from Bureau of Justice Statistics website: http://bjs.gov/content/pub/pdf/Llgsfp.pdf

Coping with racism & discrimination. (n.d.). Retrieved June 13, 2017, from UCSC Counseling and Psychological Services (CAPS) website: http://caps.ucsc.edu/pdf/coping-with-racism.pdf

11 facts about racial discrimination. (n.d.). Retrieved June 13, 2017, from Do Something website: https://www.dosomething.org/us/facts/11-facts-about-racial-discrimination

Expansive survey of america's public schools reveals troubling racial disparities. (2014, March 21). Retrieved June 13, 2017, from U.S. Department of Education website: http://www.ed.gov/news/press-releases/expansive-survey-americas-public-schools-reveals-troubling-racial-disparities

Hendriksen, E. (2015, February 13). How to deal with racism. Retrieved June 13, 2017, from Quick and Dirty Tips website: http://www.quickanddirtytips.com/health-fitness/mental-health/how-to-deal-with-racism

Levin, S. (n.d.). *Social psychological evidence on race and racism*. Retrieved June 13, 2017, from Stanford University website: https://web.stanford. edu/~hakuta/www/policy/racial_dynamics/Chapter3.pdf

QuickFacts. (n.d.). Retrieved June 13, 2017, from United States Census Bureau website: https://www.census.gov/quickfacts/table/ PST045216/00 '

Quigley, B. (2010, July 26). Fourteen examples of racism in criminal justice system [Blog post]. Retrieved from Huff Post website: http://www.huffingtonpost.com/bill-quigley/fourteen-examples-of-raci_b_658947.html

Racial disparity. (n.d.). Retrieved June 14, 2017, from The Sentencing Project website: http://www.sentencingproject.org/issues/ racial-disparity/

Racism in schools. (2015, December 22). Retrieved June 13, 2017, from No Bullying website: https://nobullying.com/racism-in-schools/

The reality of social profiling. (n.d.). Retrieved June 14, 2017, from The Leadership Conference website: http://www.civilrights.org/publications/reports/racial-profiling2011/the-reality-of-racial.html.

Sledge, M. (2013, April 8). The drug war and mass incarceration by the numbers [Blog post]. Retrieved from Huff Post website: http:// www.huffingtonpost.com/2013/04/08/drug-war-mass-incarceration_n_3034310.html

Chapter 6: Distractions – Social Media and Technology

Hess, P. (2014, July 14). The power social media has over teen lives [Blog post]. Retrieved from HuffPost website: http://www.huffingtonpost.com/patrick-hess/the-power-social-media-has-over-teen-lives_b_5582497.html

Howard, M. (2015, March 27). Distracted by technology: Focusing attention on homework. Retrieved June 13, 2017, from Beyond BookSmart website: http://www.beyond-booksmart.com/executive-functioning-strategies-blog/distracted-by-technology-focusing-attention-on-homework

Influence of mass media. (2005, June 5). Retrieved December 26, 2016, from Wikipedia website: https://en.wikipedia.org/wiki/Influence_of_mass_media

Lenhart, A., Anderson, M., & Smith, A. (2015, October 1). Teens, technology and romantic relationships. Retrieved from Pew Research Center website: http://www.pewinternet.org/2015/10/01/teens-technology-and-romantic-relationships/

Lenhart, A., & Page, D. (2015, April 9). *Teens, social media, and technology overview 2015*. Retrieved June 13, 2017, from Pew Research Center website: http://www.pewinternet.org/files/2015/04/PI_TeensandTech_Update2015_0409151.pdf

Media influence on teenagers. (2016, July 12). Retrieved June 13, 2017, from Raising Children Network (Australia) website: http://raisingchildren.net.au/articles/media_influences_teenagers.html

Rosen, L. (n.d.). iDisorder. Retrieved June 11, 2017, from Dr. Larry Rosen website: http://drlarryrosen.com/2011/03/idisorder/

Social networking's good and bad impacts on kids. (2011, August 6). Retrieved June 13, 2017, from The American Psychological Association website: http://www.apa.org/news/press/releases/2011/08/social-kids.aspx

Chapter 7: Eating Disorders

Adolescent eating disorders. (n.d.). Retrieved June 13, 2017, from The Healthy Teen Project website: http://www.healthyteenproject.com/ adolescent-eating-disorders-ca

Eating disorders. (n.d.). Retrieved June 13, 2017, from Substance Abuse and Mental Health Service Administration website: https://www. samhsa.gov/treatment/mental-disorders/eating-disorders

Eating disorders treatment. (n.d.). Retrieved June 13, 2017, from Timberline Knolls website: http://www.timberlineknolls.com/ eating-disorder

Eating disorders: Treatment options. (2017, January 23). Retrieved June 13, 2017, from Center for Young Women's Health website: http:// youngwomenshealth.org/parents/eating-disorders-treatment-options/

Higuera, V. (2016, December 5). Diagnosing an eating disorder. Retrieved June 13, 2017, from HealthLine website: http://www.healthline.com/ health/eating-disorders-diagnosis#Overview1

Mayo Clinic Staff. (n.d.). Eating disorders. Retrieved December 26, 2016, from Mayo Clinics website: http://www.mayoclinic.org/ diseases-conditions/eating-disorders/home/ovc-20182765

Swanson, S., Crow, S., & Grange, D. L. (2011, July). Prevalence and correlates of eating disorders in adolescents. Retrieved June 13, 2017, from JAMA Psychiatry website: http://jamanetwork.com/journals/ jamapsychiatry/fullarticle/1107211?maxtoshow=&hits=10&RESULT-FORMAT=&fulltext=Merikangas&searchid=1&FIRSTINDEX=0&re-sourcetype=HWCIT

Understanding eating disorders in teens. (n.d.). Retrieved June 13, 2017, from WebMD website: http://www.webmd.com/mental-health/ eating-disorders/understanding-eating-disorders-teens

What are eating disorders? (n.d.). Retrieved June 13, 2017, from The Alliance for Eating Disorder Awareness website: https://www.alliance-foreatingdisorders.com/portal/what-are-eating-disorders

What are eating disorders? (2012). Retrieved June 13, 2017, from National Eating Disorders Association website: https://www.nationaleatingdis-orders.org/sites/default/files/ResourceHandouts/GeneralStatistics.pdf

Chapter 8: Fashion

Alexander, R. (2007, July 27). 10 teen fashion tips for concerned parents. Retrieved June 13, 2017, from Life Script website: http://www.lifescript.com/well-being/articles/0/10_teen_fashion_tips_for_con-cerned_parents.aspx

Fashion. (2012, June). Retrieved June 13, 2017, from Bureau of Labor Statistics website: https://www.bls.gov/spotlight/2012/fashion/

Foust, K. (2010, September 22). 10 fashion tips for teens. Retrieved June 13, 2017, from Made Man website: http://www.mademan.com/mm/10-fashion-tips-teens.html

Gregston, M. (n.d.). What teenagers wish they could say to their parents. Retrieved June 13, 2017, from One Place website: http://www.one-place.com/ministries/parenting-todays-teens-weekend/read/articles/what-teenagers-wish-they-could-say-to-their-parents-14454.html

Piper Jafrray survey of 6,200 teens indicates optimistic economic views. (2015, April 15). Retrieved June 13, 2017, from Piper Jaffray website: http://www.piperjaffray.com/2col.aspx?id=287&releaseid=2035367

Teenage consumer spending statistics. (2016, September 4). Retrieved June 13, 2017, from Statistic Brain Research Institute website: http://www.statisticbrain.com/teenage-consumer-spending-statistics/

Teen magazines and their effect on girls. (2003, May). Retrieved December 26, 2016, from Healthy Children website: https://www.healthychildren.org/English/family-life/Media/Pages/Teen-Magazines-and-Their-Effect-on-Girls.aspx

Teen Vogue. (2013, September 25). Teen vogue and goldman sachs introduce 2013 brand affinity index research findings. Retrieved June 13, 2017, from PR Newswire Association website: http://www.prnewswire.com/news-releases/teen-vogue-and-goldman-sachs-introduce-2013-brand-affinity-index-research-findings-225196192.html

Tweens, teens, and magazines – fact sheet. (2004, September 29). Retrieved June 13, 2017, from The Kaiser Family Foundation website: http://kff.org/other/fact-sheet/tweens-teens-and-magazines-fact-sheet/

Chapter 9: Insomnia

Heffron, T. M. (2014, March 10). Insomnia awareness day facts and stats. Retrieved June 13, 2017, from Sleep Education website: http://www.sleepeducation.org/news/2014/03/10/insomnia-awareness-day-facts-and-stats

Insomnia statistics. (n.d.). Retrieved June 13, 2017, from Sleep Med of Santa Barbara website: http://www.sleepmedsite.com/page/sb/sleep_disorders/sleep_statistics

Insomnia statistics. (n.d.). Retrieved June 13, 2017, from The Better Sleep Guide website: http://www.better-sleep-better-life.com/insomnia-statistics.html

Insomnia - symptoms & Causes. (2015, March 4). Retrieved June 13, 2017, from Sleep Education website: http://www.sleepeducation.org/essentials-in-sleep/insomnia/symptoms-causes

Late-night teens 'face greater depression risk' [Newsgroup post]. (2010, January 2). Retrieved from BBC website: http://news.bbc.co.uk/2/hi/health/8435955.stm

Secrets to stealing extra sleep. (n.d.). Retrieved June 13, 2017, from The Better Sleep Council website: http://bettersleep.org/better-sleep/how-to-sleep-better/sleep-tips/

Sleep and sleep disorders. (2015, March 12). Retrieved June 13, 2017, from Center of Disease Control and Prevention website: https://www.cdc.gov/sleep/index.html

Sleep disorders & problems. (n.d.). Retrieved June 13, 2017, from National Sleep Foundation website: https://sleepfoundation.org/sleep-disorders-problems

Sleep tight! – Treating insomnia & Sleeping disorders naturally. (2014, January 10). Retrieved June 13, 2017, from Monterey Bay Holistic Alliance website: https://montereybayholistic.wordpress.com/2014/01/10/treating_insomnia/

Smith, M. S., Robinson, L. R., & Segal, R. (2017, April). Sleep disorders and sleeping problems. Retrieved June 13, 2017, from Help Guide website: https://www.helpguide.org/articles/sleep/sleep-disorders-and-problems.htm

Chapter 10: Homosexuality

Bullying and LGBT youth. (n.d.). Retrieved June 13, 2017, from Stop Bullying website: https://www.stopbullying.gov/at-risk/groups/lgbt/index.html

Gay, lesbian, and bisexual teens: Facts for teens and their parents. (2016, October 4). Retrieved June 13, 2017, from Healthy Children website: https://www.healthychildren.org/English/ages-stages/teen/dating-sex/Pages/

Gay-Lesbian-and-Bisexual-Teens-Facts-for-Teens-and-Their-Parents.
aspx

Gay-Straight alliances. (n.d.). Retrieved June 13, 2017, from GLSEN website: http://www.glsen.org/participate/student-action/gsa

LGBT youth. (2014, November 12). Retrieved June 13, 2017, from Center
of Disease Control and Prevention website: https://www.cdc.gov/lgb-
thealth/youth.htm

Lyons, L. (2003, March 18). Teens on homosexuality: Nature or nurture?
Retrieved June 13, 2017, from Gallup.com website: http://www.gallup.
com/poll/8005/teens-homosexuality-nature-nurture.aspx

*Parents' influence on the health of lesbian, gay, and bisexual teens: What
parents and families should know.* (2013, November). Retrieved June
13, 2017, from Center of Disease Control and Prevention website:
https://www.cdc.gov/healthyyouth/protective/pdf/parents_influence_
lgb.pdf

Chapter 11: Mood Swings

Bhargava, H. D. (2012, September 12). Help your teen's mood swings.
Retrieved June 13, 2017, from WebMD website: http://www.webmd.
com/parenting/features/kids-teen-moods

Goldberg, J. (Ed.). (2017, April 13). Mood swings and bipolar disorder.
Retrieved June 13, 2017, from WebMD website: http://www.webmd.
com/bipolar-disorder/guide/mood-swings#1

Halli, C. (2015, March 1). Mood disorders in teens is not normal moodiness [Blog post]. Retrieved from Healthy
Place Blogs website: http://www.healthyplace.com/blogs/
parentingchildwithmentalillness/2015/03/mood-disorders-in-teens/

Holmes and Hutchinson. (n.d.). Emotional changes during puberty: 6 things you might notice! Retrieved June 13, 2017, from Always website: http://always.com/en-us/tips-and-advice/puberty-101/emotional-changes-during-puberty-6-things-you-might-notice

Lloyd, W. C. (Ed.). (2016, October 5). What are mood swings? Retrieved June 13, 2017, from Health Grades website: https://www.healthgrades.com/right-care/mental-health-and-behavior/mood-swings

Luscombe, B. (2015, October 14). How to tell if your teen's just moody or needs therapy. Retrieved June 13, 2017, from Time website: http://time.com/4066536/teen-moods-depression-study/

Majd, S. (2011, September 11). 8 causes and treatments of mood swings. Retrieved June 13, 2017, from Quick and Dirty Tips website: http://www.quickanddirtytips.com/health-fitness/womens-health/8-causes-and-treatments-of-mood-swings

Mood disorder symptoms, causes and effect. (n.d.). Retrieved June 13, 2017, from PsychGuides website: http://www.psychguides.com/guides/mood-disorder-symptoms-causes-and-effect/

Mood swing. (2003, December 8). Retrieved June 13, 2017, from Wikipedia website: https://en.wikipedia.org/wiki/Mood_swing

Mood swings in children. (n.d.). Retrieved June 13, 2017, from Mood Swings website: http://mood-swings.bafree.net/mood-swings-in-children.php

Obiezue, A. (n.d.). Getting over your mood swings! [Blog post]. Retrieved from The Teenager website: http://zariwilde.blogspot.com/2015/08/getting-over-your-mood-swings.html

Pickrell, J. (2006, September 4). Introduction: Teenagers. Retrieved June 13, 2017, from New Scientist website: https://www.newscientist.com/article/dn9938-introduction-teenagers/

Smith, S. (2007, March 12). Raging hormones" behind teen mood swings? [Newsgroup post]. Retrieved from CBS website: http://www.cbsnews.com/news/raging-hormones-behind-teen-mood-swings/

Steingard, R. J. (n.d.). Mood disorders and teenage girls. Retrieved June 13, 2017, from Child Mind Institute website: http://childmind.org/article/mood-disorders-and-teenage-girls/

Teens and mood swings. (n.d.). Retrieved June 13, 2017, from Online Parenting Coach website: http://www.onlineparentingcoach.com/2011/06/teens-and-mood-swings.html

Witchalls, C. (n.d.). Children's and parenting health centre. Retrieved June 13, 2017, from WebMD website: http://www.webmd.boots.com/children/features/teenage-mood-swings

Chapter 12: Peer Pressure

Moffitt, B. (n.d.). Statistics & facts [Blog post]. Retrieved from Peer Pressure website: https://brooklynmoffitt.wordpress.com/statistics-facts/

Peer pressure. (n.d.). Retrieved June 13, 2017, from Family First Aid website: http://www.familyfirstaid.org/issues/peer-pressure/

Peer pressure. (n.d.). Retrieved June 13, 2017, from Women's and Children's Health Network website: http://www.cyh.com/HealthTopics/HealthTopicDetails.aspx?p=243&id=2184&np=295

Peer pressure. (2002, December 8). Retrieved June 13, 2017, from Wikipedia website: https://en.wikipedia.org/wiki/Peer_pressure

Peer pressure and influence: Teenagers. (2015, May 19). Retrieved June 13, 2017, from Raising Children Network website: http://raisingchildren.net.au/articles/peer_pressure_teenagers.html

Smith, L. K. C., & Fowler, S. A. (1984). Positive peer pressure: The effects of peer monitoring on children's disruptive behavior. Retrieved June 13, 2017, from US National Library of Medicine National Institutes of Health website: https://www.ncbi.nlm.nih.gov/pmc/articles/ PMC1307935/

Van Petten, V. (n.d.). 10 examples of peer pressure. Retrieved June 13, 2017, from Radical Parenting website: http://www.radicalparenting. com/2012/01/07/10-examples-of-peer-pressure/#sthash.WYwQ9mYp. dpuf

Chapter 13: Relationships (friendships, cliques, gangs, dating, abuse)

Dating abuse statistics. (n.d.). Retrieved June 13, 2017, from Choose Respect website: http://chooserespect.engagethecrowd.com/scripts/ teens/statistics.asp

11 facts about teen dating violence. (n.d.). Retrieved June 13, 2017, from Do Something website: https://www.dosomething.org/us/ facts/11-facts-about-teen-dating-violence

11 facts about teen pregnancy. (n.d.). Retrieved 2016, from Do Something website: https://www.dosomething.org/us/ facts/11-facts-about-teen-pregnancy

Enloe, C. (2013, April 4). Tips for A successful high school relationship [Blog post]. Retrieved from HuffPost website: http://www.huffington- post.com/chris-enloe/high-school-relationship-tips_b_3007582.html

Fritscher, L. (2013, June 15). Interesting facts on teen love. Retrieved June 13, 2017, from Live Strong website: http://www.livestrong.com/ article/1004583-interesting-teen-love/

Gangs. (2015). Retrieved June 11, 2017, from FBI website: https://www. fbi.gov/investigate/violent-crime/gangs

Kochrekar, M. (2016, February 21). How does peer pressure influence teen pregnancy? Retrieved June 13, 2017, from Mom Junction website: http://www.momjunction.com/articles/how-does-peer-pressure-influence-teen-pregnancy_00376249/#gref

Lenhart, A., Anderson, M., & Smith, A. (2015, October 1). Teens, technology and romantic relationships. Retrieved June 13, 2017, from Pew Research Center website: http://www.pewinternet.org/2015/10/01/teens-technology-and-romantic-relationships/

Measuring the extent of gang problems. (n.d.). Retrieved June 13, 2017, from National Gang Center website: https://www.nationalgangcenter.gov/survey-analysis/measuring-the-extent-of-gang-problems

Sheck, A. (n.d.). The 3 c's of relationship. Retrieved June 13, 2017, from Your Tango website: http://www.yourtango.com/experts/dr--adam-sheck/3-cs-relationship

Social groups & cliques. (n.d.). Retrieved June 13, 2017, from PBS Parents website: http://www.pbs.org/parents/education/going-to-school/social/cliques/

Teenage relationships: Romance & intimacy. (2014, November 24). Retrieved June 13, 2017, from Raising Children website: http://raisingchildren.net.au/articles/relationships_teenagers.html/context/1101

Tucker, K. (n.d.). Good things about teens dating. Retrieved June 13, 2017, from Our Everyday Life website: http://oureverydaylife.com/good-things-teens-dating-7390.html

Chapter 14: Self-Esteem

Butler, C. (2012, September 17). 7 ways to help build your teen's self-esteem. Retrieved June 13, 2017, from Quick and Dirty Tips website: http://www.quickanddirtytips.com/

parenting/tweens-teens/7-ways-to-help-build-your-teens-self-es-teem?page=all#sthash.LFlHtEMZ.dpuf

The issue. (n.d.). Retrieved 2016, from NYC Girls Project website: http://www.nyc.gov/html/girls/html/issues/issues.shtml#12

Newsome, T. (2015, September 24). 11 weird signs of low self-esteem that are easy to miss. Retrieved June 13, 2017, from Bustle website: https://www.bustle.com/articles/112199-11-weird-signs-of-low-self-esteem-that-are-easy-to-miss

Real girls, real pressure: A national report on the state of self-esteem commissioned: June 2008. (2008, June). Retrieved June 13, 2017, from The Dove Self Esteem Fund website: http://www.isacs.org/misc_files/SelfEsteem_Report%20-%20Dove%20Campaign%20for%20Real%20Beauty.pdf

Rubino, J. (n.d.). [Self esteem]. Retrieved June 13, 2017, from The Self Esteem System website: http://www.totalselfesteem.com/

The Self-Esteem Book: The Ultimate Guide to Boost the Most Underrated Ingredient for Success and Happiness in Life

Signs of low self-esteem. (2015, November 21). Retrieved June 13, 2017, from Healthy Children website: https://www.healthychildren.org/English/ages-stages/gradeschool/Pages/Signs-of-Low-Self-Esteem.aspx

Smith, M., & Segal, J. (n.d.). Dealing with loneliness and shyness. Retrieved June 13, 2017, from Help Guide website: http://www.helpguide.org/articles/relationships/overcoming-loneliness-and-shyness.htm

Ways to build your teenager's self-esteem. (2015, November 21). Retrieved June 13, 2017, from Healthy Children website: https://www.

healthychildren.org/English/ages-stages/teen/Pages/Ways-To-Build-Your-Teenagers-Self-Esteem.aspx

Neuman, M.D., Fredric. "Low Self-esteem." Psychology Today. Accessed March 3, 2014. http://www.psychologytoday.com/blog/fighting-fear/201304/low-self-esteem.

Chapter 15: Siblings

Carey, B. (2007, June 22). Research finds firstborns gain the higher I.Q. Retrieved June 13, 2017, from NY Times website: http://www.nytimes.com/2007/06/22/science/22sibling.html

15 fascinating scientific facts about siblings. (2011, May 15). Retrieved June 13, 2017, from Nursing Schools website: http://www.nursingschools.net/blog/2011/05/15-fascinating-scientific-facts-about-siblings/

Harrington, R. (2016, April 9). 7 surprising facts about siblings. Retrieved June 13, 2017, from Business Insider website: http://www.businessinsider.com/scientific-sibling-facts-2016-4/#studies-have-found-younger-siblings-can-be-funnier-and-live-longer-1

Lloyd, D. (2011, September 26). Five facts about siblings [Blog post]. Retrieved from HuffPost website: http://www.huffingtonpost.com/delia-lloyd/five-facts-about-siblings_b_963867.html

Lyon, L. (2009, July 31). 7 ways your sibling may have shaped you. Retrieved June 12, 2017, from US News website: http://health.usnews.com/health-news/family-health/articles/2009/07/31/7-ways-your-siblings-may-have-shaped-you

The sibling effect: 12 amazing facts about brothers and sisters. (n.d.). Retrieved June 13, 2017, from Business Insider website: http://www.businessinsider.com/sibling-effect-jeffrey-kluger-2011-9#sibling-traits-hold-true-across-hundreds-of-species-1

Sibling relationships reflect family dynamics. (2006, November 20).
Retrieved June 13, 2017, from The College of Health and Human
Development website: http://hhd.psu.edu/news/2006/11_20_06_sib-
lings.html

Swiger, E. (2015, September 8). The pros and cons of having siblings.
Retrieved June 13, 2017, from The Odyssey website: https://www.
theodysseyonline.com/pros-cons-siblings

Chapter 16: Substance Abuse (Drugs, Alcohol etc.)

Drug-Related hospital emergency room visits. (2011, May). Retrieved
June 13, 2017, from National Institute on Drug Abuse website: https://www.drugabuse.gov/publications/drugfacts/
drug-related-hospital-emergency-room-visits

11 facts about teens and drug use. (n.d.). Retrieved June 13, 2017,
from Do Something website: https://www.dosomething.org/us/
facts/11-facts-about-teens-and-drug-use

Epidemiologic trends in drug abuse. (2009, June). Retrieved June 13, 2017,
from National Institute on Drug Abuse website: https://www.drug-
abuse.gov/sites/default/files/cewgvol2june_web508.pdf

Guedea, G. (n.d.). Why teens turn to drugs. Retrieved June 12,
2017, from Detox Rehab website: http://www.detoxrehab.org/
why-teens-turn-to-drugs/

Hudson, C. (n.d.). 5 reasons teenagers take drugs [Blog post]. Retrieved
from Understanding Teenagers website: http://understandingteenag-
ers.com.au/blog/5-reasons-teenagers-take-drugs/

Levy, D. T., Stewart, K., & Wilbur, P. M. (1999). Costs of underage
drinking. Retrieved June 13, 2017, from National Criminal Justice
Reference Service website: https://www.ncjrs.gov/App/Publications/
abstract.aspx?ID=178228

Monitoring the future. (2016, December). Retrieved June 13, 2017, from National Institute on Drug Abuse website: https://www.drugabuse. gov/related-topics/trends-statistics/monitoring-future

NIDA. (2016, December 13). Teen substance use shows promising decline. Retrieved June 13, 2017, from National Institute on Drug Abuse website: https://www.drugabuse.gov/news-events/ news-releases/2016/12/teen-substance-use-shows-promising-decline

NIDA Blog Team. (2015, March 9). 6 tactful tips for resisting peer pressure to use drugs and alcohol [Blog post]. Retrieved from Drugs & Health Blog: https://teens.drugabuse.gov/blog/ post/6-tactful-tips-resisting-peer-pressure-to-use-drugs-and-alcohol

Payh. (2012, September 11). How easy it is for teens to get drugs [Blog post]. Retrieved from Paul Anderson Youth Home (PAYH) website: http://www.payh.org/how-easy-is-it-for-teens-to-get-drugs/

Smith, M. W. (Ed.). (2012, June 14). Teen abuse of cough and cold medicine. Retrieved June 13, 2017, from WebMD website: http:// www.webmd.com/parenting/teen-abuse-cough-medicine-9/ teens-and-dxm-drug-abuse?page=3

Teen drug and alcohol abuse facts and statistics. (n.d.). Retrieved June 13, 2017, from Teen Rehab website: http://www.teendrugrehabs.com/ facts-and-stats/

Tips for dads on talking to your teens [Blog post]. (2012, May 21). Retrieved from Parent Blog: http://www.drugfree.org/ tips-for-dads-on-talking-to-your-teens/

Vogt, A. (2013, December 18). More teens smoke marijuana reject synthetic drugs like k2 and spice. Retrieved June 13, 2017, from Bustle website: http://www.bustle.com/articles/10975-more-teens-smoke- marijuana-reject-synthetic-drugs-like-k2-and-spice